Microsoft® Money Management

Jean E. Gutmann

University of Southern Maine

Windcrest®/McGraw-Hill

NOTICES

Microsoft Windows®	Microsoft Corporation
Microsoft Money	
Microsoft Windows Calendar	
Microsoft Excel®	
Microsoft Windows Write	
Quicken®	Intuit Corporation

The products mentioned above that are manufactured by Microsoft Corporation are copyrighted products of Microsoft Corporation.

FIRST EDITION
FIRST PRINTING

© 1992 by **Windcrest Books**, an imprint of TAB Books.
TAB Books is a division of McGraw-Hill, Inc.
The name "Windcrest" is a registered trademark of TAB Books.

Printed in the United States of America. All rights reserved. The publisher takes no responsibility for the use of any of the materials or methods described in this book, nor for the products thereof.

Library of Congress Cataloging-in-Publication Data

Gutmann, Jean E.
    Microsoft money management / by Jean E. Gutmann.
      p.   cm.
    Includes index.
    ISBN 0-8306-4017-7 (pbk.)
     1. Microsoft Money. 2. Small business—Finance—Computer
programs. 3. Finance, Personal—Computer programs. I. Title.
HG4027.7.G88 1992
658.15′92′02855369—dc20   91-41785
                                      CIP

TAB Books offers software for sale. For information and a catalog, please contact
TAB Software Department, Blue Ridge Summit, PA 17294-0850.

Acquisitions Editor: Brad Schepp
Book Editor: Melanie D. Brewer
Director of Production: Katherine G. Brown
Series Design: Jaclyn J. Boone
Cover Design: Sandra Blair Design and Brent Blair Photography,
    Harrisburg, PA

WT1

Contents

Dedication
Ambition grows from strong roots.
My family has always provided that strength.
This book is dedicated to my mother,
Elizabeth M. Gutmann.

Preface

This book was written for all of you who want to have better control over your money. The new money management software for Windows, called Microsoft Money, can help you do just that. This book provides simple, yet detailed, instructions to get you started with Microsoft Money, along with detailed tutorials for all sorts of advanced features of the Money package.

The major focus of this book is on small business money management, so you will see chapters on small business management, credit management, payroll, assets, and liabilities. An individual u•er with no need to keep business records will find complete discussions of setup, transaction entry, check writing, report printing, list management, customizing Money options, credit card management, budgeting, investment accounts and more.

This book is full of computer exercises to help you learn procedures for making Money more effective. For example in chapter 4, you can learn and practice the procedure for setting up records to track several properties you own, and print reports on each property. This book also contains hints and techniques not found in the User Manual for the Money software.

I am pleased that you have chosen to buy this book, and pledge that I have given my best effort to making it worthwhile for you.

Acknowledgments

My friends, family, and colleagues provided the encouragement and support I needed to attempt and complete this major project, and I am very grateful to them. A big, hearty "THANK YOU!" goes to Linda Smith, my good friend, for reading every word and testing the computer tutorials in this book on her computer. She provided invaluable feedback and corrections that make this book user-friendly. Another big thank you to Pam Collard, my faithful student assistant, for her reading and computer verification work. Another big thank you to Susan Curtis at the University of Southern Maine for her meticulous attention to detail in the production and submission of my manuscript. I also would like to thank Brad Schepp at TAB/Windcrest for connecting me to Microsoft Corporation, and this terrific piece of software, as well as guiding me through the maze of the publishing world. Keith White, at Microsoft Corporation, became an invaluable ally in understanding the workings of Microsoft Money, and I am very grateful to him also. Melanie Brewer at TAB Books deserves a "Medal of Honor" for her outstanding editing work.

The screen images in this book were created with Microsoft Money by Microsoft Corporation, and are used with their gracious permission. These images were captured by the HiJaak package from Inset Systems of Brookfield, CT.

Typographical conventions used in this book

Registered trademarks

Windows refers to Microsoft Windows, Version 3.0 or later by Microsoft Corporation of Redmond, Washington. You must have installed Windows in order to run Microsoft Money.

Money refers to the Microsoft Money software that is the subject of this book. When the word *Money* is capitalized in the text, it refers to the Microsoft Money software, which is a money management package from Microsoft Corporation of Redmond, Washington.

Alternate font

Words or phrases displayed in an alternate font are characters that you must type at the keyboard exactly as shown in the text. For example, type Bigtime Corporation. The alternate font is also used to indicate icons, buttons, and commands that you must click on. For instance, click on Ok or select File.

Upper/lower casing

Special keys on the computer keyboard are expressed by an initial capital letter followed by lower casing. Examples of these keys are the alternate key (Alt), Control (Ctrl), Esc, and Enter. Some of these keys can be combined with other keys to form commands. For instance, if you were instructed to enter Ctrl−W, you should press and hold down the Control key while tapping the W.

Setup notes

If you haven't already set up Microsoft Money to work on your computer, follow these quick and easy instructions:

Note What you should type at the keyboard is in an alternate font. What you should look for on the screen is in "quotes."

1. Turn on your computer and access Windows 3.0. To do this, type win at the C: \ prompt and press Enter. If this doesn't work, try typing cd windows at the C: \ prompt, and press Enter; then type win and press Enter. Windows must be running in standard or enhanced mode—Money will not work in real mode.

2. You will briefly see a title screen announcing Microsoft Windows, and then you will either see a screen full of little pictures (called icons)—one for each job that Windows can handle—or you will see a small picture containing three squares topped with the C: mark and labelled "Program Manager." It looks like this:

This is called the Program Manager icon, and you should double-click on it to activate the Program Manager window, which is the one full of icons.

3. Insert your *Microsoft Money* diskette in the A: disk drive.

4. On the second line of the Program Manager Window, you will see a menu line with the words "File Options Window Help." Click on the word "File," or press Alt−F. Then click on the word "Run" in the list that drops down below "File," or press the letter R to choose this word.

5. You should now see a small box with an area labelled "Command Line." Notice that the screen is pulsing in that area, which means it is waiting for you to type something. Type a:setup and press Enter, or click the Ok button.

6. Microsoft Money will take over for a few minutes to install itself on your hard disk. You will be asked to provide your name, and to confirm that you want the Money files stored in "C:\MSMONEY." You do want them stored there so simply press Enter or click Continue to move on.

7. When the setup process is finished, a box appears to ask you whether you want to run Money right away or return to the Program Manager Window. Please take a minute to start Money now so you can begin chapter 1 in this book. Click on the "Run Microsoft Money" phrase or press ALT−R.

8. You will see a box with the title, "Setup New File." In the bottom of this box, there is a section labelled "Start With" where you can specify whether you want to use Business or Home categories. "Home Categories" is already checked (the hollow circle has a dot in it). Leave this choice as is by pressing Enter or clicking on Ok.

9. Another small box appears in the middle of your screen with the title, "Create First Account." Read this box and then press Enter or click on Ok.

10. A larger, "Create New Account" box appears where you can type an account name and choose a type of account. The account name of "Checking" is filled in for you, and a check mark (the dot within a circle) is already in place for a "Bank Account." Again you can just press Enter or click on Ok to move on.

11. Then an "Opening Balance" box appears where you can type a beginning balance amount for this account. If you know a specific balance that you want to enter go ahead and type it. Otherwise type a zero (be sure to hit the number 0, instead of the alphabetic character O). You can change this amount later if you need to. Press Enter or click Ok to be ushered into the Money Account Book. (This is the check register for your Checking account.)

12. Go ahead and say "Yes" (click on it or press Enter) to see a demonstration. It's fun and informative. During the demonstration you can press X, or click on Exit, to be returned to the Money Account Book. Go to chapter 1.

13. If you want to exit from Microsoft Money right now, click on the "File," then "Exit" menu items or press Alt−F, then X. When asked if you want to make a backup copy, click on No or press Alt−N.

1
CHAPTER

Mastering Microsoft Money in less than an hour

Small business money management does not require elaborate accounting software. Microsoft Money provides all the tools that a small business needs to control expenditures and even start tracking assets and liabilities. This unique computer package is extremely easy to use because it was designed for the Windows 3.0 environment and contains many of the features you might expect from a much more expensive accounting package.

This book will help small business users, as well as individuals, become familiar with Money and then tailor it to their own specific needs. You might be a full-time employee of a large business organization operating a small business enterprise on the side. You might be a doctor or a lawyer. You might be a consultant or other professional service provider. You might be the owner of a small retail store or construction company, or you might be involved in a small business in some other way. Whatever the case, this book will help you get a better handle on your money and make intelligent business decisions for the future.

Chapters 1 through 3 provide the basic concepts of Money for both individual and business users. Chapters 4, and 9 through 12, concentrate specifically on small business money management. The other chapters (5 through 8) might be important to both the individual and the business user, depending on the particular situation. Take a look at the Table of Contents to decide for yourself which of the chapters you'll concentrate on.

What is Microsoft Money?

Microsoft Money is a computer tool that collects money transactions in one place so that you can produce computer generated checks and have instant access to many types of historical information regarding your financial status. We'll call this tool Money throughout this book. Money can help you balance your checkbook, track credit card expenditures, maintain a budget, manage Payroll records, produce business financial statements, and many other business tasks. All you have to do is enter all disbursements and deposits in your checking accounts, or all increases and decreases in other types of accounts, and Money will do the rest. It's really as easy as that.

You can master this helpful money management software in less than an hour. You'll have instant access to various reports of the status of your accounts, and you can print checks instead of handwriting them. Once you start managing your money this way, you'll wonder how you ever maintained a manual checkbook.

Applications of Money

Money can be used by individuals to manage all personal financial affairs. Money also can be used by individuals who handle both business and personal transactions from one account. The Money Users Guide provides instructions for handling this type of application, and this book provides many more details and examples of personal use by individuals.

This book focuses on business usage of Money. The maintenance of a checkbook, or several checkbooks, the control of credit card usage, the management of a cash on hand amount, and the application of budgets to all of these are examples of the business usage that Money can handle. In addition, small businesses will be concerned about receivables, payables, payroll, loan accounts, and the net worth of the business. Money is adept at handling all of these as well.

The Windows environment

It is assumed that you have installed and have been working with Windows 3.0. When I use the word *window*, I am referring to areas of the screen contained within boldly outlined boxes. A window usually has smaller boxes within it, which you must either respond to or specify Ok to accept their contents. Money works within a window that remains inside Windows 3.0. When I use the word *Windows* (capitalized), I am referring to the Windows 3.0 software package from Microsoft Corporation. The most commonly used window in Money displays the check register that you are working with. Chapter 2 contains a full explanation of Windows terminology and activities.

Tutorial to set up some sample accounts

Let's get started right away on the simple steps needed to begin working with your first account in Money. These steps include naming the new account, entering a beginning balance, entering transactions, and printing checks. To provide you with a good overview of how Money can help you better manage your money, we'll take a quick look at budgeting and bank reconciliation. If you haven't yet installed Money with your Windows 3.0 files start with the introductory Setup notes in the preface, or refer to your Money Users Guide.

The Money screen

An example of the Money screen is shown in Fig. 1-1. Basically, the Money screen is made up of a title line, followed by a menu bar containing the words file, edit, list, report options, window, and help. A second title line follows that displays either Account Book or Checks & Forms, with the rest of the screen filled with a picture of your checkbook register or an actual check form. Near the bottom of the screen, you usually see icons, which are small pictures (graphics) that represent other windows that you can activate. The last line of the screen presents a prompt line that contains suggestions about what actions are necessary to proceed with work in the Money environment.

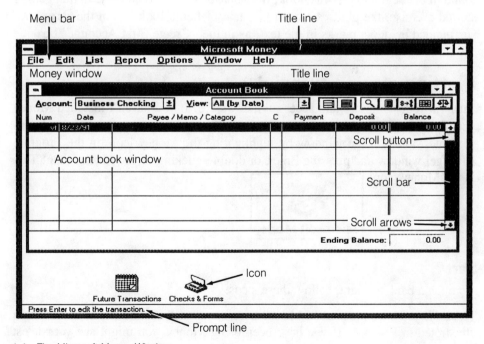

1-1 The Microsoft Money Window

Your job

This first chapter cannot include all there is to know about the Windows or Money screen layout. To get started, I will describe only the most basic features of the package and name only the action or command that is necessary to accomplish the task at hand. You will see many items on the screen that can't be covered in a fast introduction. So for starters, follow the step-by-step instructions exactly to experience the power of Money in a very short period of time.

Keyboard or mouse

In this first chapter, I will direct your actions with both keyboard and mouse notation. Keystrokes are indicated by an initial cap; for example, pressing the escape key is noted as Esc. If two keystrokes are needed, they are indicated by an expression like Ctrl−W, which means to hold down the Ctrl key while tapping the W key.

Mouse instructions are expressed by phrases such as "click the word File." This means to bring the screen arrow to the word File and click the mouse button. If a screen button should be selected, I will indicate the button with an alternate font, as in click the Ok button.

Please be sure to read the Typographical conventions section that can be found in the beginning of this book, if you haven't done so already. In this getting started exercise, the phrases or words that you should look for on the screen are surrounded by quote marks in the text, as in the "Create First Account" box.

Getting started tutorial

Turn on your computer and access Windows 3.0. If you haven't installed Money yet, first follow the procedures for setup in the introductory pages of this book. Activate Money in the window by highlighting the Money icon on the Program Manager window and pressing Enter, or double-clicking on the Money icon. This is the Money icon:

Microsoft Money

Part A

To open a bank account, follow these steps.

Note If you have never used Money before, you will see the Money window as illustrated in Fig. 1-1. If you have been using Money, you might see your latest transactions on screen. In either case, you should establish a separate play file on your disk for practice work. That's what steps 1 through 3 are for.

1. Select the File command on the top menu line by pressing Alt−F or by clicking on the word File. Then select the New option by pressing N or by clicking on that word.

2. Type the word sample to indicate that this is the name of the new file you want to create. This action causes the "∗.mny" characters in the File Name box to be overwritten. Press the Enter key or click on the Ok button to go on to the next step.

3. If you have been working with another set of accounts recently, a "Backup" box will appear to warn you to back up those accounts. Press Alt−N or click on the No button to indicate that no backup is needed at this time. More is discussed later on making backups.

4. You'll see a box in the middle of your screen labelled "Set Up New File." Press the Alt−B keys, or click on Business Categories in the Start With list. This tells Money to establish a list of categories that are appropriate for business record keeping. These categories also work fine for personal record keeping. Press the Enter key or click Ok to go on.

5. You'll hear disk noises and after a while the screen displays the "Create First Account" box. Read the message within this box and press Enter, or click Ok to go on.

Note To select commands and options on the screen using the keyboard, the Alt key is used with various letter keys. Many words and phrases on the screen have one underlined letter. For example, the B in Business Categories was underlined to let you know that pressing Alt−B will select that option.

6. In the "Create New Account" box, the screen is pulsating at the end of the line labelled "Account Name." Type Business Checking and press Enter, or click Ok, to go on. As you type the account name, the existing word "Checking" disappears.

7. Then in the "Opening Balance" box, enter the beginning balance in the business checking account. For simplicity's sake, assume you have just started a new business and the beginning balance is zero. Type the number 0 (be careful not to type the alphabetic letter o) and press Enter, or click Ok, to go on.

8. At this point, you should see the Money working window that was displayed in Fig. 1-1. If you have used Money before and modified the layout of the screen, the computer remembers the layout that you designed and your screen might look somewhat different than Fig. 1-1.

Part B   Getting help

1. Once you start experimenting on your own, you should know how to get some on-screen help as you work in Money. Press Alt−H, or click on the

menu word Help, to enter the help system. (You also can press the F1 key to access help.) Press Enter or click on the word "Index" to see a list of help topics.

2. You can press the Up or Down arrows to look through this list, or click on the scroll bar to the right of the index to move around in the list. Press the Down arrow key, or click on the scroll bar, until you see the subtitle "Reference" followed by the word "Definitions." Then press the Tab key until the word definitions is highlighted. Press Enter or click on the word "Definitions," and a complete list of defined words will appear.

3. These words are in alphabetical order from A to Z. The list is quite long, so feel free to look through it using the same technique explained in step 2. To view a specific definition, highlight the word by pressing the Tab key and then press Enter, or click on the desired word.

4. When you are finished browsing through definitions, return to the index by pressing Alt−I or by clicking on the Index box at the top of the Help window. Then press Tab to highlight "Working With Accounts" and press Enter, or click on that phrase.

5. On the next list, press Tab to highlight the phrase "Entering Transactions" and press Enter, or click on that phrase.

6. On the next list, press Tab to highlight the phrase "Introduction to Entering Transactions" and press Enter, or click on that phrase.

7. Read through the screens that describe the basic procedure for entering transactions. Use the Up and Down arrow keys, or click on the scroll bar, to move through this procedure. Any time you see a word or phrase in a contrasting color to the rest of the help text, you can Tab to that phrase and press Enter, or click on it, to reveal more specific information about it.

8. To remove the help information from your screen, press Alt−F4, or double-click on the command button. (This is the [-] symbol at the left end of the title line that reads "Microsoft Money Help - MSMONEY.HLP" at the top of the help window.)

Note If you press Alt−F4 too hard, the keys repeat themselves and you might get kicked out of Money and be back at the Windows Program Manager. If this happens double-click the Program Manager icon and double-click the Money icon again, and you'll be back in Money.

Part C Entering transactions

1. Once you remove the help window as instructed above, you should be back on the first line of the Account Book Window. Your place in this window is indicated by the reverse video used to highlight one of the lines on

the screen. You will be pressing Tab a lot to move around in your accounts, and must press Tab now to get started.

Note Our first transaction is a receipt of $2000 from the Bigtime Corporation for a consulting contract we are working on for them.

2. The first field is for a check number or reference number. We want to enter a deposit that has no number, so just type Dep to indicate a deposit, and do not press Enter. Press Tab to move to the "Date" field.

3. Money always displays the current date in the date field, which is handy when you are entering your own transactions daily. For this tutorial, however, we want to enter December transactions. Type 12/1 (for December 1) and press Tab. Money fills in the year for you. This "year" is based on the actual year and month when you are sitting at the computer and whether December is within four months of that. Money uses a date default rule that supplies the current year up to four months back and eight months forward. So if your current month is January, February, or April, Money assigns December to last year; otherwise, it assigns it to the current year. Don't be concerned about the year at this point.

4. Type Bigtime Corporation as the payee (the company you are receiving money from), and press Tab.

    If you make an error in a field, press Shift−Tab to move back to the field, then simply backspace and retype the data in that field. You also can click the mouse in any field to move there. If you want to scrap a whole transaction after you've entered a few fields, press Esc to get a clean slate. If you mistakenly press Enter before you have entered data in all fields, press the Up arrow to rehighlight the incomplete transaction, then press Tab to reach the field that needs attention, or click there.

5. Press Tab again to move from the "Payment" field to the "Deposit" field, because this is not a payment. Type 2000 in the "Deposit" field and press Tab.

6. Type For Planning Consulting in the "Memo" field and press Tab.

7. It is very important to categorize every transaction that you enter in your accounts. When you move to the "Category" field, a list of categories begins to appear below the field. You can press the Down arrow to move through the list, or click on the tiny scroll bar to the right of the category list. We want to categorize this $2000 deposit as revenue, so highlight the word "Revenue" on the list and see that the word also appears in the Category field.

8. When you are ready to record a completed transaction, press Enter. When you do, a quick beep tells you that the computer recorded that transaction.

Notice that the "Balance" column is filled in and the next section of the account book is highlighted. Money is waiting for additional transactions.

Part D   Entering checks

1. We are now ready to enter data for a check payment. In the "Num" field type a P. The word "print" is displayed in the field to indicate that an actual check is to be printed later for this transaction. This will be changed to a check number when Money prints the check. Press Tab to move on.

2. Press the + key to increment the date by one and press Tab. Pressing the + or − keys increments the date up or down. You also could have typed 12/2 at the keyboard.

3. Type Cree Advertising Agency in the Payee field and press Tab.

4. Type 720. as the "Payment" amount and press Tab twice to move past the "Deposit" field to the "Memo" field.

5. Type Ad Contract in New England in the Memo field and press Tab.

6. Press the Down arrow key until the word Advertising is highlighted and press Enter to record this transaction.

Note   The business categories that Money provides include most categories and subcategories that a typical small business needs. See Appendix C for a full list of these, and sidetrack with me at the next step to see how you can view them on screen.

7. (Sidetrack) Notice that the letter L is underlined in the word "List" on the Main menu at the top of the screen. Press Alt −L to select the "List" command or click on the word List. Press C to select the Category List or click on that choice. Press the Down arrow until the word "Automobile/Truck" is highlighted in the Category list at the upper left, or you can click on the [↓] button of the scroll bar, then click on the "Automobile/Truck" item.

   Notice that a box in the lower left corner displays a list of subcategories that have been specified for the Automobile/Truck category. Press, or click, the Down arrow slowly and observe which other categories have subcategories. This Category List window is also used to enter new categories, edit category names, enter budgets and delete unwanted categories. Press Enter, or click on the Close button to remove the Category List window and return to the account book.

8. To record a check that applies to more than one category, you can take advantage of a feature called Split Transactions. Let's assume we want to record a check to our insurance agent for $640 but part of this is for auto insurance and the rest is for liability insurance. Type a P in the Num field and press Tab. Type 12/4 in the Date field and press Tab. Type Ritter Agency in the Payee field and press Tab.

9. Press Ctrl—S to reveal the Split Transaction window. In this window, you will type a category, subcategory, and memo before the dollar amount that applies to that category.

○ Type Ins in the Category field and you will see that Money finds a category called Insurance and inserts the full name in the field. It is only necessary to type the first few letters of a category and Money will fill in the rest for you. This is a feature called SmartFill.

○ Press Tab to move to the Subcategory field and Money displays any subcategories of the Insurance category. Type Aut and "Automobile" will appear in the Subcategory field. Press Tab and type Semiannual Auto Premium in the Description field. Press Tab and type 240. in the Amount field. Press Tab to move to the next line.

○ Type a quotation mark (") in the Category field and Money repeats the category of the previous line. Press Tab to the next field, and type Lia, so Money will fill in Liability as the subcategory. Press Tab and type Semiannual Property Insurance. Press Tab and type 400. as the amount. Press Tab and notice that the total amount near the bottom of your screen has accumulated to $640.

○ Also notice that there are three buttons in the bottom of the Split Transaction window—the *D* in Done is underlined. Press Alt—D to indicate that you are done with the split categories. A Spend or Receive box is displayed with the "Spend" option already checked. Just press Enter to go on. You must press Enter one more time to actually complete this transaction. Notice that the "Balance" column has automatically been updated.

Part E

Here's a quick tour of the Money window.

1. Let's take a little break from the keyboard to explore the Money window. With your mouse, click on the 12/1 transaction and notice that you can return to any transaction by simply clicking on it and then pressing Tab and Shift—Tab to move around the fields to make changes, or click on any specific field. Press Enter or click on another transaction to complete any changes you make.

2. The Balance after each transaction is automatically calculated as you enter transactions, and recalculated when you make changes. If a transaction mentions the word Split in the Category field, you can click on that transaction and then click the icon at the upper right of the window that displays one large $ sign followed by → and two smaller $ $. This is the Split Transaction icon, and clicking on it causes the Split categories to be displayed. Click on the Done button to return to the account book.

3. You can activate any of the menu words by clicking on them. Click on the Options word and then click on the phrase Top Line View. You will see that the account book has become compressed with only the top line of each transaction in view. This helps you search your records when you have a lot of transactions. To return to full view, click on Options again and then click Entire Transaction View.

Part F

To print checks, follow these steps.

1. Because you've got the mouse at hand, we'll use it for requesting printed checks. The steps in this section also could be accomplished easily using keystrokes. Click on the word File, then Print Setup on the menus. Click on the option button in front of the words "Check Printing." Click on the option button in front of the words "Default Printer." Notice that the Check Types box contains the word "Standard." This means that standard $8^1/2$ inch wide checks will print out on continuous feed dot matrix paper. If you are using a laser printer, we will adjust for that later. Click on Ok to return to the account book.

2. Click on the word File on the Menu line; then click on the Print Checks line of the drop down menu. A "Print Checks" window appears, which is full of information about your printer and the checks that are about to be printed. Read this window.

3. Assume that all of the print information is correct and that you have checks loaded in your printer (plain paper is fine for this tutorial). Click on the Ok button and the checks will be printed.

    If there is any problem with your printer, you will see a warning message. Click Ok then Reprint, and then click Cancel to skip this step and ignore the next two steps.

4. Once your checks have printed, you will see the Confirm Printing window asking if you'd like to reprint. Click the Continue button to go on.

5. Notice that the word "Print" in the Num column has been replaced with check #101 and 102 on the entries for the advertising and insurance checks.

Part G

Unusual transactions can be handled by following these steps.

1. We have just received a notice from the bank that they are deducting $22.50 from our account for the new checks we ordered. This is a payment from our account to be recorded in the account book. Press the

Ctrl—End keys to move to the next available line in the book, or click there with the mouse.

2. Type adj and press Tab. Type 12/7 and press Tab again. Type Chase First Bank and press Tab. Type 22.5 and press Tab twice. Type New Checks and press Tab. Type Bank Charges and press Enter. Once you get the hang of it, data entry is a snap.

Part H   Producing reports

1. To print a copy of your account book thus far, press Alt—R and then press R (or click Reports and then click Register Report) on the Money Menu. The "Register Report" appears, but it covers only the period from the beginning of the current year to the current date; that is, the date you are actually reading this book. Notice the dates on the second line of the report. If the current date is earlier than December 7, the December transactions we just entered are not included on this report yet. Of course, we can remedy that.

2. Press Alt—C, or click the Customize button, and you can change the dates included on the report. In the "Customize Register Report" window, press Alt—O (or click on the box to the right of the word To in the bottom left corner) and enter 12/31. Press Enter or click on View to redisplay the Register report.

3. Because the report is too wide to fit within the window in its entirety, you might want to press the directional arrows to see the hidden columns. If you want to print a copy of this report, press Alt—P or click the Print button. A "Print Report" box appears, which you can accept by pressing Enter or clicking Ok. Press Enter or click the Close button to return to the Account Book window.

4. Probably the most important business report is the Income & Expense report. To see this report, press Alt—R then press I, or click on Reports, then Income & Expense. Again, if your current date is earlier than December 7, you won't see all of the data in your account showing on the report.

5. Press Alt—C, or click the Customize button, and you can change the dates included on the report. In the "Customize Register Report" window, press Alt—O (or click on the box next to the word To in the bottom left corner) and enter 12/31. Press Enter or click on View to redisplay the Income & Expense report. Press the Down arrow, or click on the scroll bar, to see the bottom line. This is Net Income for a business.

6. If you want to print a copy of this report, press Alt—P, or click the Print button. When the Print Report window appears, press Enter or click Ok to proceed. Experiment with the other reports if you want; they are dis-

cussed later in this book. Press Enter, or click on Close, to return to the account book.

Part I Using simple budgets

1. Budget data is entered at the Category List window. Press Alt–L, then C (or click List then Category List) to access the "Category List" window. Notice that in the bottom right hand corner of this window, there is a Budget box.

2. Press the Down arrow to highlight the "Revenue" category, or click on Revenue. Press Alt–O, or click on the box next to "Amount," to move the highlight to the budget amount field.

3. Enter 4500. and then press Alt–L to return to the list, or click anywhere on the list. This enters $4500 as the monthly budget for "Revenue," because the "Monthly Budget" option was already checked.

4. For the next and succeeding items, press the Down arrow or use the scroll bars and click to highlight the category you want to budget. Highlight the "Advertising" category, press Alt–O, or click the Amount field, and enter 800. for the monthly budget.

5. Return to the category list by pressing Alt–L, or clicking on the list, and highlight "Bank Charges." Press Alt–O, or click on Amount, and enter 20 for the monthly budget.

6. Return to the category list (Alt–L, or click on the list) and highlight "Insurance." For Insurance, we want to budget amounts in the subcategories, and only want to budget insurance payments for June and December. This requires a Custom Budget entry. Press Alt–U to get to the "Subcategory List," and then the Down arrow, or click on "Automobile." Press Alt–B, or click on "Custom Budget" to place a mark next to that option.

7. A Custom Budget window will open where you can type individual monthly amounts. Press Tab five times, or click on "Jun," to highlight the June field. Enter 240. and press Tab repeatedly again to move to the "Dec" field. You also could click on that field. Type 240. followed by Enter, or click Ok, to return to the Category List window.

8. Return to the subcategory list (Alt–U) and highlight "Liability," or click on "Liability." Press Alt–B, or click on "Custom Budget," then Tab to both the Jun and Dec fields to enter 400. in each of these two months. Press Enter, or click Ok, to go on.

9. Press Alt–L to return to the Category List box and be sure that "Insurance" is still highlighted. We also must enter the total insurance budget in the overall Insurance category. Press Alt–B, or click on "Custom Budget," to enter a custom budget. Press Alt–S, or click the Total Subcatego-

ries button at the bottom right. Notice that $640 appears in Jun and Dec, and an annual total of $1280 appears above the monthly budgets. Press Enter, or click Ok, to return to the category list. Press enter again, or click Close, to return to the account book.

10. Now let's take a look at the Budget report where these budgets are used. Press Alt−R, then B, (or click on "Reports," then "Budget Reports"). The default Budget report that appears records monthly data through your current month. December might not be on this first report. We need to customize it.

11. Press Alt−C, or click on Customize, then press Alt−M, or click on "From" in the Date Range box. Type 12/1 and press Tab to move to the To field. Type 12/31 and press Enter to view the Budget Report for only December. You might have to use the arrow keys, or click on the scroll bar to see the whole report.

12. If you want to print a copy of the report press Alt−P, or click the Print button, and press Enter or click Ok to verify the Print Report box. Press Enter or click Close to return to the account book.

Part J   Reconciling your bank statement

1. Press Alt−O, then press B (or click on "Options" and then "Balance Account") to open the Balance Business Checking window. Let's assume we have received the following simplified bank statement.

```
Statement Date:   12/10/xx
Beginning Balance: $0
Cleared Checks:    #101 $720.00
Bank Charges:      New Cks  $22.50
                   Service    8.20
Cleared Deposits:  12/2 $2000.00
Ending Balance:    $1249.30
```

2. The starting balance in this account was zero, so press Tab, or click on "Ending Balance" to move to that field. Type 1249.30 and press Tab to move to the Statement Date field. Type 12/10 and press Tab to move to the Service Charge field. Type 8.20 and press Tab. Type Bank and press Tab. We are finished with this screen so press Enter or click Continue to go on.

3. Now you must specify in your account book which transactions have been cleared by the bank. The first transaction, which was just entered by the computer based on the service charge we specified, is already marked with a "C" in the C (Cleared) column. Press the Down arrow, or click on

the "Cree Advertising" payment, to highlight this line. Press the Space-bar, or click on the C column of the Cree payment, and notice that the Cree payment has been marked "C." Press the Down arrow, and press the Spacebar (or click on the C column of the "ChaseFirst" line) to mark that transaction as cleared. Lastly, press the Spacebar, or click in the C Column, for the "Bigtime Corporation" deposit.

Note If you incorrectly mark any transactions, simply return to the line where the error is, and press the Spacebar again (or click on the C to remove it).

4. While you were performing step 3, Money was reconciling your account. Notice the status report in the lower part of the window. You are being informed that the account is in balance. The statement balance is $1249.30, and the items that you just cleared amount to $1249.30. The only outstanding item is the $640. payment to Ritter Agency.

Note If this were a more complicated account and bank statement, and the two did not balance at this stage, Money would provide a lot of help to get things balanced. More about this is discussed later.

5. Press Alt−N, or click Finish, to indicate that you are finished with this window. Then press Enter or click Ok to return to the account book. Notice that the account book now contains "R" in the cleared column to indicate that these items have been reconciled to the bank statement.

Part K

To make a backup copy of your work, follow these steps.

1. Everything we've entered in Money has been saved on your hard disk as you moved from transaction to transaction. However, it is wise to save an extra copy on a diskette frequently. Insert a formatted disk in your A: disk drive that can be used for receiving a backup copy of your Money file.

2. Press Alt−F and then press B, or else click on "File" and then "Backup." A Backup confirmation window is displayed, indicating that the backup copy will be sent to "a: \ sample.bak".

3. Press Enter to select "Yes," or click on Yes.

4. If you have performed this backup procedure before, you will be asked to confirm that you want to overwrite any existing backups. Press Alt−Y, or click Yes.

5. To exit from Money, press Alt−F, then press X, or click on "File" and then "Exit," and repeat steps 3 and 4 above to be sure you have a backup.

Congratulations! Not only have you reconciled the account, but you've finished a long and exacting tutorial. I hope you have learned a lot about Money.

Summary

Through this introductory chapter and tutorial, you have learned how to set up a new account, enter transactions and budgets, and print various reports from your records. You've also discovered that bank reconciliations are going to be a snap with Money. I hope that now you are ready to step back and absorb some of the underlying concepts about Money and Windows 3.0. Chapters 2 and 3 will build on this foundation.

2
CHAPTER

Basic Microsoft Money and Windows procedures

Now that you've got a feel for how to access Money and what to use it for, let's step back a minute to look at some of the things we've learned. The Windows environment is rich in friendly symbols and hints to lead you around. What you learn about Money today will help you in all other Windows applications, like Calendar and Notepad that come with Windows, or with Word and Excel, which are sold separately. For example, the use of a dialog box is basic to all Windows applications. You've seen them already in the overview tutorial of chapter 1. Do you remember the "dialog" that takes place in Fig. 2-1?

Also, the use of menus and the action required to make choices from them are a common technique of all computer software. Thus, understanding menus will enhance your computer skills. The understanding of basic terminology and finger actions will make all of your future computer ventures more enjoyable.

You won't need to be sitting at the computer to read this chapter. The figures included in this chapter will remind you of the screens we used in the warm up.

By the way, have you tried playing Solitaire yet? This is an excellent way to practice mouse and finger aerobics in Windows, and it lets you explore the uses of menus and dialog boxes and their contents. Just double-click Solitaire on your Windows Program Manager screen, and click Help, then Procedures when the Solitaire window opens to read the rules of the game. Have fun!

```
┌────────────────────────────────────────────────────────────────┐
│ ▄▄▄                    Print Checks                             │
├────────────────────────────────────────────────────────────────┤
│ Printer:  Default Printer (IBM Graphics)        ┌──────────────┐│
│ Check:    Voucher                               │     OK       ││
│ Account:  Business Checking                     └──────────────┘│
│ ┌─ Print Range ──────────────────────────────┐  ┌──────────────┐│
│ │ There is 1 check for $720.00 to be printed.│  │   Cancel     ││
│ │                                            │  └──────────────┘│
│ │ ◉ Print All                                │  ┌──────────────┐│
│ │ ○ Select Checks...                         │  │  Print Test  ││
│ │                                            │  └──────────────┘│
│ └────────────────────────────────────────────┘  ┌──────────────┐│
│                                                  │    Help      ││
│    1. Make sure that checks are loaded in your printer.  └─────┘│
│    2. Type the check number of the first check loaded in your   │
│       printer:                                         │ 107 │  │
└────────────────────────────────────────────────────────────────┘
```

2-1 Print Checks dialog box

What are windows?

Think of a small window that you look out of from a city apartment. Through that window, you might be able to see a corner of the building next to you, the street between you and that next building, and a tree on the corner, but there's a lot more of the city and the world beyond your view from the window. If you could enlarge your window, you'd see a lot more of your city. If you could zoom in on the next building, you might be able to see some of the activity that goes on inside it.

A computer window is just like that. It is a restricted view of a very large array of activities and possibilities beyond what you see on your screen. The computer screen is called a *Window*, and it can be split into many subwindows. In the Microsoft Windows 3.0 playground, you can look through many windows, and keep them available nearby to switch from one window to the next. Each window lets you look in on some task, document, or file. For example, when you open a window to the calculator, you can see and work with a calculator while the contents of a check register is visible nearby, and later paste the calculator results into the check register.

On a computer screen, windows are usually layered on top of one another, so you can see some part of all the windows in the background. This allows you to click on a window in the background in order to bring it to the foreground.

Application windows

There are two kinds of windows: application windows and document windows. The first Money window that you see is an example of an application window; notice the title at the top of this window, and notice that it includes a Control button, menu bar, Minimize and Maximize buttons, scroll bars, a cursor, and a mouse pointer (Fig. 2-2). I'll explain each of these in the next few pages.

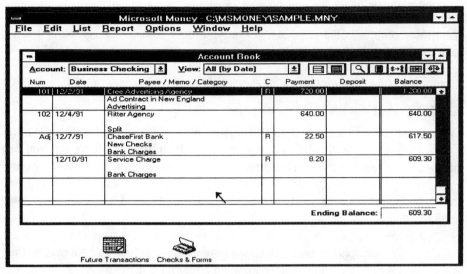

2-2 The opening Microsoft Money window

Document windows

A document window, on the other hand, has no menu bar or current file name and always appears as a subwindow inside an application window. For example, when you ask Money to display your account book, it opens the document (account book) in another window inside the Money window. In Fig. 2-3, notice that the account book does not have its own menu bar or file name, but it does have its own control menu button, minimize and maximize buttons, and sometimes a scroll bar.

Account Book							
Account: Business Checking	View: All (by Date)						
Num	Date	Payee / Memo / Category	C	Payment	Deposit	Balance	
101	12/2/91	Cree Advertising Agency	R	720.00		1,280.00	
		Ad Contract in New England					
		Advertising					
102	12/4/91	Ritter Agency		640.00		640.00	
		Split					
Adj	12/7/91	ChaseFirst Bank	R	22.50		617.50	
		New Checks					
		Bank Charges					
	12/10/91	Service Charge	R	8.20		609.30	
		Bank Charges					
				Ending Balance:		609.30	

2-3 Account Book window

Mouse pointer

The mouse pointer is the large arrow that you move around the screen by rolling your mouse on the desk. In our chapter 1 computer exercise, we had plenty of practice with it!

Doing windows

Even if you always said you didn't "do windows" you might change your mind after a few sessions with Money and Windows 3.0. In this environment, you can hide windows (even if they aren't dirty), you can resize them, move them around on the screen to suit your taste, and best of all, you can cut something out of one window and paste it into another. We'll experience some of these things in later chapters.

For a brief example of some of this window power, let's assume that we were working with our appointment calendar at the time we called up Money, but then needed to go back to the calendar to confirm an appointment. By our own choice, we can leave both the calendar and Money on the screen at the same time in two windows that we control the size of. Figure 2-4 illustrates what the screen might look like once you size the Money window and activate your appointment calendar. The Windows Program Manager is always in the background and indicated by the icon that pictures three small windows topped with a C:.

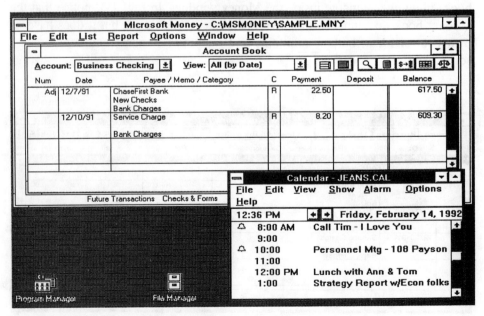

2-4 Customized Money window with calendar

Title bars

A title bar is a strip across the top of any window that contains the window's title and the document or file name that is displayed in that window. In Fig. 2-4, the Money title bar shouts its name and indicates that a file named SAMPLE.MNY is currently displayed. The characters C:\ MSMONEY \ let you know the location (directory) on your disk where the MSMONEY file is stored. The strip labelled CALENDAR-JEANS.CAL above the Calendar window is that window's title bar. The title bar of the active (selected) window is always highlighted. In Fig. 2-4, the Calendar title bar is highlighted in reverse video, because it was the selected window at that moment.

Control buttons

Each window can be enlarged (called maximized) or reduced to an icon (called minimized). At the end of this chapter, there is a full discussion of icons; you've seen them quite a bit already. They are the small pictures (graphical representations) of a program or file like the Money icon on the Windows Program Manager screen.

Controlling a window

You can control the size and location of the windows within your screen by using control buttons. A *button* on the Windows screen is a small square or rectangle that contains a symbol like an arrowhead or a bar. For example, the control button, which always appears at the left end of a title or menu bar (see Fig. 2-2 and 2-3 and 2-4), looks like this:

By pointing to this button and clicking (or pressing Alt − spacebar), you are asking that the Control Menu be displayed. In most cases this provides you with a cascading menu of window control choices (e.g., moving the window, closing the file, or switching to another application). You then can make a selection from the menu as described under the "Menus" section of this chapter. If you double-click a control button, you are asking the computer to close the active window, or completely close or exit from Windows 3.0.

I am following the convention in this book of always expressing the names of buttons in an alternate font. In chapter 1, I referred to the OK Button as Ok.

Other commonly used control buttons are:

This is the Minimize button: click on it to shrink the current window to minimum size, which usually means to an icon.

This is the Maximize button: click on it when a window is small in order to explode that window to maximum size.

This is the Restore button: click on it to restore a maximized window to its previous size.

Command buttons

Often in Money and other applications, you will see small rectangles with words within them like Ok, Cancel, Help, Print, and others. These are called command buttons, and when you click on them you are commanding the computer to take action.

A single click is all it takes. For example the Ok button is clicked when you want to confirm the contents of a dialog box and tell the computer to go on to the next activity.

In Money this would be necessary after you have requested a printed report. You'll be presented with a Print Report box naming your printer and indicating which pages will be printed. If you are satisfied with these settings you can just click on Ok to start the printing.

Focus on a button

When the words in a command button are surrounded by a dotted outline, it means that the focus is on that button. If your hands are on the keyboard, pressing Enter accomplishes the same action as clicking on that command button. This focus is provided so that you don't have to grab the mouse while entering text and numbers in your transactions. Just keep your hands on the keyboard and press Enter.

Help buttons

The Help button should be used often. Click on it whenever you want to see explanations about the current window. These explanations help you understand what is needed to continue with the activity you are working on, and will lead you to discoveries about related parts of the application as well.

Just point to this and click; you'll find a book open to just the right page to help you through an activity. While you are using the Help windows, you'll see Index, Back, Browse, and Search command buttons, which you can click to move you around the help topics.

Microsoft menus

A menu is a list of choices that are available to you. In Money these choices are usually listed across the first line of a window (called the main menu), or they cascade below one of the menu words on the first line, once you choose a menu word. Choose a main menu word by clicking on that word, then choose your next option from the cascading menu that is revealed.

For example, Fig. 2-5 shows the menu we used to access the split transaction feature of Money. After you clicked on the word Edit of the main menu line, you then clicked Split Transaction on the cascaded list.

2-5 The Edit menu for transaction editing

Edit	List	Report	Options
Undo			Ctrl+Z
Cut			Ctrl+X
Copy			Ctrl+C
Paste			Ctrl+V
Delete Transaction			
Void Transaction			
Split Transaction...			Ctrl+S
Schedule in Future...			Ctrl+E
Mark as Cleared			Ctrl+M
Find...			Ctrl+F

One thing leads to another and . . .

Sometimes a selection from one menu will lead to further menus or boxes. Notice that some items on the Edit menu in Fig. 2-5 have three periods after them. When you see menu items like this (e.g., Split Transactions) it means that choosing this item will cause a dialog box to appear (explained in the next section).

When a menu item is followed by a key notation (e.g., Ctrl−S), you can press the Ctrl and S keys together to access this menu item without displaying the menu at all. For example, once you've been around Money for a while, you'll want to use the shortcut of pressing Ctrl−S while working in the account book, instead of fumbling the mouse to point around the top of the screen. Don't you hate it when the mouse pointer jumps off the edge of the screen?

If a menu item appears dim, like the Undo item in Fig. 2-5, it means that this item is not available at the current time. In this case, the dimmed Undo choice simply means that no transaction has been cut or pasted, so there is nothing to be undone or changed. Once you cut or paste a transaction, the Undo item will not be dimmed.

To cancel a menu choice click anywhere outside the menu in the active window, or press the Esc key.

Keyboard notes

If your hands are on the keyboard anyway, because you have been typing transaction data, you might want to leave them there when using a menu. To choose an item from the Money Main Menu hold down the Alt key while pressing the first letter of the menu word (e.g., press Alt−R to select the Reports menu word). Once a cascading menu appears, you can press the underlined letter of your menu choice (e.g., press the S key to choose Summary Report). Notice in Fig. 2-6 that a letter is underlined in each of the menu items of the cascading menu. It is also handy to note that when you get to a dialog box that requires no changes, like the one that would appear after you have selected the Reports option described above, the Close button is already highlighted. This means that the button appears brighter than the other buttons, or on a color screen, it is displayed in a different color. Pressing the Enter key while the Close button is highlighted yields the same results as clicking on it. Appendix A provides a handy list of keystrokes used for various Money menu items.

2-6 The File menu

Dialog boxes

A dialog box is used just as its name implies. We use them to have a dialog or conversation with the computer. In other words, the computer is asking you for information, and you reply by typing something or clicking a button in a dialog box. Both the File Open window and the Print Report window in Money are good examples of dialog boxes. Dialog boxes can contain command buttons, List boxes, Text boxes, Option buttons, and/or Check boxes. Command buttons were explained previously, but we'll explore each of these other items now. Examples of dialog boxes are shown in the next few figures (Figs. 2-7, 2-8).

List boxes

The File Open dialog box that appears when you ask Money to call up a specific checking account contains a list of items for you to choose from. This is a list box. You would see a window similar to the one in Fig. 2-7. In this case there are three accounts to choose from. They are listed in what is called a list box appearing inside the dialog box. Point to the account in this list box you want, for example the Personal file, and double-click the mouse.

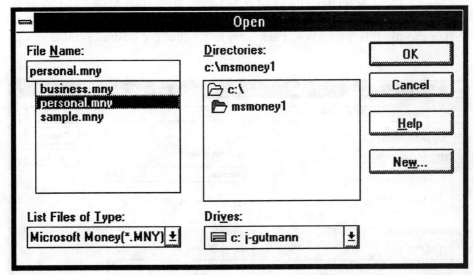

2-7 File Open list box

If a List box contains a longer list than will fit in the current window, you will see a scroll bar at the right border of the box. You can view the rest of the list by clicking on that bar, or pressing the Down Arrow key. More about scroll bars is discussed further on.

Sometimes you will see a field, or an item on a list, that is followed by a button that contains a down arrow with a line below it like this:

This means that there are more choices available than just the one showing on that line. Click on this button and a list box will drop down from that button. Then click on other choices in the list, or scroll further down the list if a scroll bar appears. An example of this is the Money Category List that appears below the category field when you are entering transactions.

Text boxes

The Customize Report box is an example of another type of box that sometimes appears within a dialog box. This is called a text box because it displays textual information that you can alter. You might want to change some information by entering text in some of the fields within the dialog box. For example, if you wanted to restrict the printing of a register report to the dates that fall between August 1, 1992 and August 14, 1992, you would need to alter the From and To dates in the Date Range text box shown in Fig. 2-8. To do this you would first click anywhere within the From box and observe that the cursor has just changed to a solid vertical bar at the left of that box. Delete the displayed date and type 8/1. Press the Tab key and type 8/14 in the To box. If you do not need any more changes within this dialog box, click View to produce the desired printed report.

2-8 Customize Report dialog box

Check boxes

Another way that options are presented to you within a dialog box is with check boxes. These boxes differ from the option buttons discussed above in that they provide you with two or more options that can all be engaged (or checked) at the same time. With option buttons, it's an either/or situation; with check boxes you can check as many choices as you'd like.

Items to be checked

As an example, the Include Fields box in Fig. 2-9 lets you specify which fields to

2-9 Include Fields dialog box

```
┌─ Include Fields ──────────────────────┐
│                                        │
│   ☐ M̲emo          ☒ C̲ategory          │
│                                        │
│   ☐ Accou̲nt                            │
│                                        │
│   ☒ Cleared Fla̲g                       │
│                                        │
└────────────────────────────────────────┘
```

include on a report. This box is just a small part of the Customize Report dialog box.

Notice that the Include Fields box lists four items preceded by open squares. Some of the boxes have X's in them. In this example, the Category field and the Cleared field will appear on the custom report, because each of these have a check in front of them. If you want to add an X to an empty check box, just click on that box. If you want to delete the X from any item, point to the X and click on it to turn it off. On the keyboard you can press the Spacebar to turn the X on and off.

Single check marks

Once in a while you will find a solo check box that allows only a yes or no (X or no X). Click the box to add or remove an X. You see this type of check box when you exit Windows completely. Just above the Ok and Cancel buttons, you can see the Save Changes check box. Click it if you want to save any Windows design changes you made during your work session or leave it blank if you don't need to save them. Don't worry about saving Money changes and additions as you exit Windows, because all work you do in Money is saved automatically as you move around within Money. You don't have to tell the computer to save these things again as you exit from Windows.

Report boxes

Often in Money you will work within a special type of box called the report box. The report box, as you might have guessed, displays a Money report that you requested. These reports contain various views of your data, either in detail or summarized at your request. The unique thing about them is that they have a tall, skinny dialog box attached to them on the right that contains option buttons for your use, like Fonts or Customize. See Fig. 2-10.

After viewing a report, simply click on the Close option button to return to a previous window or proceed with a task like printing or customizing. If your hands are already on the keyboard, just press Esc to return to your previous work.

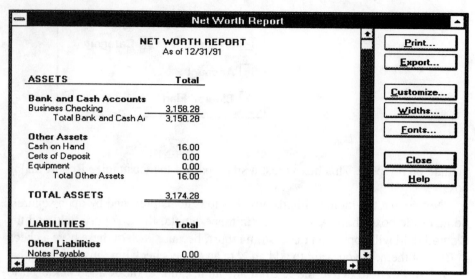

2-10 Net Worth report in the Report box

Option buttons

Sometimes, as in the Customize Report dialog box, you might choose between several options that are available. You do this using option buttons. For example, you can specify whether you want to include all transactions or just selected transactions on a custom report. The Include Transaction box in Fig. 2-11 contains two round option buttons. Notice how one of the buttons is already on (that is, it has a dot inside it). To choose the Select Transactions option, simply click on the round button in front of that phrase. The button will appear to be turned on, while the All Transactions button is turned off. You would then proceed to specify which transactions you wanted to select for your custom report.

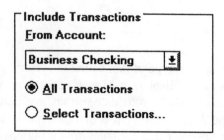

2-11 Include Transactions Options box

Scroll bars

The scroll bars within a window appear as thick bars to the right and at the bottom of a window. The bars usually have arrow buttons on the ends of them, with a small blank box somewhere along the bar, called a scroll box. You'll see the meaning of these terms by referring to the labels in Fig. 2-12. These tools are fun to use, because they are the key to looking beyond just a tiny window into a very big "city" or "world."

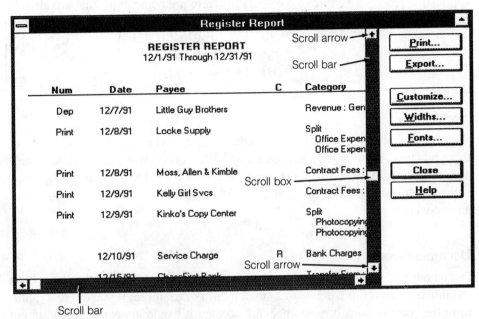

2-12   Register report in the middle of a month's transactions

Single clicks

The window in Fig. 2-12 shows just a tiny portion of a register report, which happens to be two printed pages long. Only about 1/3 of each printed page can be displayed in the window at one time. Clicking on either arrow button of the scroll bar moves the window display in that direction. The display moves a line at a time, unless you press and hold the mouse button to move it continuously.

Dragging

Clicking and dragging the scroll box allows you to jump to a specific point in the entire document or list without seeing each line. For example, if I dragged the scroll box to about the middle of the vertical scroll bar and then released the mouse button, lines from the middle of the report would be displayed. The report used in Fig. 2-12 contains categories from all of my accounts for one month. After dragging the scroll box half way down the scroll bar, the categories in the middle of the report are then revealed. These same principles apply to the horizontal scroll bar.

Icons

Icons are small pictures used to represent applications (like Money, the Notepad, or Microsoft Excel), documents, programs, or tools. An icon presents a picture that resembles the task performed by that application; for example, the Calculator application icon is a picture of a calculator. Here are some icons that are already familiar to you:

Application icons

When you first access Windows 3.0, the Program Manager window is full of these pictures. You can see icons for every application that Windows makes available to you. As you add applications to the Windows Applications group, new icons appear for you to choose from. The Microsoft Money icon is an example of an application icon.

Document icons

Document icons are symbols that represent documents (or files) that have been minimized from a full window to a small icon. For example, if you chose to minimize the account book of your checking account it would appear at the bottom of your screen as an icon that looked like this:

This indicates that a document, your account book, has been shrunk to an icon, while you went on to look at something else. You can retrieve the check register at any time by clicking on this icon.

Program icons

Within an application like Money, you often will encounter icons that represent subapplication. The following icon is used to represent the Bank Reconciliation package on the Tool Bar:

This is called a program icon because it represents a program (procedure) that can only be started from within the current application. In other words, the bank reconciliation procedure is a separate program that only can be accessed from within the Money window. Thus, icons are a helpful way to represent choices within the computer environment, and they provide a button to click when you want to make a choice.

Closing a window

Whether you are working in the Money window or in a Windows window, the procedure for exiting from your work is the same. This can be done in one of three ways. Adopt one of these methods, and it will become a habit to you.

☐ Click the File menu word, and then the Exit menu item. On the keyboard, press Alt−F, then X.

☐ You can activate the Control menu by clicking the Control Menu button ([-]) in the upper left corner of the window; then click the Close menu item. On the keyboard, press Alt−Spacebar, then C.

☐ The fastest way is to double-click the Control Menu button, which serves to automatically choose the Control Menu and then the Close item. On the keyboard, press Alt−F4).

Summary

We've just taken a quick tour of the tools you'll be using repeatedly in Money and Windows. Taking action with command buttons and your mouse, choosing items from lists or menus, conversing with the computer using dialog boxes, and scrolling the display are the major tasks that you will perform each time you use Money. If you've got the time, and need Windows practice, play the tutorial that follows this chapter. While you're in Money, feel free to exercise all the new skills you've learned thus far but, don't add too much to your sample file because we will be using that file in later chapters.

Next I'll try to solidify your base of knowledge about Money by taking the time to thoroughly explain the basic money management concepts.

Window aerobics tutorial

This tutorial is completely optional. You can go on with subsequent chapters without using the tools practiced in this tutorial, but the exercise provided here will help you learn more about the Money window layout and how to customize it to your tastes. It is assumed that you have completed the chapter 1 tutorial before beginning this one. If you have used Money for anything more than the chapter 1 tutorial, the layout of your screen might be slightly different from the *default* layout—the layout that Microsoft designed as the startup setting. You still should proceed with this tutorial.

Manipulating windows is best done with a mouse, so this tutorial assumes almost exclusive use of the mouse. Directions will be oriented toward pointing the screen arrow to an area of the screen and clicking, double-clicking, or dragging the arrow.

We'll be using many symbols on your screen that were illustrated in chapters 1 and 2. The following sums up many of them for you to use as reference as you complete this tutorial.

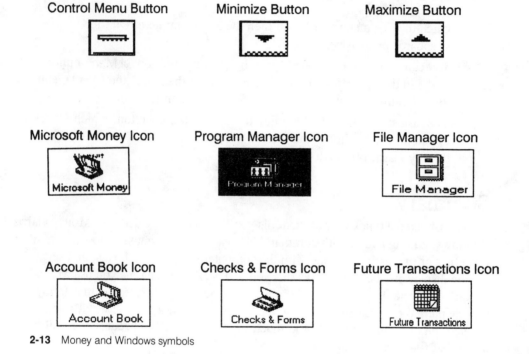

2-13 Money and Windows symbols

Part A

You've already opened at least three windows as you accessed Windows 3.0 and Money, and within the Money window, you can see the Account Book window. In this first part, we'll open and close several windows within the Money window and then learn to minimize and maximize them.

- ☐ Access the Windows 3.0 Program Manager window
- ☐ This window contains many icons for all your applications
- ☐ Double-click on the Money icon
- ☐ You have just opened the first three windows

○ Program Manager window is underneath the Money window
○ The Money window fills the entire screen now
○ The Account Book window is open inside the Money window

Note If you also can see a Checks & Forms window somewhere on your screen, skip this next step.

☐ Double-click on the Checks & Forms icon (bottom of the window)

☐ Now there are four windows open

☐ Visually locate the Checks & Forms title bar

☐ Click on the Minimize button at the far right of the Checks & Forms title bar

If you miss the Checks & Forms Minimize button and hit the Minimize button on the Money title bar instead, you'll feel like you just lost the whole shooting match, but you didn't. You'll see that Money has become an icon at the bottom of the screen. Restore any window by double-clicking on its icon. Double-click on the Money icon now if you've made this mistake. Then click on the Minimize button of the Checks & Forms title bar.

☐ The Checks & Forms window has returned to an icon

☐ Double-click on the Future Transaction icon at the bottom of the window

☐ You also can close a window by clicking the Control Menu button of the specific window you want to close

☐ Double-click the Control Menu button on the Future Transactions title bar

☐ The Future Transactions window has returned to an icon

Note If you mistakenly double-click the Control Menu button of the Money title bar, you've asked to close the entire Money program. If this happens, you'll see the Backup box. Select No to skip the backup procedure. Then double-click the Program Manager icon and double-click on the Money icon again to reopen the Money window.

☐ We can reduce all the Money windows to icons

☐ Click on the Minimize button of the Account Book title bar

☐ There should be three icons at the bottom of the window

Part B

It is possible to change the size of any window so that you can fit more windows on the screen at once, thus enabling you to see the parts of those windows that are important to you. This part of the tutorial leads you through sizing and moving windows.

- ☐ Double-click on the Account Book icon
- ☐ Move the mouse arrow to the bottom border of the Account Book
- ☐ Finesse the mouse until the arrow changes to a double arrow
- ☐ This is the *sizing arrow*
- ☐ Drag the double arrow about an inch up the screen (this means to click and hold down the mouse button while the double arrow slides up the screen an inch, then release the mouse button)
- ☐ Move the mouse arrow to the right border of the Account Book window, being careful not to touch the right edge of the Money window border
- ☐ Finesse the mouse until the arrow changes to a double arrow
- ☐ Drag the double arrow to the left about an inch
- ☐ The Account Book has now shrunk to your specifications

You also can activate the Control Menu button using keystrokes. Let's do this now.

- ☐ Press Alt −- and the Control Menu appears
- ☐ Click the Move item on this cascading menu
- ☐ The arrow has changed to a four-pointed arrow, which is the *move pointer*
- ☐ Place this move pointer on the Account Book title bar
- ☐ Drag the move pointer to the right about one inch (an outline of the Account Book window should move with you)
- ☐ When you release the mouse button, the Account Book moves over (Similar actions can be performed on any window.)
- ☐ Double-click the Future Transactions icon
- ☐ Move the mouse arrow until it is exactly at the lower right corner of the Future Transaction window
- ☐ Finesse the mouse until the arrow changes to a double diagonal arrow
- ☐ You now can drag the vertical and horizontal border together
- ☐ Drag the diagonal arrow about two inches toward the middle
- ☐ The Future Transaction window changes to your specifications

Part C

Although the Program Manager window is still open, it has been reduced to an icon in the background. This would be true of any other applications within Windows that you had open but did not exit from. To see the icons of any of these applications, we need to shrink the Money window a little.

- ☐ Move the mouse arrow to the extreme bottom of the Money window
- ☐ Finesse the mouse until the arrow changes to a double arrow
- ☐ Drag the double arrow about one inch up the screen
- ☐ The bottom border of the Money window has moved up and now you can see the Program Manager icon
- ☐ Double-click on the Program Manager icon
- ☐ The Money window is still in the background
- ☐ The Program Manager window has been brought to the foreground

Note   The Money package has not been closed. It simply has been overshadowed by the Program Manager window. To close Money, press Alt−F4, or double-click the Control Menu button on the Money title bar. Don't do this now.

- ☐ Double-click on the Money icon to return there
- ☐ The Money window still should contain the reduced Account Book Window and the reduced Future Transactions window
- ☐ The Checks & Forms icon is visible at the bottom
- ☐ Double-click the Checks & Forms icon
- ☐ With the Checks & Forms window large, the Futures window is almost lost—at the far left you can see the edge of the Futures window
- ☐ Click on that edge of the Futures window to select it

Part D

If a window is not used often, it might be better to keep it reduced to an icon. We'll do this with the Future Transaction window, but the icon might get lost behind some other window. We can move its icon to an empty corner, so it will always be visible. Any icon can be dragged to a convenient location.

- ☐ Click the Minimize button on the Futures title bar—the Future Transaction icon cannot be seen at this point
- ☐ Click the Minimize button on the Checks & Forms title bar

- □ Now you can see the Future Transaction icon at the bottom
- □ Drag the Futures icon to the upper left corner of window
- □ Double-click the Checks & Forms icon
- □ Select the Account Book window by clicking anywhere within it
- □ Select the Checks window by clicking anywhere within it
- □ Select the Account Book window again by clicking anywhere in it

Part E

The possibilities are endless. With these few skills, you can customize your windows to your liking. Go ahead and experiment. The pattern that you leave within your Money window when you exit will be saved for you in a file called "MSMONEY.INI". The next time you access Money, your window design will be restored. If you want to get rid of this design and start over with the Microsoft default design, perform Part F after Part E. These last few steps are to close the Money window and exit.

- □ Double-click the Control Menu button on the Money title bar
- □ Insert a diskette in your A: drive
- □ Choose Yes in the Backup box—if you are asked about Overwrite?, choose Yes again
- □ You are now back in the Windows control area
- □ Double-click the Program Manager icon to access this

Part F

Do not perform this last part unless you want to start from scratch in designing your money window layout.

This section describes how to delete the MSMONEY.INI file from your disk using the Windows File Manager utility. This deletes your custom design of the Money window layout. The next time you access Money, the MSMONEY.MNY file will be loaded. You can access the sample file of chapter 1 by selecting File, then Open from the menu and selecting sample.mny from the list of files.

- □ Double-click the File Manager icon from Program Manager
- □ Double-click the disk symbol next to the letter C
- □ Double-click the MSMONEY item on the list that appears (scroll the window if you can't see this item at first)
- □ Select the file named MSMONEY.INI on the next list (in other words, be sure you highlight the MSMONEY.INI file, because now you are going to ask that it be deleted)

- ☐ Select the File, then Delete, menu items
- ☐ Choose Delete in the Confirm Delete box
- ☐ Choose Yes in the File Manager Delete box
- ☐ Double-click the Control Menu button on the File Manager title bar, and choose Ok to close the File Manager
- ☐ Double-click the Program Manager icon to return there
- ☐ Double-click the Control Menu button to close Windows

Note At this point you can access Money again and open one of your files. Customize the screen if you desire.

3
CHAPTER

Underlying concepts of Microsoft Money

This chapter asks you to step back for a moment from the tricks of Windows and what you already know about Money, and try to fully understand the underlying concepts upon which the Money package is built. In this chapter, we will take a closer look at the contents of the Money window and the various ways in which you can use it. We also will explore the basic definitions of Money terminology, learn how your files are managed on computer disk, study transaction entry in more detail, and understand what SmartFill can do for you.

As noted in chapter 1, this book serves both individual users and those who want to use Money in a small business setting. It is important for both of these audiences to understand some basic terminology and transaction entry concepts that will apply throughout all your uses of Money. Mastery of the material in this chapter is essential to your success in using this software to its maximum capacity.

Now that you are familiar with both the use of the mouse and the use of the keyboard, the remainder of this book will provide you with the key words, menu words or buttons that need to be used to accomplish a task, without naming both the mouse and keyboard action for each procedure. This should make your reading a little easier. Appendix A (Keyboard reference) and Appendix B (Menu map) will help you make selections using either the mouse or keyboard.

Detailed tour of the Money window

In Fig. 1-1 of chapter 1, you were introduced to the layout of the Money window as it appears when you first use the Money package. Take a look at that figure again and notice that the account book fills most of the screen, while the Checks

& Forms window and the Future Transactions window, appear only as icons at the bottom of the window. Using the techniques discussed in chapter 2, I have customized my Money display so that all three of these document windows shows within the larger Money window at the same time; see Fig. 3-1. In this illustration, each part of the window is labelled and described for your information.

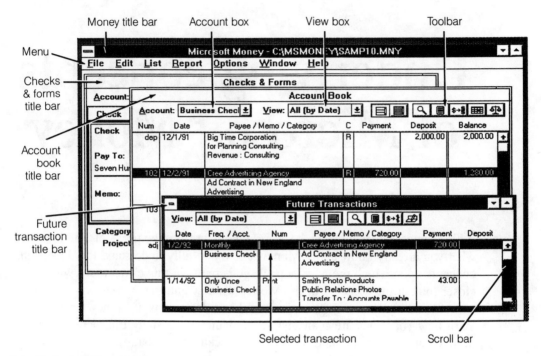

3-1 Customized Money window

Selected transaction

Notice in Fig. 3-1 that the first line of the transaction dated 12/2 for Cree Advertising appears in reverse video; that is, it seems to be highlighted by appearing in a contrasting color to the rest of the screen. This transaction is said to be the *selected* transaction, and any action that you take by using a menu word or an icon from the toolbar will take effect on this selected transaction. When you want to edit a transaction, you first must select it by clicking on it or by pressing the directional keys to highlight it. The term *selected transaction* will be used henceforth to mean the transaction that is highlighted in this way.

Basic parts

Let's review the most basic parts of the screen layout. The Money title bar is followed immediately by the Menu line: File Edit List Report Options Window

Help. When you select an item from the menu (by clicking on it or pressing Alt plus the underlined letter), a second menu list cascades below the menu word you have chosen. You already know that each window within the Money window is labelled with a title bar (e.g., Checks and Forms appears on a highlighted bar at the top of the window that looks like a check from a checkbook). The bottom of the Money window usually contains a *prompt line*, which provides hints on what your next action should be.

Each of the three windows that you see in Fig. 3-1 display several boxes near the top. The Account box tells what account within your file is active in the window, and this box can be used to list your other accounts and choose from that list. The View box tells what set of transactions is being shown in the window, and can be used to change to other views within the selected account. For example, you could view the transactions in order by number, instead of by date.

The Toolbar

The Toolbar is the collection of icon style buttons that appears in the upper right corner of each window. These icons represent different screen display options and tools (like the calculator or split transaction feature) that you can access easily by clicking on this toolbar. Figure 3-2 magnifies one of the toolbars from Fig. 3-1, so you clearly can see the pictures (icons) contained on the toolbar. Please understand that the toolbar gives you instant mouse access to some of the menu items without need for the keyboard and several keystrokes. All of the tools available through the toolbar, however, also can be accessed using menu items like Options then Calculator, or Edit then Find, or by a combination of keystrokes involving the Ctrl key.

3-2 Toolbar of the Account Book window

The first icon at the far left on the toolbar shows a form with several lines widely spaced (as compared to the picture on its right where the many lines are closely spaced). This first icon is the Entire Transaction View tool; click it to display the current window with only a few transactions, each of them taking up three or more lines. The next icon on the toolbar shows a form with many tightly spaced lines. This is the Top Line View tool; clicking it changes the Account Book or Future Transactions window so that each transaction occupies just a single line. Many more transactions can be seen at one time this way. These first two icons do not apply to the Checks and Forms window, so they do not appear on the toolbar of that window. The action accomplished by these two tools also can be accomplished by selecting Options, Top Line View or Entire View from the menu, or Ctrl−T.

Once your account contains a lot of transactions, you'll need the next tool to get around quickly. The icon that contains a picture of a hand-held magnifying glass is the Find tool; click on it to specify some criteria for a transaction you want to look at. This also can be accomplished by selecting Edit then Find from the menu, or Ctrl−F.

The next icon pictures a miniature calculator. This is the Calculator tool; clicking on it brings up the calculator for your use. Selecting Options then Calculator, or pressing Ctrl−K does the same.

The next icon on the toolbar shows one large $ sign with two smaller $ signs to its right. This is the Split Transaction tool; clicking it takes you to the Split Transaction window for the currently selected transaction. Selecting Edit then Split Transaction or Ctrl−S also accomplishes this.

The icon that pictures a small calendar with one of the days on the calendar blocked out is called the Schedule Future Transactions tool; click on this to enter the currently selected transaction in the Future Transaction list. This is the same as selecting Edit then Schedule in Future, or Ctrl−E.

The last icon on the far right shows a set of scales with equal weights on each side, so it looks balanced. This is the Balance Account tool; clicking on it leads to the procedure for balancing the currently active account. You also can select this procedure with Options then Balance Account from the menu.

There's just one more toolbar icon that has not been illustrated yet. Figure 3-3 shows the toolbar from the Future Transaction window. This figure is slightly different than the illustration in Fig. 3-2. The last icon on the far right of this toolbar looks like an open checkbook with a pen poised to begin writing. This is the Pay Bills icon; click on it to begin the process of specifying a date and items from the Future Transaction list to be recorded in the account book. Clicking this icon is the same as selecting Options then Pay Bills from the menu, or Ctrl−P.

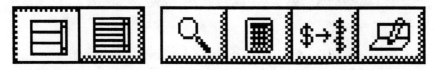

3-3 Toolbar of the Future Transaction window

Checks & Forms window

Figure 3-4 provides a closeup of just one of the windows within Fig. 3-1, the Checks & Forms window. You can see that in addition to the boxes and toolbar described above, there are also four buttons that can be selected to change the form for data entry of a check, deposit, payment, or transfer. The window in Fig. 3-4 is filled with a Check form. If you wanted to enter a Transfer transaction, you

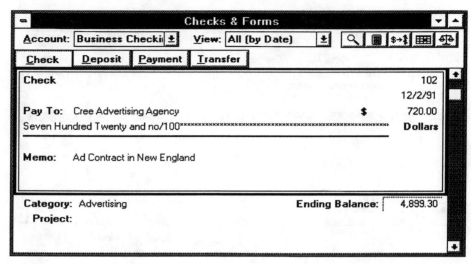

3-4 Checks & Forms window

would need to select the Transfer button so that a Transfer form is displayed in the window. The advantage to using the Check form displayed in Fig. 3-4 is that fields for payee address and a comment are included that do not appear in the account book. However, you can add a payee address and comment field (and a telephone number) if you monitor and maintain your payee list in the Account List window (covered in chapter 5). These fields usually are not used when entering a deposit, transfer or adjustment, so it is easier to enter these types of transactions in the account book.

Account Book window

The Account Book window is shown again in Fig. 3-5. You have already entered transactions in this format, so we don't need to dwell on any of the columns on this form. It is intended to look similar to the check register that accompanies a manual checkbook. Although the Memo field is totally optional, the Category field should be considered mandatory if you want to have full control over your finances. The Balance field contains the sum of all payments and deposits and is continually updated by Money as you enter and edit transactions. When you scroll back through previous transactions, the final ending balance always remains displayed in the bottom right hand corner of this window.

Future Transactions window

We will discuss how future transactions are stored and then used to pay bills a little later in this chapter. A future transaction is generally one that occurs regularly. By placing a transaction of this type on the Future Transactions list, you will

Account Book window

Num	Date	Payee / Memo / Category	C	Payment	Deposit	Balance
dep	12/1/91	Big Time Corporation for Planning Consulting Revenue : Consulting	R		2,000.00	2,000.00
102	12/2/91	Cree Advertising Agency Ad Contract in New England Advertising	R	720.00		1,280.00
103	12/4/91	Ritter Agency Split Split		640.00		640.00
adj	12/7/91	Chase First Bank new checks	R	22.50		617.50

Ending Balance: 4,899.30

3-5 Account Book window

not have to retype the data details every time you want to enter the payment or deposit. Figure 3-6 shows the detailed view of this window from Fig. 3-1.

The most important thing to note here is that the Future Transactions window almost always contains dates in the future, and does not contain a Balance column, because these items have not been deducted from, or added to, your account balance yet. In effect, they are waiting to be paid or deposited.

Also in Fig. 3-6, the Freq/Memo/Category column is used to denote the frequency with which this transaction will be recorded in the checkbook (weekly, monthly, bimonthly, or only once on the specified date, etc.), the memo to be used each time (optional), and the category to be assigned.

Date	Freq. / Acct.	Num	Payee / Memo / Category	Payment	Deposit
1/2/92	Monthly Business Check		Cree Advertising Agency Ad Contract in New England Advertising	720.00	
1/14/92	Only Once Business Check	Print	Smith Photo Products Public Relations Photos Transfer To : Accounts Payable	43.00	
1/15/92	Only Once Business Check	Print	Mobil Portland, Inc. Tune up Transfer To : Accounts Payable	82.00	
1/15/92	Monthly	Print	Coastal Computer Center	131.67	

3-6 Future Transactions window

The calculator

A calculator is also readily available. Click on the Calculator icon of the toolbar, or select Options then Calculator from the menu (Ctrl−K). When the calculator appears, use it just like any old calculator. Press numeric keys interspersed with arithmetic symbols. The ∗ symbol is used for multiplication and the / symbol is used for division. Press = or Enter to view the results.

You can save the calculated results to be pasted into a field in Money. After you get the result on the top of the Calculator window, press Ctrl−Ins to save the result in memory. Then remove the calculator from the screen (usually by pressing Alt−F4, or double-clicking the Control Button of the calculator title bar). When you get to the field in Money where you want to place the results from the calculator, press Shift−Ins.

SmartFill and SuperSmartFill

Transaction entries are the basis of all that happens in Money, and they are the most tedious, key-oriented chores that you will have to endure. Because Microsoft knew that most computer users detest the drudgery of data entry, they made it super easy to fill in the data fields in Money. As soon as you type in the first few letters of a payee or category name, a feature called SmartFill causes the computer to find a payee with those characters that was used before and fill in the rest of a field. For example, when you receive your next contract payment from the Bigtime Corporation that we used in the chapter 1 tutorial, all we have to type is Big before the computer displays the whole name, Bigtime Corporation.

SuperSmartFill is even more helpful. Once you enter the payee name on a transaction and Tab to the amount field, the data for the last transaction involving that payee is filled in for the remaining fields and all you have to do is review that data, type over it if necessary, and then press Enter to go on to the next transaction. This means that once you get a data bank of a few months' transactions entered in your Money file, most of the data you need for new transactions will pop up automatically after you enter a payee name.

One note of caution: the first time you enter a payee and associated information, you should be careful about proper spelling and capitalization. This data becomes part of your payee list. Subsequently, you can forget about capitalization; just type big and Bigtime Corporation will be found. If you have several payee names that begin with the letters B I G, then you would have to type four or five letters before SmartFill recognizes the name.

Chapter 5 describes the procedures for editing and maintaining a payee list.

Important definitions

The "account" where we recorded a few beginning transactions is the checking account that you would maintain with your bank. Within this account, we assigned each transaction or part of a transaction to a *category*. We could assign transactions to an even finer level of detail called *classifications*. These three places where transactions can be recorded are all contained within one *file* in your computer's memory and on computer disk. The understanding of each of these terms is essential to understanding how data is stored by Money.

Accounts

In the tutorial of chapter 1, we created an account by naming it Business Checking and entering a beginning balance. This account was then used to enter a few basic transactions. When we printed reports, the data from that single account was shown on the reports. It is possible to maintain records for many accounts simultaneously and to switch back and forth between these accounts as needed. This is illustrated in greater detail in upcoming chapters.

To be perfectly clear, an *account* is the collection of data that relates to one element of your financial transactions. Your checking account is just one element of your finances. If you also have a credit card, this is another element of your finances and could be managed using an additional account in Money. If you own real estate, this could be managed in an additional account. If you have a mortgage on that real estate, that would necessitate yet another account titled Mortgage Payable. The possibilities are endless. I even maintain a separate account for the few certificates of deposit (CDs) that I own. Each of these elements for a person's finances are called an *account*.

Files

A *file* is a group or collection of accounts that are related to one another. Continuing with my example of the previous paragraph, my Money *file* would contain my checking account, credit card account, CD account, real estate account, and mortgage payable account. If you used Money for both your business accounts and personal accounts, you would want to store each of these sets of accounts in a separate file.

When I asked you to name your new file Sample in the tutorial of chapter 1, this would ensure that any sample accounts we created as a result of your work with this book would be stored on your computer in a separate place from the "real" files you created for yourself.

A file that contains all the accounts you create in Money is stored on your computer disk and updated whenever you finish a transaction. Unless you specify otherwise, the file that is placed on your disk is labelled "MSMONEY.MNY." The file we created in chapter 1 was labelled as "SAMPLE.MNY" when it was placed on your disk, because we selected the File then New menu words and typed in the name "sample" as the file name. Any file created by Money is uniquely identified with the last three letters "MNY." This is called a file extension. Most popular software uses this technique; the file extension is used to identify the files that work with the specific software package being used. For example, all Windows Write files carry the extension of "WRI."

This process of saving or storing your work happens automatically, and an extra copy is made when you exit from a file if you answer Yes when asked if you want to back up your work. We'll talk more about backup copies later.

Categories

The term *category* is used in Money to refer to the descriptive groupings of transactions that are similar in nature. For example, purchases of stationery, envelopes, cards, staples, tape, and note pads would be best grouped together as Office Supplies for reporting purposes. Transactions that happen within a group of related accounts stored in one file all can share the same category list. For example, transactions in your checking account and transactions in your credit card account both can·be charged to (or categorized as) Office Supplies. In other words, each file contains one category list.

Appendix C contains the three built-in category lists that Money provides. You might choose one of these lists when you first set up a new file, or you might start from scratch and design your own category list. Chapter 5 discusses the maintenance of category lists in detail. Categories and subcategories are discussed in further detail later in this chapter.

Classifications

A *classification* allows for further breakdowns of transactions than·would be possible with just categories. Classifications allow you to group transactions into major areas of financial dealings like business versus personal, if both of these types of transactions are administered from one account. Another common need for classifications arises when an individual owns several rental properties and wants to classify transactions by property owned (e.g., 100 State Street, 10 Main Street, and 20 Broadway).

A small business might want to use classifications to group transactions by major functions performed by the business. For example, a construction company might need classifications for home, industrial, and road construction. Then they could assign transactions to categories like Revenue and Salaries, and further specify that these items relate to home construction or road construction projects. The use of classifications allows businesses to track individual projects, like the Smith Home, Jones Building, or Scott Paper Road.

Chapters 4 and 5 provide detailed illustrations for the use of classifications.

More about categories

Your ability to produce meaningful reports with Money is dependent on your faithful use of categories. At the very least, each transaction should be assigned to a category from the category list. When you produce an income and expense report, your income and expense categories are automatically summarized for you. When you request a summary report or register report, you can specify that data be summarized by category. The contents of the categories in these reports rely on how completely you categorized transactions as they were entered.

You can customize a category list in any way you wish. You can add categories to the list at any time by simply typing a category that Money cannot find on the existing list. When you do this, Money asks whether you'd like to add the new category to the list. You also can select List then Category from the menu and choose New, Delete, or Rename to edit the current list. These procedures are discussed in detail in chapter 5.

Subcategories

Money provides you with *subcategories* within some categories. For example, in the chapter 1 tutorial we found that the Insurance category included a further

INCOME AND EXPENSE REPORT
12/1/91 Through 12/31/91

Subcategory	Total
INCOME	
Revenue	2,000.00
TOTAL INCOME	2,000.00
EXPENSES	
Advertising	720.00
Bank Charges	30.70
Entertainment	
Meals	45.00
Total Entertainmen	45.00
Insurance	
Automobile	240.00
Liability	400.00
Total Insurance	640.00
Office Expenses	
Furnishings	65.00
Supplies	20.00
Total Office Expen	85.00
TOTAL EXPENSES	1,520.70
INCOME LESS EXPENSES	479.30

3-7 Single-month Income and Expense report

breakdown to Automobile, Health, Liability, and Life insurance. Subcategories provide a finer level of detail than categories. If you specify it, subcategories can be listed separately on reports, with subtotals for each category. On the other hand, an income and expense report can be produced in a summarized form, if you specify that you want to see only categories. Figures 3-7 and 3-8 show a comparison between a single-month report and a multiple-month report. If you prefer, you can ignore the subcategories totally and only assign transactions to categories. You also can add more detailed subcategories for each category. The mechanics of this process are discussed in chapter 5.

INCOME AND EXPENSE REPORT
10/1/91 Through 12/31/91

Subcategory	10/1/91 - 10/31/91	11/1/91 - 11/30/91	12/1/91 - 12/31/91	Total
INCOME				
Revenue	1,675.00	1,900.00	2,000.00	5,575.00
TOTAL INCOME	1,675.00	1,900.00	2,000.00	5,575.00
EXPENSES				
Advertising	680.00	680.00	720.00	2,080.00
Bank Charges	27.00	29.75	30.70	87.45
Entertainment				
Meals	67.75	112.35	45.00	225.10
Total Enterta	67.75	112.35	45.00	225.10
Insurance				
Automobile			240.00	240.00
Liability			400.00	400.00
Total Insuran			640.00	640.00
Miscellaneous	48.98			48.98
Office Expenses				
Furnishings			65.00	65.00
Repairs	45.60	18.50		64.10
Supplies		75.10	20.00	95.10
Total Office	45.60	93.60	85.00	224.20
TOTAL EXPENSES	869.33	915.70	1,520.70	3,305.73
INCOME LESS EXPENS	805.67	984.30	479.30	2,269.27

3-8 Multiple-month Income and Expense report

Splitting transactions

Sometimes a transaction should be assigned to more than one category and/or subcategory. For example, when you register for a professional conference and pay your annual membership dues in the professional organization at the same time, you would want to categorize part of this payment as Travel and part of it as Memberships. This can be accomplished in Money by using the Split Transaction window. At any point during the entry of this transaction, you can press Ctrl−S or click the Split Transaction icon and you will have as many lines as you need to break down the total amount of the transaction into separate categories. Figure 3-9 shows the split transaction used in the chapter 1 tutorial for the payment of insurance premiums to the Ritter Agency.

Split Transaction		
Category	Description	Amount
Insurance : Automobile	Semi-annual Auto Premium	240.00
Insurance : Liability	Semi-annual Liability Premium	400.00

| Done | Cancel | Help | Unassigned Amount: | 0.00 |

3-9 Split Transaction window

Three windows for transaction entry

Transactions can be entered in any one of the three windows presented earlier: the Account Book window, the Checks and Forms window, or the Future Transactions window. The question is; when should each of these be used? From experience, I have found that the first time you make a payment to a payee that you haven't used before, it is best to use the Checks and Forms window because this form will remind you to enter an address for the payee. For subsequent payments to this same payee, enter the transaction in the account book and type just the first few letters of the payee name. SuperSmartFill will fill in the rest of the data for the transaction and even though you don't see the address in the account book, a payee address will be printed on the check if you entered one previously. You can edit the transaction as necessary before or after you enter it in the account book.

Because deposits and adjustments in the checking account rarely need to contain more than a payee and a memo, it is probably more efficient to enter these types of transactions in the account book. When using accounts where there is no need to actually print checks, like credit card accounts, asset accounts, and other payable accounts, transaction entry is most efficient using the account book.

If a transaction occurs on a regular basis, like rent payments, or if it is a one-time item that you want to schedule in the future, you should enter it in the Future Transactions window.

Future transactions

A *future transaction* is any transaction that is going to need to be recorded in your account on some future date. The most common example of this is the rent or loan payments that have to be made on a specific date each month. A less common example would be the inevitability of paying the balance due on your Federal Income tax obligation on April 15. You might become aware of this future transaction on March 10, but you might not want to write the check or mail it until a minute before midnight on April 15.

Scheduling into the future

You can handle these future transactions by copying them into the Future Transactions window after entering them in the account book (best for the example of rent), or you might enter a transaction directly in the Future window (best for the Income Tax example).

Copy a transaction to the Future Transaction window by selecting it in the account book and pressing Ctrl−E, or by clicking the Future Transaction icon. You will be asked to specify what date the next payment is due and whether this transaction will reoccur daily, weekly, monthly, annually, at some interval between these, or only once. Figure 3-10 shows the future scheduled payment of advertising fees to the Cree Agency that we paid in the first tutorial. This contracted fee is due on the second of each month, and it was entered on the Future Transactions list by selecting Schedule in the Future from the menu.

Date	Freq. / Acct.	Num	Payee / Memo / Category	Payment	Deposit
1/2/92	Monthly		Cree Advertising Agency	720.00	
	Business Check		Ad Contract in New England Advertising		

3-10 Future transaction for Cree Advertising

A transaction can be entered directly into the Future Transaction window by typing data in each field according to the label for that field, tabbing to the next field, and pressing Enter when finished. A scheduled April 15 income tax payment, illustrated in Fig. 3-11, was entered directly into the Future Transactions list.

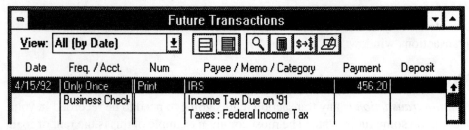

3-11 Future transaction for income tax owed

The reminder system

A nice feature of Money is the reminder feature for transactions that have been scheduled in the future. As future transaction dates come near, a warning message is displayed as soon as you access the Money window announcing that some transactions are coming due and asking if you want to deal with them. The Reminder window is illustrated in Fig. 3-12. If you close this window by selecting Yes, each of the scheduled transactions that should be recorded before your specified date will be displayed.

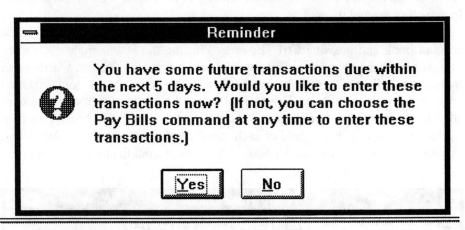

3-12 Pay Bills Reminder window

Figure 3-13 illustrates just one of the transactions that was scheduled to be paid on December 15 in our sample account. Choose Enter to record this transaction in the account book, or choose Don't Enter to handle it later. If you choose not to enter a scheduled transaction when you see it, or choose not to pay any future transactions when presented with a reminder, you can pay them at any time by selecting the Pay Bills icon, or selecting Options then Pay Bills from the menu.

Maintaining the futures file

There's nothing to it. When you first enter a transaction that you know will reoccur, select it and press Ctrl−E to put it on the Future list. You can review and edit

```
┌─────────────────────────────────────────────────────────────────┐
│ ▬            Enter Scheduled Transactions                        │
├─────────────────────────────────────────────────────────────────┤
│ Enter In:  [Business Checking  ] ↧   Remaining Balance: 1,409.30 │   [  Enter   ]
│                                                                  │   [Don't Enter]
│  Num      Date       Payee/Memo/Category      Spend    Receive   │   [Reschedule ]
│ [      ] [1/2/92  ]  Cree Advertising Agency [720.00] [       ]  │
│                      Ad Contract in New England                  │
│                      Advertising                                 │
│                                                                  │   [  Cancel  ]
│ [Split...]                                                       │   [   Help   ]
└─────────────────────────────────────────────────────────────────┘
```

3-13 Enter Scheduled Transaction dialog box

the Future Transaction list at any time by selecting Window then Future Transactions from the menu and selecting any transaction that you want to edit. Press Tab to access any field that needs changes and Enter to complete the edit, or use Edit then Delete to get rid of a scheduled transaction entirely.

Transfers between accounts

A *transfer* is a transaction that is not categorized as income or expense, but is categorized as charged to another account. For example, when a deposit is made in your checking account that resulted from the sale of a CD that had been recorded in an asset account titled Certs of Deposit, the deposit should not be categorized as income, but as a Transfer. When a transfer is recorded, the subcategory field is used to name the account where the amount should be transferred. Figure 3-14 illustrates the necessary entry for the example just cited. This transfer causes an addition to the checking account balance and a deduction from the Certs of Deposit account balance. This gives us the basis for a double entry system of accounting that might be very important to the small business readers of this book. You'll hear much more on this topic in the next chapter.

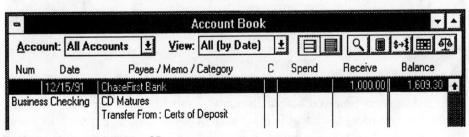

3-14 Transaction to redeem a CD

Transfers to a Cash on Hand account

Both business and personal users will understand the need for a Cash on Hand account. All of us withdraw money from our checking accounts once in a while for pocket cash. ATM machines have made this more popular than ever before. Businesses call this Petty Cash and should keep strict control of where the money goes.

Let's assume we do this for about $200 each week. When these transactions are recorded in the checking account, they need to be categorized somehow. If we plug them into Miscellaneous, the fairly large amounts we spend on food, gasoline, gifts, supplies, and other major items will go uncategorized unless we return to the $200 withdrawal and use the split transaction procedure to categorize all significant amounts. A good way to track these $200 withdrawals is to establish a Cash on Hand account. This is considered an asset account and should be started with a beginning balance of zero.

The first transaction in this new account wouldn't be recorded in Cash on Hand, but it would be recorded in the account book of the checking account and categorized as a Transfer to Cash on Hand. Figure 3-15 shows the entry in the account book for a withdrawal of $200. Figure 3-16 shows the entry that then would appear automatically in the Cash on Hand account as a result.

Num	Date	Payee / Memo / Category	C	Spend	Receive	Balance
ATM	12/16/91	Working Cash			200.00	1,609.30
Business Checking		Trans to Cash on Hand				
		Transfer To : Cash on Hand				

Account: All Accounts · View: All (by Date)

3-15 ATM withdrawal for pocket cash

Num	Date	Payee / Memo / Category	C	Decrease	Increase	Balance
	12/16/91	Working Cash			200.00	200.00
		Trans to Cash on Hand				
		Transfer From : Business Checking				

Account: Cash on Hand · View: All (by Date)

3-16 ATM withdrawal in the Cash on Hand account

Receipts should be saved for any cash expenditures that you want to categorize, and the next time you have a chance you should update the Cash on Hand account by recording decreases in it for each of your receipts. Figure 3-17 shows the recording of cash expenditures in the Cash on Hand account, followed by a

```
┌─────────────────────────────────────────────────────────────────────────┐
│  ⊟                            Account Book                         ▼  ▲   │
├─────────────────────────────────────────────────────────────────────────┤
│  Account: │Cash on Hand│ ±│   View: │All (by Date)│ ±│  ▣ ▤ ▥ |Q| ▣ |$→‡| ▦ ▨ │
├─────────────────────────────────────────────────────────────────────────┤
│  Num    Date       Payee / Memo / Category   C  Decrease  Increase  Balance│
│  ┌──────────────────────────────────────────────────────────────────────┐│
│  │     12/16/91  Working Cash                            200.00   200.00 ▲││
│  │               Trans to Cash on Hand                                    ││
│  │               Transfer From : Business Checking                        ││
│  ├──────────────────────────────────────────────────────────────────────┤│
│  │     12/17/91  Rock Road Cafe               45.00               155.00 ││
│  │               Lunch with Client                                        ││
│  │               Entertainment : Meals                                    ││
│  ├──────────────────────────────────────────────────────────────────────┤│
│  │     12/18/91  Locke Supply                 85.00                70.00 ││
│  │               Stationery & book case                                   ││
│  │               Split                                                    ││
│  │               Split                                                   ▼││
│  └──────────────────────────────────────────────────────────────────────┘│
│                                               Ending Balance: │   70.00  │ │
└─────────────────────────────────────────────────────────────────────────┘
```

3-17 Spending transaction in the Cash on Hand account

Miscellaneous entry to categorize the small change that you didn't keep receipts for. It is possible to balance this account using the Balance Account procedure on the Options menu and charge any unreconciled balance to Miscellaneous Expense. The procedure for balancing accounts is presented in chapter 12.

Dates

Money always displays the current computer system date in the date field so you don't have to type it while entering data. You can overtype this date with whatever date you need. If you type just a month and a day, as in "12/7," Money will supply the year. It supplies this year on a four months back, eight months forward basis. For example, if it is actually March 21, 1993 when you type in 12/7 as a date, Money will assign the year as "1992," but if it is August 21, 1993 when you type in 12/7 as a date, Money will assign a year of "1993."

Maintaining backup files

After all your hard work in entering data, you should guard against loss by making a backup copy of this work. Make backup copies onto a diskette or the hard disk drive. Have a formatted diskette ready when you exit from Money if you want your backup on diskette, because you will be presented with a Backup dialog box, with a suggested file name and disk drive. Don't ignore this procedure. Simply insert a diskette and choose the Yes button to make a backup copy on diskette (A: or B:), or no disk drive letter to store the backup on the hard disk. More details about making backup copies can be found in chapter 12.

Summary

This chapter has provided you with the underpinnings of a successful relationship with Money. The basic terminology of Money was carefully defined. You should now have a better understanding of the use of accounts, files, categories, subcategories, split transactions, future transactions and transfers. We've seen how SmartFill and SuperSmartFill are going to make your life easier. To further your mastery of these topics, you also have learned how a CD account and a Cash on Hand account should be used. Let's practice what we've just learned with a quick tutorial.

Money magic tutorial

This tutorial builds on the concepts learned in chapter 1, and assumes that you have completed the chapter 1 tutorial and that you have read chapter 2. Access Money from the Program Manager window of Windows 3.0.

Part A

First we must recall the sample file we worked with in chapter 1. Then we will review and edit some of the entries we made. Most importantly, we will experience the power of SmartFill and SuperSmartFill to make future transaction entry a quick and easy experience.

- ☐ Be sure that the Money window appears on your screen
- ☐ Select File, then Open from the Menu (this is Alt−F, then O on the keyboard)
- ☐ Select sample.mny from the list of files, then choose Ok
- ☐ When asked about backup, choose Yes and follow the further screen prompts
- ☐ The window now contains the sample file from chapter 1
- ☐ Press Ctrl−Home or scroll up to review the Bigtime deposit
- ☐ Press Ctrl−End or scroll down to select the next available transaction line
- ☐ Type Dep in the Num field, then Tab
- ☐ Type 12/11 in the Date field, then Tab
- ☐ Type big in the Payee field
- ☐ SmartFill has found and entered Bigtime Corporation for you
- ☐ Tab to the Amount field

☐ SuperSmartFill has found and entered all the data from the most recent Bigtime transaction

☐ Press Tab and typeover 2400 in the Deposit field

☐ Press Enter to record this transaction

☐ Type p in the next Num field

☐ Type – in the Date field

☐ Tab to the Payee field and type Rit

☐ SmartFill has found and entered Ritter Agency for you

☐ Press Enter to fill in the rest of the fields

☐ Super SmartFill has completed the transaction for you

Note This is how easy transaction entry can be after you have established a data base of payees and amounts. We didn't mean to enter Ritter again, so let's delete it. Select the last Ritter Agency transaction. Select Edit, then Delete Trans from the menu. Choose Yes to verify this deletion.

Part B

Our lawyer just sent us a bill for $385, which we hesitate to pay in one lump sum. After discussing this with her, she verbally agreed to a 20% installment now, with the balance to be paid later. This is a chance to use the Money calculator and insert the results in the Amount field of a transaction. You understand now that you must press Tab to move from field to field, so I'll dispense with instructing you with every needed Tab.

☐ Be sure you are on a blank transaction line in the account book

☐ Type p in the Num field, then 12/12 as the Date

☐ Type Rand, Hoyt, Associates as the Payee

☐ Tab to Payment amount and select the Calculator tool
(You can select the Calculator tool by pressing Ctrl–K, or by selecting Options, then Calculator, or by clicking on the Calculator icon of the toolbar)

☐ Type 385 and press the multiplication symbol (∗)

☐ Type .20 and press the = sign

☐ The result appears at the top of the calculator

☐ Press Ctrl–Ins to save this result in memory

☐ Press Alt–F4 to remove the Calculator window

Note If you press Alt–F4 too hard or too long, you might be asking to close the

Money window completely. If this happens just double-click the Program Manager icon, and double-click the Money icon to return to where you were.

- ☐ You are back in the Payment field of the transaction
- ☐ Press Shift—Ins and the result of the calculation appears
- ☐ Tab to the Memo field
- ☐ Type 20% of Legal Services in the Memo field
- ☐ Categorize as Services, Legal
- ☐ Press Enter to record this transaction
- ☐ Select File, Print Checks
- ☐ Type 104 as the Check Number
- ☐ Choose Ok to print this check
- ☐ Choose Continue to return to the account book

Part C

This section provides practice for scheduling transactions in the future and then paying future transactions. The Cree Advertising Agency contract payment will be due on the 2nd of every month.

- ☐ Select the Cree Advertising transaction of 12/2
- ☐ Select the Schedule in Future icon from the toolbar, or Ctrl—E
- ☐ Select Monthly in the Frequency list box
- ☐ Type 1/2 in the Next Date box
- ☐ Choose Ok to proceed
- ☐ Select Window, Future Transactions
- ☐ Notice how the Cree payment is scheduled for payment on 1/2/9x
- ☐ Select Options, then Pay Bills from the menu, or Ctrl—P
- ☐ Type 1/2 in the Date box, then choose Ok
- ☐ Read the Enter Scheduled Transactions window
- ☐ Choose Enter to enter this in the account book
- ☐ The beep you hear indicates that this is now recorded
- ☐ Select the Account Book window—notice that a 1/2 Cree payment has been entered here
- ☐ This was just an experiment; we don't want to enter this yet, so select the 1/2 Cree payment, Edit, and Delete Transaction
- ☐ Choose Yes to confirm the deletion

Part D

Up until now we've been working only within a single checking account. This section leads you through the process of setting up a new account for Cash on Hand within our sample file, and introduces the concept of transferring amounts between accounts. The transaction to establish the funds in the Cash on Hand account comes from an ATM withdrawal from the checking account.

☐ Select the Account box at the top of the account book

☐ Select the New Account item from the Account list box

☐ Type Cash on Hand in the Account Name box

☐ Check the Cash Account option on the Account Type list

☐ Choose Ok to proceed

☐ Type a zero for the beginning balance in this account

☐ Choose Ok to proceed

☐ The window now displays the account book for this new account

☐ We want to return to the checking account to record a transfer

☐ Select the Account box at the top of the account book

☐ Select the Business Checking item from the Account list box

☐ Now you're back in the account book of the Checking account

☐ Select the next available transaction line in the account book

☐ Type ATM in the Num field, then 12/12 as the Date

☐ Type Working Cash as the Payee, and 100 as the Payment Amount

☐ Type For Cash Needs as the Memo

☐ Select Transfer from the category list, and select Cash on Hand from the account list that appears under the subcategory column

☐ Press Enter to record this transfer transaction

Part E

The transaction we just recorded in the Business Checking account also has been automatically recorded in the Cash on Hand account. We'll work within the Cash on Hand account in this next section, so you'll see the original $100 entry, and enter some typical cash expenditures.

☐ Select the Account box, and select Cash on Hand

☐ You now should see the $100 transfer transaction in the account book of the Cash on Hand account

- The Deposit in this account is termed an increase
- Select the next available transaction line
- Leave the Num field blank
- Type 12/13 as the Date, and Locke Supply as the Payee
- Type 42 as the Decrease, and Stationery as the Memo
- Categorize this as Office Expenses, Supplies
- Press Enter to complete the transaction
- Begin another transaction, leaving the Num field blank
- Type 12/14 as the Date, and Rock Road Cafe as the Payee
- Type 41.5 as the Decrease, and Lunch with Prospects as the Memo
- Categorize this as Entertainment, Meals
- Press Enter to complete the transaction
- The $16.50 balance in this account was spent on miscellaneous items not worth classifying separately
- Begin another transaction, leaving the Num field blank
- Type 12/14 as the Date, and Miscellaneous Cash as the Payee
- Type 16.5 as the Decrease, and Misc as the Memo
- Categorize this as Miscellaneous Expense
- Press Enter to complete the transaction
- This is just one method of accounting for your miscellaneous cash expenditures
- We need more cash in our pocket.
- Type ATM in the Num field, then 12/14 in the Date field
- Type Work in the Payee field, and Tab
- SuperSmartFill fills in the rest of the data
- Type 200 over the 100 in the Increase field
- Press Enter to complete this transaction
- This also has been entered in the Business Checking account
- Now just one more transaction; delete the ATM in Num field
- Type 12/16 as the Date, and West Side Mobil as the Payee
- Type 108 as the Decrease, and Tune Up as the Memo
- Categorize this as Automobile and Maintenance
- Press Enter to complete the transaction

Part F

Now that you have quite a few transactions in your account books, it won't be as easy to find items quickly. Money provides the Find tool to help you get around. This section tests that tool to quickly locate the deposits from Bigtime Company and the payment to your lawyer.

- ☐ In the Account box, select the Business Checking account
- ☐ Select the Find tool from the toolbar by selecting Edit then Find from the menu, or Alt−E then F (you also can use the shortcut key Ctrl−F, or click the Find icon on the Toolbar)
- ☐ Type Bigtime in the Find What box
- ☐ Notice the settings of Look in All Fields and Up Direction
- ☐ Choose Find Next and the highlighter jumps to the transaction
- ☐ Press Esc to remove the Find box
- ☐ The highlighter is on the 12/11 Bigtime transaction
- ☐ To search further, select Find again (Ctrl−F)
- ☐ Choose Find Next and the highlighter jumps again
- ☐ Press Esc to remove the Find box
- ☐ The highlighter is on the 12/1 Bigtime transaction
- ☐ Now we are at the top of the account book
- ☐ Select the Find tool again
- ☐ Type 20% in the Find What box
- ☐ Select Memo in the Look In list box
- ☐ Check Down in the Direction box
- ☐ Choose Find Next to move the highlighter
- ☐ Press Esc to remove the Find box
- ☐ The highlighter is on the 12/12 Rand, Hoyt transaction

Part G

When you need to make a correction to a previous transaction, the Find tool is an excellent way to find the transaction that needs to be edited. Let's assume our lawyer called to say that the $77 check we sent should have been for $87 due to a $10 processing fee that we overlooked. We want to void check #104 and write a new check to Rand, Hoyt. This section describes the process of voiding checks.

- ☐ The 12/12 Rand, Hoyt transaction is already selected
- ☐ Select Edit, Void Transaction from the menu

- [ ] The transaction is marked void, and 77 is added back to the balance in this account (Hint: You also can use this method to unvoid a check. Notice how the Edit menu now has an Unvoid option on it.)
- [ ] Select the next available blank transaction line
- [ ] Type p then 12/14, then Rand and Tab
- [ ] The data of the previous Rand transaction appears
- [ ] Type 87 in the Payment field
- [ ] Press Enter to record this new transaction
- [ ] Select File, Print Checks, then Ok
- [ ] Choose Continue after the new check is printed

Part H

This chapter discussed the concept of saving separate files for business versus for personal affairs. Because the sample accounts used thus far have assumed the existence of a small business, you now should experience the procedure for setting up a separate file for your personal financial transactions.

- [ ] Select File, then New
- [ ] Type Personal in the File Name box, and choose Ok
- [ ] Insert a diskette in your A: disk slot
- [ ] Choose Yes in the Backup box
- [ ] If you are asked if you want to overwrite, choose Yes again
- [ ] In the Setup New File box, check the Home categories option
- [ ] Choose Ok then Ok again in the Create First Account box
- [ ] Type Personal Checking for Account Name
- [ ] Choose Ok and type a zero for Opening Balance
- [ ] The screen now displays a blank account book for your new personal checking account
- [ ] Notice that the title bar includes the PERSONAL.MNY file name
- [ ] Take a careful look at the categories in the Home list
- [ ] Select List, then Categories
- [ ] Scroll slowly through the categories and subcategories
- [ ] Choose Close to return to the account book
- [ ] Enter a $1000 startup deposit in this account
- [ ] Categorize it as Other Income, Gifts
- [ ] Enter a $450 rent payment to Landlords, Inc.

- ☐ Categorize this as Housing, Rent
- ☐ Schedule this monthly rent payment as a future transaction
- ☐ Use the Pay Bills option to pay next month's rent
- ☐ Delete these transactions so this account will be ready for your own personal records

Part I

Now we can exit from Money and make a backup copy of the new file. Remember that you now have two sets of accounts on your disk; the sample business file, and the personal file we just created. Use the File, then Open menu items to recall whichever of these files you want to work with.

- ☐ Press Alt–F4 to exit from Money
- ☐ Be sure there is a diskette in drive A:
- ☐ Choose Yes to make a backup of your new personal file

4
CHAPTER

Small business Money principles

This chapter is especially for users who want to employ Money for business financial management. We will explore the concept of cash versus accrual basis accounting, review the procedures for setting up a separate business file, and learn how to customize the category list for business use. The use of classifications is introduced here, along with some sample transactions that would require using this feature. Producing and using business financial statements, such as the income statement, the balance sheet, journals and summary reports, completes this chapter.

Small business financial management

Financial management encompasses all the procedures employed by a business to plan and control its finances. The most important procedure within this realm is the accurate and timely recording of all financial transactions. You already experienced how Money can provide excellent control over this process. The use of categories and classifications, split transactions, future transactions and SmartFill are all intended to help you record transactions in an accurate and timely fashion.

Comprehensive financial management also includes procedures for planning/budgeting, periodic analysis of results, and complete financial reporting. Each of these topics are introduced in this chapter, and financial reporting and budgeting are further detailed in chapters 6 and 7 respectively.

Separating business and personal records

Good small business management requires that the personal records of the owner are kept entirely separate from the business records. This is referred to as the *separate entity* principle in the world of accounting. For income tax reasons, as well as for legal reasons, all businesses abide by this principle. It is assumed in this book that you are doing just that.

It was briefly mentioned in the last chapter that a separate file should be set up for personal versus business records. In the tutorial of the last chapter, we created a New file to hold your personal records. This starts you on the right route to sound business management.

Follow the procedure of Part H in the chapter 3 tutorial to set up a separate business file. To summarize, first select the File, then New menu items and type in a file name (e.g., business). Check the option box for Business Categories, and then proceed to set up the first account within this file. Type a name for your business checking account and specify its type (e.g., Bank Account), then enter a beginning balance. This checking account is just the first account in a group (file) that applies to your business. The next section of this chapter presents some ideas for other business accounts that you might want to maintain.

Each time you access Money, the file that you were working in most recently appears in the window. If you want to work in a different file, execute the File, then Open, menu items and select the file name of that other file. This is the way you would switch back and forth between your business accounts and your personal accounts, or the sample file we will continue to use in the tutorials for this book.

A minimum set of business accounts

The business checking account forms the basis for most transactions that a small business engages in. You then might create accounts for petty cash, loans payable, equipment, investments, accounts receivable, accounts payable, payroll taxes payable, or many other possibilities that apply to business management. Figure 4-1 presents a net worth report for a small business to give you a sample list of accounts. A net worth report is intended to summarize the ending balances in a set of accounts. By studying this figure, you also can compare and contrast assets and liabilities. This net worth report is discussed further in chapter 11.

Your decision to maintain business records on a cash basis, or on an accrual basis, will determine whether you need payable and receivable accounts.

Cash versus accrual basis recordkeeping

In cash basis accounting, transactions are not recorded in your records until cash

```
                        NET WORTH REPORT
                         As of 12/31/91


ASSETS                                          Total

Bank and Cash Accounts
Checking Cash                                   845.50
Petty Cash                                      125.00
        Total Bank and Cash Accounts           970.50

Other Assets
Accounts Receivable                           1,265.00
Building                                    134,000.00
Equipment                                     8,800.00
Other Assets                                  1,200.00
        Total Other Assets                  145,265.00

TOTAL ASSETS                                146,235.50


LIABILITIES                                     Total

Credit Cards
American Express                                845.90
VISA at Key Bank                                622.45
        Total Credit Cards                    1,468.35

Other Liabilities
Accounts Payable                              3,498.40
Equip Loans Payable                           7,105.00
Mortgage Payable                             87,500.42
Payroll Taxes Payable                           655.87
        Total Other Liabilities              98,759.69

TOTAL LIABILITIES                           100,228.04


NET WORTH                                    46,007.46
```

4-1 Net Worth report with typical Business accounts

actually changes hands. With accrual basis accounting, transactions are recorded in your records when a financial obligation occurs, whether cash changes hands or not. For example, when you buy supplies on account, a financial obligation to pay for them has occurred. With accrual basis accounting, this transaction would be recorded in an Accounts Payable account and categorized as Office Expenses. In effect, the Accounts Payable account is increased so that Office Expenses are increased at the time of the purchase. When payment is made for these supplies, it is recorded in the Checking account. At that time the checking balance is decreased, and the Accounts Payable account is decreased. Accounts Payable and Accounts Receivable are discussed in detail in chapter 10.

Cash basis accounts

If you intend to maintain cash basis records you probably only need the following accounts:

- ☐ Business Checking
- ☐ Cash on Hand (petty cash)
- ☐ Credit Cards (one for each credit card)
- ☐ Inventory (if you are a retail business)
- ☐ Equipment (or separate accounts for Auto, Computer, Tools)
- ☐ Investments (savings, CD's, IRA, etc.)
- ☐ Other Assets (Prepaid Expenses, Deposits on Contracts)
- ☐ Loans Payable (or a payable for each loan)
- ☐ Other Liabilities (Taxes Payable, Legal Judgments)

Accrual basis accounts

If you intend to maintain accrual basis records, the following list of accounts is suggested:

- ☐ Business Checking
- ☐ Cash on Hand
- ☐ Accounts Receivable
- ☐ Credit Cards
- ☐ Inventory
- ☐ Equipment
- ☐ Investments
- ☐ Other Assets
- ☐ Loans Payable
- ☐ Accounts Payable
- ☐ Payroll Taxes Payable
- ☐ Taxes Payable
- ☐ Other Liabilities

Business categories and subcategories

The business categories that are supplied by Money are a good starting place for the categories that you will use in your business. Appendix C provides you with the full picture of these business categories and subcategories. Chapter 5 discusses how you can customize these categories as you wish. You generally can rename or delete existing categories, or add new categories. You also can add categories at any time by typing a new category name in the Category field of a transaction entry. You'll be asked to verify what you've done and whether the category is an income or an expense. All of these actions also can be taken on subcategories and classifications.

Expense categories

Just to get you thinking about ways that the categories can be molded to your business, let me make a few customizing suggestions. If you contract with support people for regular services, set up a Contract Fees category; this might be further broken down into Clerical, Building, and Answering Service subcategories. If you belong to professional organizations or subscribe to professional publications, you'll need a Dues & Subscriptions category. If the rent you pay applies to more than office space, delete the Rent subcategory under Office Expenses, and set up a new category for Rent. Within the new category, you can establish subcategories for Office Rent and Store Rent. If you sell goods on account, you inevitably will have some customers who never pay; you'll need a Bad Debt expense category.

Take a look at a Federal Schedule C for some ideas. You might need a Commissions and Fees or Employee Benefits category. Establish a Repairs and Maintenance category to coincide with the Schedule C; then remove the Repairs subcategory from Office Expenses. Even if you rely on your accountant at the end of a year for figures on Depreciation or Depletion, you'll need these categories in Money if you want to see the full picture on your income and expense report. Depreciation is covered in chapter 11.

When you purchase goods on account, you are sometimes offered a discount for paying early. The Purchases category includes a Discounts subcategory for this. The discount amount should be recorded as a minus. The Returns & Allowances category also should be a subcategory of Purchases. I suggest adding this as a subcategory to the Purchases category, and deleting Returns & Allowances as a category.

Income categories

If the revenue you earn comes from several major sources, you might want to insert subcategories in your Revenue category. For example, a person like myself who writes books, provides computer training, and performs small business accounting consulting might create subcategories under Revenue for Consulting, Training and Royalties. If you sell products, you might want to rename the Revenue category as Sales. This might be subcategorized with the major types of products you sell (e.g., Flowers, Plants, Cards, Accessories).

If you have no Rental Income, delete this category. It might be appropriate for you to have a Dividend Income category if the business invests in security instruments that pay dividends, or you could classify this in the catch-all Other Income category.

Net income

Net income is the remainder of total income after subtracting total expenses. Money easily produces an income & expense report that summarizes income and expenses and calculates net income. Business managers call this the *bottom line*. The transactions that you assign to income and expense categories are what determines this net income. It is important to understand, however, that not every cash outlay or deposit should be categorized as expense or as income. If you buy an automobile, for example, you shouldn't charge it to Automobile Expense. An automobile is what we call a fixed asset, because it benefits the business over many years. This type of item should be categorized as an asset, and depreciated over the years that we use it in the operation of the business. More is discussed about fixed assets in chapter 11, but at this point you simply need to know that many transactions occurring in a checkbook are transfers, not just categorized as income or expense. Several of these transfer transactions are illustrated later in this chapter.

Classifications for business

Money provides *classifications* to allow further breakdown of your transactions, but they are not just additional subcategories. Think of classifications as major groupings of data that cross category lines. For example, if your consulting business served several major clients, you might want to set up a classification titled Clients, enter a list of clients, and categorize transactions by these clients. Begin this process by selecting List, then Other Classification, from the menu and choosing the New button in the Other Classification dialog box. You are presented with a list of classification types where you can check Clients.

Figure 4-2 illustrates a sample of the window contents as you set up classifications. Figure 4-3 illustrates the creation of items within a classification. You

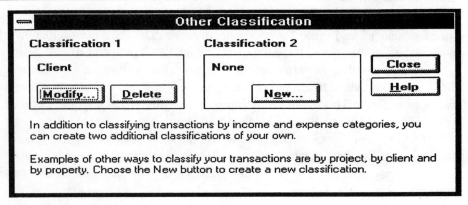

4-2 Classifications Setup dialog box

4-3 Items within a classification

even can include subitems within an item. For example, with a list of clients as items, you could create subitems within clients for location or type of service being performed (planning, training, implementation, etc.). You can include a shortcut code, comments, telephone numbers and other notations. If you include addresses and phone numbers, you can later print a client list that includes either or both of these.

Figure 4-4 illustrates a few transactions that involve classification by client. Notice that once you've created any classification, the space allocated in the account book to display a transaction has expanded from three lines to four lines.

Num	Date	Payee / Memo / Category		C	Payment	Deposit	Balance
Dep	12/7/91	Little Guy Brothers				120.00	
		Computer Consulting					
		Revenue	General				
		Little Guy Brothers					
Print	12/8/91	Locke Supply			132.50		3,013.78
		Forms for Big & Little					
		Split					
		Split					
Print	12/8/91	Moss, Allen & Kimble			420.00		2,593.78
		Preparation 5 yr plan financials					
		Contract Fees : Tech Writing					
		Bigtime Corporation					

Account: Business Checki — View: All (by Date)

4-4 Transactions involving client classifications

The fourth line is reserved for classification. With this design, it would be best if every transaction categorized as Revenue, Consulting, also be assigned to a classification. The first transaction in Fig. 4-4 is an example of this. The second transaction in Fig. 4-4 illustrates an expenditure that is split between several clients.

With classifications by client, you would want to classify as many expenditures as possible, but some payments, transfers, and deposits simply could not be assigned appropriately to a client.

The reason for sorting data by classification is seen in Fig. 4-5. This client summary was created by customizing a summary report for a specific date range to display rows by category and columns by client, including data from all accounts and transactions. This provides you with the information to analyze the progress and profitability of servicing each client. This concept of setting up classifications also can be used for managing costs by property, job, project, location, or even departments. Chapter 5 contains all the procedures you need for creating and maintaining a classification list.

CLIENT SUMMARY REPORT
12/1/91 Through 12/31/91

Category	Bigtime Corp	Little Guy Bro	Middle Company	Blank Client	Total
INCOME CATEGORIES					
Revenue	4,400.00	450.00	1,400.00		6,250.00
TOTAL INCOME CATEG	4,400.00	450.00	1,400.00		6,250.00
EXPENSE CATEGORIES					
Advertising				720.00	720.00
Automobile/Tru				108.00	108.00
Bank Charges				30.70	30.70
Entertainment				41.50	41.50
Insurance				640.00	640.00
Miscellaneous				16.50	16.50
Office Expense	280.00			73.00	353.00
Professional F	848.90		112.00		960.90
Training Mater	124.25	22.50	55.55		202.30
Travel	727.50	35.00	127.50		890.00
TOTAL EXPENSE CATE	1,980.65	57.50	295.05	1,629.70	3,962.90
GRAND TOTAL	2,419.35	392.50	1,104.95	(1,629.70)	2,287.10

4-5 Client summary report

Sample transactions

We have practiced several business transactions in chapter 1 and chapter 3 already. The deposit of business revenue, payment of expenditures, adjustments for bank charges, transfer of funds to a Petty Cash account, and payments from the Petty Cash account are all examples of simple business transactions.

Once you have set up a group of accounts for your business, you will begin to see how transfers between accounts allow a business to track some important asset and liability accounts. For example, the balance you owe on a credit card is a liability. When items are charged on a credit card, they become increases in the credit card account—your liability to pay increases. When payments are made on the credit card, the transaction is recorded in the checking account and transferred to the credit card account; payments decrease your liability. These credit card transactions are covered in detail in chapter 8, but there are many types of transfers that are important for business records, which we will explore now.

Buying equipment

When you purchase equipment or an automobile, you are making an investment in a fixed asset. If you pay cash, the transaction can be recorded in the checking account but should be categorized as a transfer to Equipment. You could set up accounts for office equipment, automobiles, computers, maintenance equipment, etc. Figure 4-6 illustrates the proper entry for purchasing equipment for cash. This equipment should be depreciated eventually; we'll get to that in chapter 11.

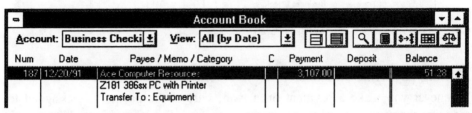

Num	Date	Payee / Memo / Category	C	Payment	Deposit	Balance
187	12/20/91	Ace Computer Resources		3,107.00		51.28
		Z181 386sx PC with Printer				
		Transfer To : Equipment				

4-6 Purchase of equipment for cash

If you purchase equipment or other assets on a time or credit plan, the transaction cannot be recorded in the Checking account because no cash was paid. Record this type of purchase in a Loans Payable account and categorize the amount as a transfer to Equipment, as shown in the previous figure.

If you pay a down payment when you buy equipment, part of the purchase price is paid with a check and the balance will be paid over time. You can record a split transaction for this in the Checking account. Figure 4-7 shows how this is a

Split Transaction

Category	Description	Amount
Transfer To : Equipment	Z181 386sx PC with Printer	4,107.00
Transfer From : Loans Payable	Bal Owed on Z181 386sx PC	(3,600.00)

Done   Cancel   Help   Unassigned Amount: 0.00

4-7 Purchase of equipment on credit

transfer to both Loans Payable and Equipment. The Loans Payable transfer must be recorded as a minus, while the Equipment cost is positive, so the net amount of the check is the down payment. The Loans Payable account receives an increase during this transfer process. Figure 4-8 shows the automatic effect on the Loans Payable account as a result of this transaction.

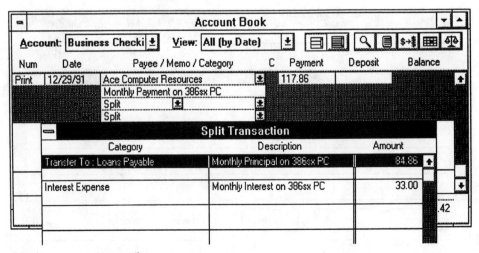

4-8 Purchase of equipment in the Loans Payable account

Making payments on loans

Whenever you make a payment on a loan, part of the payment is assigned to reducing the principal and part is interest expense. The loan officer at your bank can provide you with what is called an amortization schedule to detail what part of each of your payments is interest, and what part is principal repayment. Let's assume that the $3600 loan for the equipment in our previous example was going to be paid over 3 years, at an annual interest rate of 11% and in equal monthly installments of $117.86. The first monthly payment is comprised of $33.00 in interest and $84.86 towards the principal.

Figure 4-9 illustrates how this payment should be recorded in your Checking account. Notice that the interest portion of the payment is categorized as Interest

4-9 Loan payment transaction

Expense and the principal portion of the payment is a transfer to the Loans Payable account. The positive transfer amount in the checking account results in a decrease in the Loans Payable account.

The monthly loan payment should be scheduled on the Future Transaction list so that you will be reminded to make a payment each month. Each successive payment applies a slightly larger portion toward the principal, and less towards interest. When each future payment is made, you should edit the amounts applied to interest and principal. After three years many "decrease" transfers will have been made to the Loans Payable account, and it will have a zero balance in relation to this $3600 loan.

Other types of loans

An automobile loan, or any other loan taken out for the purchase of an asset (including the purchase of real estate with a mortgage), would be handled like it was in the previous equipment example. If you borrow money from the bank or any other source, the loan is handled in a similar manner. When the money is borrowed and deposited in your Checking account, make a deposit entry that is categorized as a transfer to Loans Payable. A deposit causes an increase in your Checking account and an automatic increase in the Loans Payable account (similar to the decrease in your checking account and the decrease in the loan account when you make a payment on a loan). A transfer transaction for the borrowing of money is illustrated in Fig. 4-10. A payment on this loan would be recorded exactly as previously shown in Fig. 4-9, with appropriate amounts for the second loan.

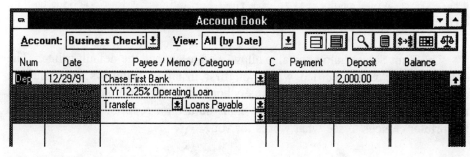

4-10 Receipt of proceeds from loan

Printing business checks

There is a Print Setup option under the File menu. You should select this option before you try to print checks or reports for the first time, because it allows you to specify the default printer to be used, optional layouts for reports, and a check style. A Print Setup dialog box appears where you must indicate whether you want to set up for printing reports or printing checks. Choose the Printing Checks option and explore the list in the Check Style list box. A voucher style check is illustrated in Fig. 4-11. This is recommended for business use because of the remittance advice that follows the actual check.

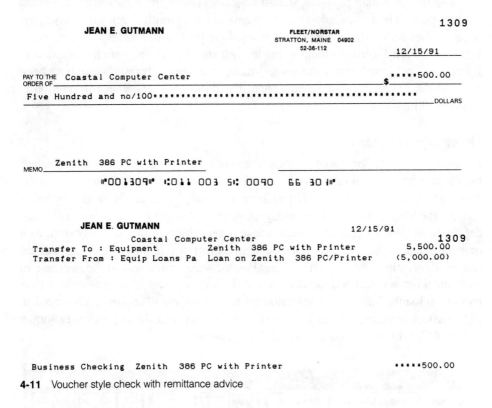

4-11 Voucher style check with remittance advice

The Print Setup dialog box also allows you to change the default printer. The default printer was specified when you first installed Windows, but you can change it here if you have several printers hooked to your computer and you want to print checks with a different printer than you use for reports. Experiment with the printer choices to see what works for you.

Print the checks

The process of printing checks for either personal or business use is the same. You must place the word Print in the Num field of any payments you want to print checks for. To begin the printing process, select the File, then Print Checks menu items. A Print Checks dialog box appears where you have an opportunity to specify the starting check number and which specific checks to print. If you check the Select Checks option, a list of checks from your account book is presented. These would be all payments with a Print indicator in the Num field. Choose checks from this list by highlighting each of them (either click on them or use the arrow keys to move to them and press the Spacebar). Unless you specify otherwise, checks are printed in a standard 11 inch wide format, with no remittance advice. Voucher style checks are preferable for business use, because they include a perforated remittance advice. You can order business checks that are designed for Money from Deluxe Business Systems, 1-800-328-0304.

Financial statements

Meaningful and accurate reports are the desired outcome of all financial record keeping. In a business setting, the most commonly used reports are the *Income Statement* and *Balance Sheet*. Although Money does not produce a business style balance sheet, the Net Worth Report serves this purpose. In addition, most businesses want to maintain a complete audit trail of all of their transactions, usually called a *Journal*. Business managers produce summary reports for various accounts and categories to analyze performance of some aspect of the business. Business budgets are an added management tool that yields helpful financial information. Budgets are covered in detail in chapter 7.

Income statements

Income statements summarize income earned and expenses incurred during a specific period of time. Expenses then can be deducted from income to determine the business net income. Money provides the Income & Expense Report for this purpose. An income statement should be produced and analyzed each month. Some businesses only do this quarterly, and sometimes very small businesses only do it annually. With Money, however, you'll find that income statements are so easy to produce, you'll want to do them weekly.

To prepare an income statement, select Reports, then Income & Expense, and customize the report for a specific period. At the bottom of the Customize Report dialog box are three options within a Report Transfers By box. Check the Income Statement option button to suppress transfers on this report. If you want to summarize in a cash-flow format, there also is an option for that. Figure 4-12 illustrates a single month income statement with rows for every subcategory. After you've accumulated data for several months' worth of transactions, you undoubtedly should compare one month's performance to previous months. Do this by preparing a multimonth income statement. Figure 4-13 shows an example with rows for each category (subcategories are summed into the categories). Customize an Income & Expense report by specifying a three month date range, a row for every category, and a column for every month. Check Income Statement in the Report Transfers By box, and experiment with Fonts to compress the printed characters on the report.

SAMPLE INCOME STATEMENT
12/1/91 Through 12/31/91

Subcategory	Total
INCOME	
Revenue	
Consulting	2,000.00
Training	2,800.00
Total Revenue	4,800.00
TOTAL INCOME	4,800.00
EXPENSES	
Advertising	720.00
Automobile/Truck	
Maintenance	108.00
Total Automobile/Truck	108.00
Bank Charges	30.70
Entertainment	
Meals	41.50
Total Entertainment	41.50
Insurance	
Automobile	240.00
Liability	400.00
Total Insurance	640.00
Miscellaneous	16.50
Office Expenses	
Supplies	42.00
Total Office Expenses	42.00
Training Material	120.00
TOTAL EXPENSES	1,718.70
INCOME LESS EXPENSES	3,081.30

4-12 Single month income statement

Balance sheets

A balance sheet summarizes the ending balances in all of your accounts at a specific date. This differs from the income statement, which lists accumulated amounts in categories for a period of time that you specify. The balance sheet presented in Fig. 4-1 at the beginning of this chapter is a comprehensive example that uses all of the accounts we have discussed thus far. Look at that balance sheet again and notice that the net worth is calculated by subtracting Total Liabilities from Total Assets.

COMPARATIVE INCOME STATEMENT - NOV & DEC
11/1/91 Through 12/31/91

Category	11/1/91 - 11/30/91	12/1/91 - 12/31/91	Total
INCOME			
Revenue	3,600.00	4,800.00	8,400.00
TOTAL INCOME	3,600.00	4,800.00	8,400.00
EXPENSES			
Advertising	695.00	720.00	1,415.00
Automobile/Truck	92.50	108.00	200.50
Bank Charges	22.50	30.70	53.20
Entertainment	88.95	41.50	130.45
Insurance	102.00	640.00	742.00
Miscellaneous	12.13	16.50	28.63
Office Expenses	194.95	73.00	267.95
Training Material	82.30	120.00	202.30
TOTAL EXPENSES	1,290.33	1,749.70	3,040.03
INCOME LESS EXPENSES	2,309.67	3,050.30	5,359.97

4-13 Multimonth income statement

Generally in the business world, what your business is worth is determined by the remainder left when the things you owe (liabilities) are subtracted from the things you own (assets). In other words, it is the owners' equity in the business. Equity refers to the owners' investment plus or minus net income, or losses over the life of the business.

Money balance sheets cannot be customized much, except for the date, but your accountant will appreciate them as they are. If you want to make more changes to the layout of the balance sheet, you can export the report to a file to be used in a spreadsheet or word processing package. Look in chapter 12 for the procedures for doing this.

Journals

A business journal is a chronological record of all financial dealings of the organization. The report includes transactions of all kinds in all accounts. It is a matter of personal preference whether the journal includes the payee, memo, category, subcategory, and classification (if any). A simplified journal is illustrated in Fig. 4-14.

This report was produced by customizing a register report so that it includes the Memo field, displays split transactions, includes all transactions from all accounts, and so that it is restricted to a specific date period.

Num	Date	Payee	Account	Category	Amount
Month Ending 12/31/91					
	12/10/9	Service Charge	Business Checking	Bank Charges	(8.20)
dep	12/11/9	Bigtime Corporation	Business Checking	Revenue : Training	2,400.00
	12/12/9	Pocket Money	Cash on Hand	Transfer From : Bus	100.00
atm	12/12/9	Pocket Money	Business Checking	Transfer To : Cash	(100.00)
	12/13/9	Locke Office Supple	Cash on Hand	Office Expenses : S	(42.00)
	12/14/9	Orson Eatery	Cash on Hand	Entertainment : Mea	(41.50)
	12/14/9	Misc	Cash on Hand	Miscellaneous	(16.50)
	12/15/9	First National CD	Certs of Deposit	Transfer To : Busin	(1,000.00)
	12/15/9	Pocket Money	Cash on Hand	Transfer From : Bus	200.00
	12/15/9	Coastal Computer Ce	Equipment	Transfer From : Bus	5,500.00
	12/15/9	Coastal Computer Ce	Equip Loans Payable	Transfer To : Busin	(5,000.00)
atm	12/15/9	Pocket Money	Business Checking	Transfer To : Cash	(200.00)
dep	12/15/9	First National CD	Business Checking	Transfer From : Cer	1,000.00
Print	12/15/9	Coastal Computer Ce	Business Checking	Split	(500.00)
	12/16/9	West Side Mobil	Cash on Hand	Automobile/Truck :	(108.00)
	12/16/9	City Bank	Note Payable	Transfer To : Busin	(2,000.00)
Dep	12/16/9	City Bank	Business Checking	Transfer From : Not	2,000.00
Dep	12/17/9	Middle Company	Business Checking	Revenue : Training	400.00
Print	12/17/9	Kinko's Copy Center	Business Checking	Split	(120.00)
	Total Month Ending 12/31/91				2,463.80
GRAND TOTAL					2,463.80

4-14 Journal for one week

If you want to print a list of transactions within a specific account, or transactions in various categories for some period, you can customize a register report even further. Figure 4-15 is an example of a restricted business register report of this type. In this example, I wanted to analyze the transactions in one category for a three month period. I selected Reports then Register Report and customized it to include a descriptive title, Memo, Account and Client fields, subtotal by month, and All Accounts. I also specified a date range and restricted it to Select Transactions—specifically one category. This is a form of Journal report restricted to one category. You might need to experiment with width and fonts to get the report to fit across one page.

Num	Date	Payee	Account	Memo	Amount
Month Ending 10/31/91					
88	10/22/9	USPS	Business Checking	Envelopes	(18.50)
94	10/31/9	High Street Party S	Business Checking	Halloween Party at	(12.50)
	Total Month Ending 10/31/91				(31.00)
Month Ending 11/30/91					
Dep	11/1/91	Locke Office Supply	Business Checking	Report Pads	(56.00)
	11/17/9	Downeast Office Mat	Cash on Hand	Misc Office Supplie	(56.50)
	11/18/9	Ace Computer	Business Checking	Fix Platen on Print	(82.45)
	Total Month Ending 11/30/91				(194.95)
Month Ending 12/31/91					
	12/13/9	Locke Office Supply	Cash on Hand	Binders & Folders	(42.00)
	Total Month Ending 12/31/91				(42.00)
GRAND TOTAL					(267.95)

4-15 Transaction register for office expenses for three months

Summary reports

An example of a summary report was shown in Fig. 4-4 to illustrate the collection of client data. Summary reports can be prepared for any subset of data that you've entered, because the customize option for summary reports presents unlimited possibilities. Figure 4-16 shows a summary report that tracks which accounts were used to enter transactions in various categories. For this report, select Report then Summary Report from the menu and customize for a descriptive title. Select row for every category, column for every account, specify a date range, and include all accounts and all transactions. This report could be customized further by selecting transactions for a specific payee, client, or category.

ACCOUNT SOURCE AUDIT TRAIL
12/1/91 Through 12/31/91

Category	Business Checking	Cash on Hand	Total
INCOME CATEGORIES			
Revenue	4,800.00		4,800.00
TOTAL INCOME CATEGORIES	4,800.00		4,800.00
EXPENSE CATEGORIES			
Advertising	720.00		720.00
Automobile/Truck		108.00	108.00
Bank Charges	30.70		30.70
Entertainment		41.50	41.50
Insurance	640.00		640.00
Miscellaneous		16.50	16.50
Office Expenses		42.00	42.00
Training Material	120.00		120.00
TOTAL EXPENSE CATEGORIE	1,510.70	208.00	1,718.70
GRAND TOTAL	3,289.30	(208.00)	3,081.30

4-16 Summary report by category and account

Other reports

For small business reporting, all categories are tax related. Because of this, the income statement, balance sheet, and summary reports all serve as tax reports. The Tax Reports option on the Reports menu is not used. The budget report is the only other report on the Report menu, which is covered in a special chapter on budgeting—chapter 7.

Summary

In this chapter, we covered the bare essentials of using Money for small business record keeping. We've discussed using a separate file for business records, establishing a basic set of accounts to use, customizing categories, and using classifications, as well how to obtain many useful reports. To further your repertoire of transactions, some common business transactions were explored. We will cover much more on small business procedures in chapters 5 through 12.

Small business basics tutorial

This tutorial builds on the concepts learned in chapters 1 through 3, and assumes that you have completed the tutorials of chapters 1 and 3. The chapter 2 tutorial was optional, but this exercise assumes that you are familiar with Windows terminology. Access Money from the Program Manager window of Windows 3.0.

Part A

When the Money window appears, it contains the transactions of the last file that you were working on. To ensure that you have a separate file for business records, we'll create one now. Then we'll return to the sample file that you created in the chapter 1 tutorial, which you expanded in chapter 3.

- ☐ With the Money window open, select File then New
- ☐ Type business in the File Name box and choose Ok
- ☐ Make a backup copy of the file you were previously using by following the screen prompts
- ☐ In the Setup New File box, check the Business Categories option
- ☐ Choose Ok and Ok again in the Create First Account box
- ☐ Type your own bank name for Account Name
- ☐ Choose Ok and type a zero for Opening Balance, then Ok
- ☐ The screen now displays a blank account book for your new Business Checking account
- ☐ Take a careful look at the categories in the Business list
- ☐ Select List then Category List
- ☐ Scroll slowly through the categories and subcategories
- ☐ Choose Close to return to the account book
- ☐ Select File then Open from the menu
- ☐ Select sample.mny in the list of file names, then Ok
- ☐ Choose No in the Backup box
- ☐ The sample file we used previously is now in the window

Part B

This section describes how to customize categories and subcategories for a specific business.

- ☐ Select List then Category List from the menu
- ☐ The Category List dialog box appears
- ☐ Select Rental Income in the Category List box
- ☐ Notice that there are two boxes on the left side of the window: one labelled Category List, and the other labelled Subcategory List
- ☐ Be careful which of these you choose as you proceed below
- ☐ Choose Delete from below the Category List box (Alt−D)
- ☐ The highlighted category is deleted with no warning
- ☐ Select Revenue in the Category List box
- ☐ Choose New below the Subcategory List box (Alt−W)
- ☐ Type Training in the New Subcategory box, then Ok
- ☐ Choose New below the subcategory list again
- ☐ Type Consulting in the New Subcategory box, then Ok
- ☐ The Revenue category now contains two subcategories
- ☐ Scroll further through the category list to select Office Expenses

Note   You can move back and forth from the category list to subcategory list with Alt−L for Category and Alt−U for Subcategory. Always look for the underlined letter of the area of the screen you want to move to, and press Alt+ that underlined letter.

- ☐ Select Equipment in the subcategory list
- ☐ Choose Delete below the subcategory list (Alt−E)
- ☐ Select Furnishing in the subcategory list
- ☐ Choose Delete below the subcategory list
- ☐ Select Services in the category list
- ☐ Choose Rename below the category list (Alt−R)
- ☐ Type Professional Fees in the New Name box, then Ok
- ☐ Choose Report at the upper right (Alt−T)
- ☐ Choose Print at the upper right (Alt−P), then Ok
- ☐ Choose Close to return to the Category List box
- ☐ Choose Close again to return to the account book

Part C

This section leads you through one of the ways that you can set up a new account. Part F will guide you through setting up a new account by typing it when an account name is called for within a transaction.

- ☐ Select List then Account List from the menu
- ☐ Choose New in the Account List dialog box (Alt−N)
- ☐ Type Equipment in the Account Name box
- ☐ Check the Asset Account option (Alt−A), then Ok
- ☐ Type a zero in the Opening Balance box, then Ok
- ☐ Choose New in the Account List dialog box (Alt−N)
- ☐ Type Equip Loans Payable in the Account Name box
- ☐ Check the Liability Account option (Alt−L), then Ok
- ☐ Type zero in the Opening Balance box, then Ok
- ☐ Choose Close to return to the Account Book window

Part D

We are now ready to enter some equipment and loan transactions in these new accounts. First we'll record the purchase of a $5500 computer system, paying $500 down, with the balance to be financed over 4 years at 12%—resulting in monthly payments of $131.67.

- ☐ Select the next blank transaction line (Ctrl−End)
- ☐ Remember to press Tab to move between fields
- ☐ Type p in the Num field, and 12/14 in the Date field
- ☐ Type Coastal Computer in the Payee field
- ☐ Type 500 in the Payment field
- ☐ Select the Split Transaction tool (Ctrl−S)
- ☐ Select Transfer from the category list
- ☐ Select Equipment from the Account list (this appears in the Subcategory field)
- ☐ Type ComTech PC with Printer in the Description field
- ☐ Type 5500 in the Amount field and Tab to the next line
- ☐ Select Transfer from the category list
- ☐ Select Equip Loans Payable from the account list
- ☐ Press " in the Description field

- [ ] Type – 5000 in the Amount field and press Tab
- [ ] The net amount of these two lines is the $500 down payment
- [ ] The net amount of the split transaction is now 0
- [ ] Choose Done to return to the account book
- [ ] Press Enter to complete the transaction
- [ ] Select File, Print Checks, then Ok
- [ ] The $500 down payment check to Coastal is printed
- [ ] Select Equip Loans Payable in the Account box
- [ ] The balance of Equip Loans Payable should be $5000
- [ ] Select Equipment in the Account box
- [ ] The balance of this account is $5500
- [ ] Return to the account book for the Checking account

Part E

In this part, we will schedule the monthly loan payment for this computer loan. The loan payment of $131.67 is comprised of $81.67 payment toward the principal and $50 in interest.

- [ ] Switch to the Future Transactions window
- [ ] Select the next available transaction line
- [ ] Type 1/16 in the Date field
- [ ] Select Monthly in the Frequency field
- [ ] Type p in the Num field
- [ ] Type Coas in the Payee field
- [ ] Type 131.67 in the Payment field
- [ ] Select the Split Transaction tool or Ctrl – S

Note The data you see in the window now is from the previous Coastal transaction. It will be necessary to type lines for the loan payment over the existing computer purchase data. In the Category and Subcategory fields in this window, the Down Arrow button indicates that a list is available to you. Press Alt – Down Arrow to activate these lists. To make selections from these lists, press Down Arrow to highlight your choice, then Tab to the next field. With a mouse, click on the arrows and then on your selection.

- [ ] Press Tab, or select the Category field on the first line
- [ ] Select Transfer in the category list
- [ ] Select Equip Loans Payable in the account list

- ☐ Type Monthly Payment on PC Loan in the Description
- ☐ Type 81.67 in the Amount field
- ☐ Press Tab to begin the next line
- ☐ Select Interest Expense in the category list
- ☐ Press " in the Description field
- ☐ Type 50 in the Amount field and press Tab
- ☐ Notice that the Net Amount of the split is now 0
- ☐ Choose Done to return to the Future Transaction window
- ☐ Press Enter to complete this transaction

Note   When the middle of January rolls around, the Money reminder box will let you know that this payment is due.

Part F

This section describes the procedure for recording loans directly from a bank. This time we'll set up a new account (Notes Payable) during the transaction entry instead of editing through the account list. Let's borrow a couple thousand from City Bank.

- ☐ Return to the account book for the Checking account
- ☐ Select the next available transaction line
- ☐ Type Dep in the Num field
- ☐ Type 12/16 in the Date field
- ☐ Type City Bank in the Payee field
- ☐ Tab past the Payment amount field
- ☐ Type 2000 in the Deposit field
- ☐ Type 1 Yr, 12% Operating Loan in the Memo field
- ☐ Select Transfer in the category list
- ☐ Type Notes Payable in the Account Field, and press Tab (this initiates the Create New Account process)
- ☐ Note that the account name Notes Payable is filled in
- ☐ Press Alt−L, or click to check Liability Account
- ☐ Choose Ok
- ☐ Type 0 as the opening balance, then Ok
- ☐ You're back in the transaction entry
- ☐ Press Enter to complete this transaction
- ☐ Switch to the account book of the Notes Payable account

- ☐ Notice the $2000 increase transferred here
- ☐ Return to the account book of the Checking account

Part G

This section provides practice in setting up classifications. For our sample business, we will set up a system of classification for two major training projects we are working on. Then, we will enter a deposit from Middle Company for a project we are working on for them.

- ☐ Select List then Other Classification from the menu
- ☐ Choose New within the Classification 1 box
- ☐ Check the Project item on the Type list (Alt−P)
- ☐ Choose Ok, and a Project List dialog box appears
- ☐ Choose New in the Project List box
- ☐ Type Middle Co-Spreadsheets and choose Ok
- ☐ Choose New again for a second project
- ☐ Type Bigtime-Basic PC Course and choose Ok
- ☐ Choose Close to return to the account book
- ☐ Notice that each transaction section now has an extra line
- ☐ Select the next available transaction line (Ctrl−End)
- ☐ Type Dep, 12/17, then Middle Company
- ☐ Skip the Payment field and type 400 as the deposit
- ☐ Type Deposit on Spreadsheet Course as the Memo
- ☐ Select Revenue from the category list
- ☐ Select Training from the subcategory list
- ☐ Select Middle Co-Spreadsheets in the project list
- ☐ Press Enter to record this transaction

Note   During all future transaction entries, you will be presented with the project list. To track the Middle Company and Bigtime Corporation projects, you should categorize all appropriate transactions associated with each project. Many other transactions, however, will not use the Project field.

Part H

In this part, we will edit Bigtime's payments to show that they should be applied to subcategories and the Basic PC Course project we just created. We also will record an expenditure transaction that applies to our two projects.

- [ ] Select the Find tool on the toolbar (Ctrl−F)
- [ ] Type Bigt and choose Find Next (Alt−F)
- [ ] The highlighter moves to the 12/11 Bigtime transaction
- [ ] Press Esc or choose Cancel to remove the Find box
- [ ] Move to the Subcategory field, to the right of Revenue
- [ ] Select Training as the subcategory
- [ ] Move to the Project field
- [ ] Select Bigtime-Basic PC Course from the project list
- [ ] Press Enter to record the transaction
- [ ] Execute Find again
- [ ] Move to the 12/1 Bigtime Transaction
- [ ] Tab to the Subcategory field and select Consulting
- [ ] Select the next available transaction line
- [ ] Type p, 12/17, then Kinko's Copy Center, and 120 in the Payment field
- [ ] Type Course Handouts as the Memo
- [ ] Choose the Split Transaction tool
- [ ] Type Training Materials as the category, then Tab
- [ ] This is a new category, so the Create New Category dialog box appears
- [ ] Choose Ok to establish this new category
- [ ] Type 80 as the amount
- [ ] Select Bigtime-Basic PC Course from the project list
- [ ] Tab to the second section of the Split Transaction
- [ ] Press " to repeat Training Materials as the category
- [ ] Press " to repeat Course Handouts as the description
- [ ] Type 40 as the amount
- [ ] Select Middle Co-Spreadsheets from the project list
- [ ] Choose Done, then Enter to finish this transaction

Part I

This section helps you see the results of some of the actions taken in this tutorial. We will customize and print some financial statements. First let's look at a summary of our project revenue & expenditures.

- [ ] Select the Reports then Summary Report, menu items
- [ ] Choose Customize

- [ ] Type Project Summary in the Title box
- [ ] In the Row for Every box, select Category
- [ ] In the Column for Every box, select Project
- [ ] In the Date Range box, select From and type 12/1
- [ ] Tab to the To box and type 12/31.
- [ ] Make sure that All Accounts and All Transactions is selected
- [ ] Choose View and scroll through the report
- [ ] Choose Print, then Ok to print this on paper
- [ ] Choose Close to return to the account book

Note This report shows only the few transactions we classified in Parts G and H, so it isn't too meaningful yet. Once you classify all transactions that apply to a project, a project report like this can be very revealing.

Part J

Lastly we'll print the basic business financial statements—the income statement and balance sheet.

- [ ] Select the Reports, then Income & Expense menu items
- [ ] Choose Customize
- [ ] Type My Company Income Statement in the Title box
- [ ] In the Date Range box, select From and type 12/1
- [ ] Tab to the To box and type 12/31
- [ ] Be sure that All Accounts and All Transactions is selected
- [ ] Check the Income Statement option on the last line within this Customize Report dialog box
- [ ] Choose View and scroll through the report
- [ ] This summarizes all revenue recorded in December as well as all expenses from all accounts in December
- [ ] Choose Print then Ok to print this on paper
- [ ] Choose Close to return to the account book
- [ ] Select the Reports then Net Worth menu items
- [ ] Choose Customize
- [ ] Type My Company Balance Sheet in the title box
- [ ] In the Date box type 12/31
- [ ] Choose View and scroll through the report

- □ This report lists ending balances in all the accounts
- □ Choose Print then Ok to print this on paper
- □ Choose Close to return to the account book

Part K

Although everything we've done was saved as we progressed through this tutorial, it's always a good idea to make a backup copy.

- □ Select File then Backup from the menu
- □ Insert a disk in your A: disk drive and choose Yes
- □ If the Confirmation Overwrite box appears, choose Yes
- □ Hang around and experiment!

5
CHAPTER

Maintaining lists

This chapter focuses on the list structure that Money relies on for organizing data and reporting results. The category list, payee list, account list, and the classifications list form the basis of all user files. When transactions are recorded, at least one of these lists must be used by the computer in order to properly store the data. This chapter details the techniques for creating lists, entering items on lists, changing items on lists, and deleting unnecessary items from lists.

Maintaining an account list

The *account list* contains items that describe groups of related transactions. For example, your Checking account is the item that contains all transactions resulting from the flow of money into and out of your Checking account with a bank. If you have several checking accounts each of these would be listed in Money as separate items (accounts). An account list is created automatically when you first use Money and are required to create your first account. We've done this at the end of each chapter tutorial in previous chapters.

Personal account lists

After defining the term *account* in chapter 3, it was suggested that the basis for personal recordkeeping was formed by a few basic accounts for bank checking, credit cards, loans, and property owned. To be specific, the following titles are suggested as a set of personal accounts:

- ☐ Checking account (several if necessary)
- ☐ Cash on Hand (pocket cash)
- ☐ Savings accounts (any bank account other than checking)
- ☐ Real Estate (any real property)

☐ Motor Vehicles (cars, trucks, vans, motor homes, trailers, etc.)
☐ Equipment (power tools, small tools, sports equipment, boats, computers, etc.)
☐ Appliances (kitchen, heating, generator, etc.)
☐ Investments (securities, annuities, CDs, bonds, etc.)
☐ Credit Cards (one account for each VISA, American Express, etc.)
☐ Bank loans (car loans, consumer loans, major purchase loans)
☐ Mortgage payable (any real estate loans, home equity loans)

The last three items on the above list are personal liabilities (your obligations to pay some creditor), and the rest are personal assets (what you own). Maintaining these types of accounts enables you to determine your net worth. This concept was introduced in chapter 3 and will be discussed further in chapter 6.

Each individual situation calls for modification of the titles suggested by this list. For example, the equipment item listed above might be replaced by several accounts; sports equipment, computers, or tools (of all kinds, from the electric drill to the lawn mower). In each of these accounts, the Payee or Memo field could be used to identify which specific piece of equipment was involved. When you purchase a modem for your computer, the Memo field could begin with the word Computer, so that reports could later be customized based on the Memo field to group all Computer transactions in the Equipment account.

Transactions in personal accounts

Many personal transactions should be recorded in one of the accounts suggested above, instead of being categorized to the revenue or expense categories found on the Money Category list. For example, when you buy a new boat, the cash outlay should probably be recorded as a payment in your Checking account, but what do you use for the category? If you buy the boat outright for cash, categorize the whole amount as a transfer to the Sports Equipment account. If you make a down payment and set up a loan for the rest, categorize the full cost of the boat as a transfer to Sports Equipment, categorize the amount of the loan as a negative transfer to a Loans Payable account and the net amount of this transaction is the down payment. This example is illustrated in Fig. 5-1.

The idea here is that you will end up with a more accurate picture of your financial status if you maintain these asset and liability accounts as well as charging true expenses to expense categories. Other examples of nonexpense transactions are provided in chapters 3 and 4.

Business account lists

Several complete lists of suggested business accounts were given in the section on the minimum set of business accounts in chapter 4. The importance of maintaining asset and liability accounts and categorizing every item of revenue and

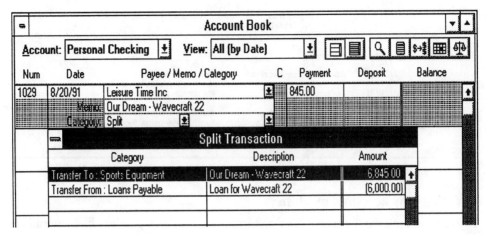

5-1 Personal purchase of a major asset

expense was discussed. This is so business owners and managers can determine an accurate picture of their net income each period and the status of the business' net worth, which is the ultimate goal of all business recordkeeping.

Don't let this concept overwhelm you. Micro businesses begin by gaining control of the revenue versus expense picture. You can do this by religiously categorizing every transaction as either Revenue, Expense, or Other. Other should be an account (not a category) that you create outside of your checking account to catch any transactions that should not be categorized as revenue or expense. This Other account then collects data about your net worth without the breakdown into assets and liabilities. Put loans, purchases of assets and investments, proceeds from sale of assets, etc. in the Other account just to keep them out of the revenue/expense picture. By doing this, you will ensure that the bottom line of the Income and Expense report delivers the true story of net income—profit.

An example of the use of a catch-all Other account is illustrated in Figs. 5-2 and 5-3. Figure 5-2 illustrates a business transaction that should be handled as a transfer to the Other account. Figure 5-3 presents a sample Register report for the Other account. It should be clarified, however, that this suggestion about an Other account is an inferior alternative to the sound business management principles presented in chapter 4 and in the upcoming chapters.

⊟	Account Book	▼ ▲
Account: Personal Checking ⬇	**View:** All (by Date) ⬇	⊟ ▤ 🔍 ▤ $→$ ▦ ⚖

Num	Date	Payee / Memo / Category	C	Payment	Deposit	Balance
Dep	7/5/91	Key Bank			2,000.00	5,275.00 ▲
		1 year loan				
		Transfer From : Other - Non Inc/Exp				

5-2 Sample transaction categorized to "Other" account

Num	Date	Payee	Memo	Amount
	7/5/91	Key Bank	1 year loan	(2,000.00)
	7/17/91	Downeast Communications	Car Phone System	522.60
	8/7/91	Key Bank	Monthly Payment on Loan	88.50
	8/20/91	Leisure Time Inc	Our Dream - Wavecraft 22	6,845.00
	8/20/91	Leisure Time Inc	Loan for Wavecraft 22	(6,000.00)
	8/21/91	Ferris Credit Union	Monthly Payment on Car P	45.50
	8/23/91	Fidelity Mortgage Co.	Monthly Mortgage Payment	57.70
	8/31/91	Old Town Canoe Co	Tripper Canoe	782.00
GRAND TOTAL				341.30

5-3 Register report for an "Other" account

Creating new accounts in Money

If you've completed the tutorials of previous chapters, you're already a veteran at creating new accounts. The process takes place by naming a nonexistent account during the entry of a transfer transaction, or through the List command on the Main Menu. With the latter procedure, select the List then Account List menu items, and then select the New button in the Account List dialog box.

In either case, a Create New Account dialog box appears where you must type an account name and indicate a type of account. Money includes provisions for the following types of accounts: bank account, credit card, cash or other, asset, and liability accounts. Figure 5-4 shows this dialog box, so you can review the descriptions of each of these account types. Then you are asked to enter an

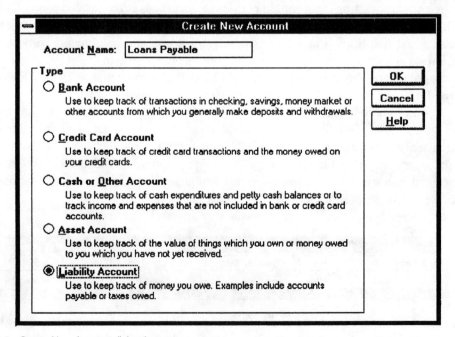

5-4 Create New Account dialog box

opening balance for your new account. I suggest that you start with a zero balance and enter transactions to build a balance in the account. When these two steps are complete, you are returned to the transaction you were entering, or to the Account List dialog box, with your new account displayed as the selected account. In the Account List dialog box, you then might indicate a shortcut code, bank name, account number, and comment.

If you created a new account during the middle of a transaction, you can recall the new account listing for editing by selecting the List then Account List menu items to reach the Account List dialog box and scroll to the account you want to work with.

Shortcut, bank name, account number, and comment

An example of the Account List dialog box for a Mortgage Payable account is shown in Fig. 5-5. The Shortcut code is a very brief reference for the account that can be entered when an account name is needed by Money. During transaction entry, the shortcut Pay can be entered instead of Mortgage or instead of scrolling to the Mortgage Payable account in a long list. The shortcut field also can be used to identify how items are transferred to a tax preparation program. The Opening Balance can be changed at any time; however, this is not recommended because it could render earlier reports invalid if they contained this figure, and it also could affect the balancing of accounts that you reconcile periodically.

Use the Bank Name field to identify your bank, if you are using a bank account. Enter a company or organization name here, if this is a nonbank mortgage, loan, or credit card.

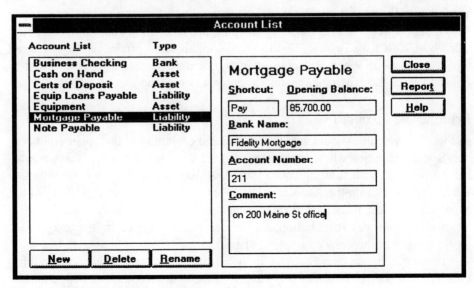

5-5 Account List dialog box for mortgage payable

The Account Number field can contain the account number that the bank has assigned to you, or a small business might want to assign numbers to each account in keeping with a chart of accounts. This method calls for a pattern where 100 through 199 might be assigned to assets and 200 through 299 to liabilities.

The Comment field could serve a number of purposes. Small businesses could effectively use this field for a description of the types of transactions that should be assigned to the account, as shown in Fig. 5-5.

Editing existing accounts

The Account List dialog box illustrated in Fig. 5-5 is the work area where you will do all your maintenance of accounts, other than transaction entry. You can see that this box contains buttons for Delete and Rename, as well as the New option. All of the fields discussed in the previous paragraph can be edited at any time by selecting an account in the account list, and changing data in any field within that account.

Use the Delete button if you want to completely remove an account, and any transactions in that account, from your files. Be sure the correct account is selected when you take this action. If the account has no balance, you will not be warned to confirm the deletion. If there is a balance in the account, from an opening balance or from transactions, you will be warned that this is true and asked "Are you sure?" before the deletion is completed. When you select Yes, all the transactions in the deleted account will be erased. (If you do this accidentally, refer to the section on using backup copies in chapter 12.)

Use the Rename button if you want to change the name of an account to be more descriptive. For example, you might have started using Money with one account for all loans, Loans Payable. Later you might want to change that name to Auto Loan Payable after establishing separate accounts for Equipment Loan Payable and Credit Line Payable. Spelling and capitalization errors can be corrected this way as well. When you choose Rename, a Rename dialog box opens to remind you of the existing name and asks for a new name.

Printing the account list

In Fig. 5-5, you also should take notice of a Report button in the upper right corner. Select this option when you want to print a list of your accounts. The list automatically prints with shortcut codes included. You can customize it to eliminate the shortcut codes on the Account List report and to include the balances in the accounts, the bank name, and account number. The Customize Account List dialog box includes an Export button, so you can create a tab-delimited text file for use in your word processor or spread sheet.

If you specify Account Balances in the customize box, you'll get both opening balances and current balances. Figure 5-6 presents an account list with balances

Account	Opening Balance	Current Balance
Business Checking	0.00	5,459.30
Cash on Hand	0.00	92.00
Certs of Deposit	1,000.00	0.00
Equip Loans Payable	0.00	5,000.00
Equipment	0.00	5,500.00
Mortgage Payable	85,700.00	85,700.00
Note Payable	0.00	2,000.00

5-6 Account list report

in the accounts. This is similar to a net worth report, but you have no opportunity to specify a date range, so be aware that the amounts shown are as of the current date. Also the balances are not shown as positive and negative numbers, so it's hard to see their relationship to one another. I recommend not using this report for business purposes. Rely on the Net Worth report instead.

If you specify Bank Name in the customize box, you get both the bank name and the account number on your report. This would be the way to print a business Chart of Accounts with account numbers.

Maintaining a payee list

As you enter transactions, Money builds a list of payees automatically. SmartFill relies on this list to help you enter additional data for these payees. The term *Payee* includes both parties you pay money to and parties you receive money from. You can be somewhat unaware of the *payee list*, unless you activate the list arrow in the Payee field of a transaction entry. Instead of typing a payee name, you can select a name from the list that cascades from the Payee field. An example of this is shown in Fig. 5-7.

The procedures for entering new payees, editing payee information, and printing payee lists are similar to the procedures presented for maintaining accounts.

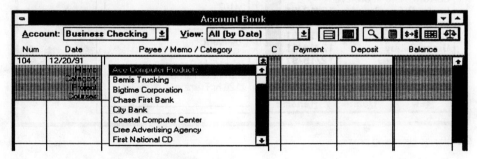

5-7 Payee list dropped down from the payee field

Entering new payees

You automatically enter a payee on the payee list when you type a name in the Payee field of a check, an account book transaction, or a future transaction, and when the payee name has not been entered before. For this reason, you should be very careful to spell and capitalize a payee name correctly the first time you use it. During subsequent data entry, you can use all caps or all small letters and only have to type a few characters before SmartFill finds the payee. If you want to enter an address for a payee, you might want to enter early transactions in the Checks & Forms screen, because that window includes a field for such data. If you want to enter addresses later, you can do this from the Payee List dialog box, discussed below.

An alternate, and more complete, procedure for entering payees is the selection of List, then Payee List, from the menu to access the Payee List dialog box. This dialog box is shown in Fig. 5-8. In a similar fashion to creating a new account, you can choose the New button here and fill in the Payee information box shown below the large heading for Bigtime Corp. Enter a phone number so you can later print a phone list. Enter an address if you want to use window envelopes to mail checks to the payee. Use the Comment box to maintain notes about the payee, such as contact names, pay rates, contract dates, credit terms or other helpful notations.

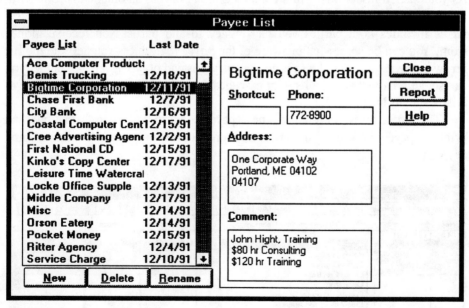

5-8 Payee List dialog box

Editing existing payees

First access the Payee List dialog box by selecting List, then Payee List from the menu. Then select the payee you want to edit in the Payee List. Existing information for that payee will be displayed in the information box. Select any field you want to edit and type in your changes. The Rename and Delete buttons in the Payee List dialog box are used to make changes in your existing payees in the same way these options work on an account. Use the Rename button to make any corrections to a payee name that you entered earlier. Use the Delete button to remove payees that you no longer need. You can delete a payee whose name is included on completed transactions without affecting those transactions—no transactions or payee names within them will be deleted. You can restore a payee name by typing it on a new transaction.

Printing the payee list

The phone numbers and shortcut codes that you enter for each payee can be printed on a Payee List report. Produce a payee list by choosing Report from the Payee List dialog box (you can see this in Fig. 5-8), and a two column list will be displayed showing Payee Name and Shortcut. Customize this report to include Phone Numbers for a handy calling list. The data from your payee list also can be exported to a tab-delimited text file to be used with a word processor. Choose Export and enter a file name to create a file on disk. Access your word processor and load in this file of payee names from Money.

Maintaining category lists

Categories and subcategories are maintained in one window, the Category List dialog box. The procedures that are used are the same as those used for the payee and account list maintenance, with a few extra twists.

Entering new categories and subcategories

You can enter a new category or subcategory by naming a nonexistent category (or subcategory) during the entry of any transaction, or by using the New button in the Category List dialog box. With the latter procedure, select the List then Category List menu items to access the Account List dialog box and then choose New. A Create New Category (or Subcategory) dialog box appears where you can enter or verify the category name and indicate whether it is an income or expense category. If you are creating a subcategory, you are asked to verify which category it applies to.

The Category List dialog box is illustrated in Fig. 5-9. Take careful note of the two list boxes within this dialog box. When you select a category in the Category List box, the subcategory list changes to display the subcategories of the category selected in the upper box. The category information box in the middle of this dialog box displays the additional information that is stored for the selected category. When you create a new category, or by later editing, you can enter a shortcut code, a comment, budget amounts, and a notation to include the category on Tax reports.

Editing categories

You can Rename or Delete categories and subcategories using these buttons in the Category List dialog box in the same manner as you rename or delete accounts. Take a look at Fig. 5-9 and notice that there are two sets of New, Delete and Rename buttons—the upper set belongs to the category list and the lower set belongs to the subcategory list. A name must be selected on one of the lists in order for the Delete and Rename buttons to be usable. When they are not usable, they are blurry (referred to as *grayed out*), indicating that they cannot be selected at that moment.

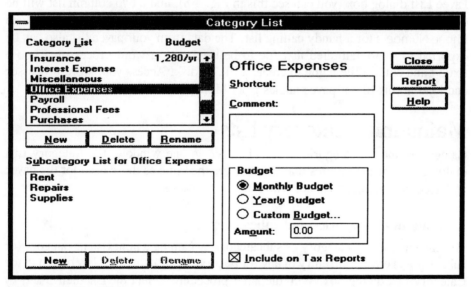

5-9 Category List dialog box

If you rename a category, all transactions that use that category are updated with the new name. When you delete a category or subcategory, you will be asked for confirmation if there are amounts assigned to that category. A Delete Category dialog box will appear where you will be asked where you would like to reassign the transactions. If you insist on deleting a category or subcategory with amounts without reassigning the transactions, the deleted categories and subcategories will be changed to blank categories in the associated transactions. If you delete a category that contains subcategories, you will be warned of this and asked for confirmation; then the subcategories are deleted along with the category you've specified.

Once you understand this process, you can use this delete action to combine transactions from two categories into one, or move transactions from a category to a subcategory. For example, let's say you wanted to combine the transactions in the Freight category with the transactions in a subcategory under Purchases named Transportation In. Delete the Freight category, and in the Delete Category dialog box, indicate that you want any transactions reassigned to the Transportation In subcategory.

Edit the shortcut, comment, budget, or tax report flag by selecting a category or subcategory and typing in the field you want to change. Entering and editing budgets is complex, so an entire chapter expands upon it—chapter 7.

Printing the category list

Categories and subcategories are printed together on one list when you choose the Report button in the Category List dialog box. You can see this button in the upper right corner of Fig. 5-9. Without customization, the category list will be broken down by subcategories and include shortcuts. Choose the Customize button once the report is displayed to include basic or detailed budgets. This is the procedure that must be used to print a full year budget plan with no actual spending amounts. Refer to chapter 7 where budgets are discussed in detail.

You also can create a tab-delimited text file to be used in your word processor by choosing the Export button in the Customize Category List dialog box. You'll find more about Export in chapter 12.

Maintaining classification lists

The procedures for maintaining classification lists are similar to those discussed earlier for accounts and categories. We practiced entering one type of classification, *projects*, in the chapter 4 tutorial. Refer to sections on classifications in chapters 3 and 4 if you need an explanation of how classifications are used.

Creating a classification

You must first establish a classification by selecting List then Other Classification from the menu, and then choosing New in the Classification 1 box of the Other Classifications dialog box. This is followed by a Classify By list where you can select from client, department, job, project, property, work order, or a unique type that you enter yourself. If you check the Allow Sub Items? option, each item (client or job) can have subitems (like projects being worked on for one client). After these first setup steps, you will be presented with a Client List dialog box (or Job, Project, etc.) as illustrated in Fig. 5-10. Choose the New button to enter

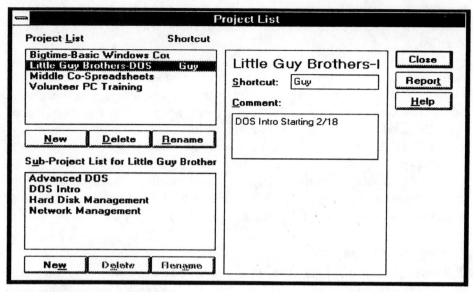

5-10 Item List dialog box for classifications

the name of each item in this classification, and select the Subitem, Shortcut, or Comment box to enter more detailed information.

You can maintain up to two classification types, but each of the classifications can contain as many items as you need. If you set up two different types of classifications the transaction entry area of the Account Book expands to five lines. Summary reports can be produced by any classification that you invent. If you create a unique classification name, like Trips offered by a travel agency, you will see the word Trips on the customize choices within a report.

Editing classification items

Once you establish a classification type of client, department, job, project, property, work order, or a unique name, these terms appear as part of the titles on the Create and List boxes. For purposes of example, the following few paragraphs use the word *client* when referring to a sample classification. Think of replacing that word with *Project, Job*, or whatever classification you want to create.

The Client List dialog box that was illustrated in Fig. 5-9 is the work area where you will do all your maintenance of classification items. Access this box by selecting List then 1 or 2 from the menu. The List dialog box contains buttons for Delete and Rename, as well as the New option. All of the fields discussed in the previous section can be edited at any time by selecting an item in the client list and then selecting and changing data in any fields for that client.

Use the Delete button if you want to remove a client and the client reference in any transactions assigned to that client. If the client has no balance, you will not be warned to confirm the deletion. If there is a balance for that client, you will be warned that this is true, and asked if you are sure before the deletion is completed.

Use the Rename button if you want to change the name of any client. Spelling and capitalization errors can be corrected this way, as well as adding a descriptor for each client after its name. When you choose Rename, a Rename dialog box opens to remind you of the existing name and to ask for a new name.

You also might rename or delete an entire classification in the Client Classification dialog box. Access this box by selecting List then Other from the menu and then choose Modify or Delete. The modify option allows you to change the name and add subitems to a classification. When you delete a classification, the reference to that classification will be deleted in all transactions that contained such a reference. The transactions themselves will not be deleted from your file.

Printing classification lists

Notice a Report button in the upper right corner of Fig. 5-10. Select this option when you want to print a list of your clients. The list automatically prints with shortcut codes included. You can customize to eliminate the shortcut codes, but no other modifications are offered. If you have entered subitems, these will be displayed on the client list. You also can choose to Export this data to a text file.

Figure 5-11 is a sample classification list offered as a model for how extensively the classification concept can be carried. This classification includes both items and subitems. I hope it inspires you.

```
                COURSE OFFERINGS - 1992-3


        Courses                              Shortcut
        Excel Spreadsheet                       Ex
        Lotus 1-2-3 Beginner                    123
            1 Day
            2 Three Hr sessions
        Lotus Advanced                          Ad
            12 hr Split
            2 Continuous Full Days
        MS-DOS Introdcution                     DOS
            1 hr Demo
            2 hr Tutorial
            3 hr Tutorial
        PC Paint Intro                          Paint
        Windows Basics                          Win
            12 hr Hands-on
            2 hr Demo
            6 hr Hands-on
        Wordperfect Begin                       WP
        XYWrite Overview                        XY
            2 hr Demo
```

5-11 Sample classification list with subitems

Summary

This chapter presented the procedures for entering, editing, and printing reports from the major lists around which your data is organized in Money. Accounts, categories, subcategories, payees, and classifications were discussed in detail with some suggestions for how these can be customized for your specific situation. Additional examples of the use of these lists can be found throughout this book.

On the list tutorial

This tutorial builds on the concepts learned in chapters 1 through 4, and assumes that you have completed the tutorials of chapters 1 and 4. The chapter 2 tutorial was optional, but this exercise assumes that you are familiar with Windows terminology. Access Money from the Program Manager window of Windows 3.0.

Part A

This first section is designed to review all the previous lists that have been created while we were working with the sample file in the tutorials in chapters 1, 3 and 4. We will browse the account list, the payee list, the category list, and the classification list.

- ☐ If the Money title bar does not display SAMPLE.MNY as the filename, select File, Open, and then sample.mny; make a backup copy of the file you were working on when asked to do so
- ☐ Select List then Account List from the menu
- ☐ You see the Account List dialog box
- ☐ Select each account in turn and notice how the large title changes in the information box at the right
- ☐ Choose the Report button to view the entire list
- ☐ Choose the Customize button
- ☐ Check the Include Account Balances option
- ☐ Choose View to see the list with balances
- ☐ Choose Close twice to return to the account book
- ☐ Select List then Payee List from the menu
- ☐ Scroll slowly through the payee list (we haven't included addresses or phone numbers when we created Payees in our sample file, so there's not much to look at)
- ☐ Choose Close once to return to the account book
- ☐ Select List then Category List from the menu

- ☐ You see the Category List dialog box
- ☐ It's easier to see this whole list as a report
- ☐ Choose the Report button to view the entire list
- ☐ Scroll slowly through the list, reading the item names
- ☐ Choose Close to return to the category list
- ☐ Select the Insurance expense category
- ☐ Notice that this category has subcategories and budgets
- ☐ Choose Close to return to the account book
- ☐ Select List then 1. Projects from the menu
- ☐ You see the Project Classification List dialog box
- ☐ Choose the Report button to view the entire list
- ☐ Choose Close once to return to the project list

Part B

While we're in the classification list, let's edit it to include a few more projects, and add comments and shortcuts. Then we'll print the full project list on paper.

- ☐ Be sure you are still in the Project List dialog box
- ☐ Choose New to bring up the Create New Project box
- ☐ Type Little Guy Brothers-DOS and choose Ok
- ☐ Select the Shortcut box and type Guy
- ☐ Tab to the Comment box
- ☐ Type DOS Intro starting 2/18
- ☐ Choose New to add another project
- ☐ Type Volunteer PC Training and choose Ok
- ☐ Select Bigtime-Basic PC Course in the project list (on the keyboard, you need to press Alt−L and then scroll Up Arrow to Bigtime)
- ☐ Choose Rename and the Rename Project box appears
- ☐ Don't type anything yet
- ☐ Press the Left Arrow to move the cursor to PC
- ☐ Press Del twice to erase PC
- ☐ Type Windows and choose Ok

Note This is a good thing to know about editing a field. If you press BackSpace or type new characters, the whole field is erased. If you press the directional keys, however, you can move the cursor (vertical bar) to the exact position where you want to make a change. This could save a lot of retyping.

- ☐ Although the project name is too long to see in its entirety on the Project List, it is all stored in memory
- ☐ Choose Report to view the full project list
- ☐ Choose Widths and select the Extra Wide option
- ☐ Choose Ok
- ☐ Now you can see the full Bigtime project name
- ☐ Choose Close twice to return to the account book

Part C

In this section we will add to the account list and enter helpful data in the Comment field of some accounts. Your account list should already include accounts for Business Checking, Cash on Hand, Equipment, Notes Payable, and Equip Loans Payable if you have completed all the earlier tutorials. If you don't have all these accounts, try adding them at the end of this part.

- ☐ Select List then Account List from the menu
- ☐ You see the Account List dialog box
- ☐ Select the Notes Payable account
- ☐ Select the Opening Balance box and type 5000
- ☐ This is a loan from last year to get the business started
- ☐ Select the Bank Name box
- ☐ Type Boston Five and First Chase
- ☐ Select the Comment box
- ☐ Type Use this account for all bank loans; put other loans in specifically labelled Payable accounts based on the purpose of the loan
- ☐ You can type up to 256 characters here, and you don't need to press Enter between lines
- ☐ Choose New
- ☐ Type Office Building
- ☐ Select Asset Account, then Ok
- ☐ Enter 0 for Opening Balance, then Ok
- ☐ Choose New
- ☐ Type Mortgage Payable
- ☐ Select Liability Account then choose Ok
- ☐ Enter 0 for Opening Balance, then Ok
- ☐ Choose the Report button to view the entire list

☐ Print the list on paper if you'd like

☐ Return to the Account Book window

Part D

In this section, we will explore and edit the payee list. We need to add some mailing addresses and comments and correct the spelling of the Bigtime Corporation.

☐ Select List then Payee List from the menu

☐ Press the k key to jump to Kinko's

Note Remember that you can Tab between fields

☐ Move to the Phone field and type 775-9000

☐ Move to the Address field and type 120 Forest Avenue
Portland, ME 04013

☐ Move to the Comment field and type Contact: Pam Collard

☐ Select Middle Company in the payee list

☐ Move to the Phone field and type 780-8950

☐ Select Bigtime Corporation in the payee list

☐ Move to the Phone field and type 772-1000

☐ Select the Rename button

☐ In the Rename Payee box the cursor is at the end of the name

☐ Use the Left Arrow, Spacebar and Del keys to correct the spelling here
to: Big Time Corporation

☐ Choose Ok

☐ Choose Report then Customize

☐ Choose the Include Phone Numbers option, then View

☐ Choose Print, then Ok

Note This would make a good phone contact list once we entered phone numbers for each of our payees

☐ Choose Close twice to return to the account book

☐ Select the Find tool (click on it or Ctrl−F)

☐ Type big t, and verify that Direction is Up

☐ Choose Find Next

☐ Press Esc to return to the account book

☐ Notice that the old name Bigtime has changed to Big Time in this
transaction

Part E

In this section we will explore and edit the category list. We will delete some unnecessary names from this list, add a category, and print a complete list of the customized category list. A category or subcategory name must be highlighted before you can work with it.

- ☐ Select List then Category List from the menu
- ☐ You see the Category List dialog box
- ☐ Select the Interest Income category to move to the top of the list
- ☐ Press the e key
- ☐ This moves you quickly to the first Expense category
- ☐ Press the e key again
- ☐ This moves you quickly to the first category that begins with the letter e (Entertainment)
- ☐ Press the t key to move quickly to Taxes
- ☐ This selects the Taxes category

Note As you have seen, you can move quickly around a list by pressing the first letter of a name you want to select. This also works in an Account list, a Payee list, and a Classification list.

- ☐ We want to delete the Permits and Sales Tax subcategories
- ☐ Select the Permits subcategory (on the keyboard you need to press ALT−U for subcategory list, then arrow keys)
- ☐ Select Delete under the subcategory list (Alt−E)
- ☐ Select the Sales Tax subcategory
- ☐ Select Delete under the subcategory list
- ☐ Return to the category list (Alt−L)
- ☐ Select the Interest Income account
- ☐ Select the Comment box
- ☐ Type For Savings and Checking Interest Earned
- ☐ You can type up to 256 characters here, and you don't need to press Enter between lines
- ☐ Select New from below the category list
- ☐ Type Computer Supplies
- ☐ Notice that the Income Category option is checked in the Create New Category box, because we were last working on an income category. The new category is an expense.

☐ Check the Expense Category option, then choose Ok

☐ Choose Report

☐ Choose Print, then Ok

☐ Choose Close twice to return to the account book

☐ Exit from Money and make a Backup copy, or stay around and play

6
CHAPTER

Customizing views, reports, and setup

This chapter describes the many ways that you can customize Money. For starters there are several ways to customize what your Money window displays, and in what order it displays it. Reports were briefly discussed in earlier chapters, and more customization features for reports are presented in this chapter. Also discussed are setup options that can be manipulated to provide you with the means for customizing the display size, some screen colors, the warning beeps during transaction entry, the reminder for scheduled transactions, and a few other features.

Customizing screen views

Unless you specify otherwise, the Account Book and Future Transactions window display transactions in a multiple line format. You've seen this in many of the illustrations in this book thus far. Figure 4-4 is a good example. The entire transaction view presents three to five lines per transaction, depending on whether you have created classifications as discussed in the last two chapters.

Choose the Top Line View tool from the toolbar, or select Options then Top Line View from the menu, and the window that is active will change to a single line view. That is, just the top line of each transaction will be shown in the window. You can see many more transactions this way. Figure 6-1 illustrates the Account Book window with Top Line View allowing about 15 transactions to be seen at once. You could maximize the Account Book window to fill the entire screen and see even more transaction lines.

If you are in the account book when you select Top Line View, the account book changes to a single line per transaction. If you are in the Future Transactions

Account:	Business Checking		View:	All (by Date)										

Account Book

Num	Date	Payee / Memo / Category	C	Payment	Deposit	Balance
dep	12/1/91	Big Time Corporation	R		2,000.00	2,000.00
102	12/2/91	Cree Advertising Agency	R	720.00		1,280.00
103	12/4/91	Ritter Agency		640.00		640.00
adj	12/7/91	Chase First Bank	R	22.50		617.50
104	12/9/91	Boston Regency		125.60		491.90
adj	12/10/91	Service Charge	R	8.20		483.70
atm	12/12/91	Pocket Money		100.00		383.70
105	12/15/91	Coastal Computer Center		500.00		(116.30)
atm	12/15/91	Pocket Money		200.00		(316.30)
dep	12/15/91	First National CD			1,000.00	683.70
Dep	12/16/91	City Bank			2,000.00	2,683.70
106	12/17/91	Kinko's Copy Center		120.00		2,563.70
Dep	12/17/91	Middle Company			400.00	2,963.70
107	12/18/91	Computer Land		82.00		2,881.70

					Ending Balance:	2,931.70

6-1 Account book in top line view

window when you select Top Line View, it is that window that changes, and the account book is not affected. After you take this action, the Options menu changes to Entire Transaction View, so that you can switch back to that style. The toolbar always contains both the Top Line View tool and the Entire Transaction View tool, so you can switch back and forth quickly.

The View box

The View box that appears at the top of each of the windows in Money gives you the flexibility to change the makeup of transactions that are displayed together in the window. For example, the default View shows all transactions in one account (usually the checking account) in order by date. The list that cascades from the View box tells you your other choices. This View box is illustrated in Fig. 6-2.

Account Book

View:	All (by Date)

lemo / C

All (by Date)
All (by Num)

Unprinted Checks
Unreconciled (by Date)
Unreconciled (by Num)

A Payee...
A Category...
A Client...

Other...

6-2 Viewing options in the View box

You can choose to view all transactions by date or by number, just the unprinted checks, unreconciled items by date or by number, a specific payee, category, or project, and much more because the Other option leads to many more choices.

It is important to be aware that this View box works in conjunction with the Account box to its left. Use the Account box to specify which specific account you want to see in the window, then you can specify in which order you want the transactions with the View box. You also can view all accounts at once, and again rely on the View box to specify which transactions you want to see and in what order. For simplicity sake, we will assume that you are viewing one account in the next few examples.

Another important fact about changing the view is that the Balance column within the altered window is recalculated to include only the transactions in the current view. This is very helpful when viewing all transactions in one category or for one payee, but it can be confusing or misleading when you are viewing combined accounts and selected transactions.

View by number   Choose the All by Number option in the View box when you want to see the transactions in order by the Num field. Transactions with blank in the Num field are listed first. Transactions with a check number (in order by number) are listed next, followed by transactions with alphabetic characters in the Num field (i.e., Dep, ATM, Adj, or Print). This is helpful when you want to browse through all transactions of one type, followed by all of another type. For example, all transactions with a Dep in the Num field are listed by date within that group.

View unreconciled transactions   Choose the Unreconciled by Date or Unreconciled by Number option from the View box when you want to see only the transactions that do not have an R in the C column. This is the Cleared column, which indicates that the transaction has not yet appeared on a statement (usually a bank statement) and marked as reconciled when the Balance Accounts procedure was applied. These views are especially helpful when you are marking items as cleared or outstanding after you receive a statement associated with the account being viewed. More about this is discussed in chapter 12.

View a specific payee, category, or classification   The Payee, Category, and Classification options in the View box are all very similar. When you choose A Payee in the View box, you will be presented with a list of all your payees so you can select one of them. For example, if you were displaying an Accounts Payable account and wanted to know how much you owed to a specific payee, the View by Payee option would tell you just that. There is a more detailed example of this in chapter 10.

The Category and Classification options work in the same manner. With the Category option, you can select a specific subcategory without viewing a whole category. When you are trying to analyze all expenditures in a category or subcategory (i.e., Ground Transportation under Travel) for a whole year, this option can be a real time saver. Figure 6-3 provides an example of a view of transactions restricted to one category.

Once you've set up a classification and chosen Job, Project, or Client (etc.) as the type, the View box will present options using those types. For example, because I have a classification for Clients, the View box contains an option labelled A Client.

6-3 Restricted view for just one category

Really custom views The Other option in the View box opens up all kinds of other possibilities. Figure 6-4 illustrates the Other View dialog box that appears when you select this option. The Sort By box gives you the option to sort by date, number, account, payee, category, or classification. This sort can apply to all types of transactions, for all payees, categories, and classifications (whether reconciled or unreconciled)—or you might want to make choices in each of these boxes on the Other View dialog box. You also can restrict the view to a specified date range, a designated number range, and/or to a selected dollar amount.

For example, when you select the Category list box, the categories you have designed cascade below this box. Figure 6-5 illustrates this set of options. You can select one or multiple categories, and at the end of the list, you can select a group of categories, like income categories, expense categories, or blank categories. If you select the Multiple Categories option, another dialog box is displayed where you can choose the ones you want, even down to a specific subcategory.

Here are some ideas. Customize the View to include only transactions with a blank in the category field, so you can identify and correct (or delete) items that were accidentally entered without being categorized. Select transactions from just the Expense categories and specify Amounts, From: 500 to view all expense items

6-4 Other View dialog box

6-5 Category list in the Other View dialog box

in excess of $500. This will help you focus on big dollar pay outs. Restrict the view to an earlier month by indicating Date, From: 2/1/92, To: 2/28/92 in the Other View dialog box. This is convenient when you are analyzing activity in an earlier period and want to have a smaller list represented on the scroll bar so you can jump around more efficiently.

Restoring the old standard view Choose the All by Date option in the View box when you want to return to the default view.

Customizing reports

The general procedure for customizing reports is to select the Report menu item, then specify the report type (e.g., Net Worth Report) and view the default report on screen. The default report is produced based on the current system date with a "plain Jane" approach to rows and columns. When a report is in the window, you will see a Customize button, which brings up a host of customizing options when selected. For example, the default Income & Expense Report has that phrase for a title, and it presents rows for each subcategory with a single column containing amounts that are accumulative for the entire current year to date. If you'd like an income and expense report that contains rows for each category instead, customize it by specifying Rows For Each and selecting Category in the drop down list.

Printer setup

Before you print reports or checks for the first time, you must let Money know what printer you will be using and some other settings for paper size, orientation, and source. Select File then Printer Setup from the menu, and the Print Setup dialog box appears. On the first line, you need to check either the Check Printing option or the Report Printing option. The settings are slightly different for each of these. Please refer to the section on printing business checks in chapter 4 for more details on check printing.

Once you specify the Report Printing setup option, the Print Setup dialog box appears as shown in Fig. 6-6. The Printer box contains a choice of using the default printer (which is the one that you have chosen in your Windows setup) or indicating an alternative printer, if you have listed any other printers in your Windows setup.

You can see in Fig. 6-6 that you have the option of printing in Landscape or Portrait orientation. Portrait orientation is the default and it means that the rows will be written across the $8^1/2''$ width, assuming an $8^1/2$ by $11''$ paper size. Landscape orientation means that the rows are written across the $11''$ width. You can specify various paper sizes and indicate the source of the paper as Upper Tray, Lower Tray, or Manual Feed for laser printers.

Refer to your Windows documentation for more specific instructions about choosing printer types and installing a printer that is not already on your list.

Once a report is customized to your satisfaction, simply use the Print button in the upper right of any Report window to initiate the print process. A Print box appears where you can specify the number of copies you want to print, the range of pages to print, and whether you want draft or letter quality output—then choose Ok. Before you print, however, here's how you customize.

6-6 Print Setup dialog box for report printing

Customize Report dialog box

The Customize Report dialog box is somewhat different for each report. The Customize Net Worth Report dialog box provides only the option of changing the date. We discussed this report in chapter 4, so we'll focus on the customize options of other reports here.

Customizing Register reports The Customize Register Report dialog box is shown in Fig. 6-7. If you want to produce a complete audit trail of your transactions (this is the journal discussed in chapter 4), you should leave all of the report settings at their defaults except for inserting an appropriate title and date range,

6-7 Customize Register Report dialog box

and including All Accounts. If you don't change the From date, the report will include everything back to the beginning of the current year.

As you can see in Fig. 6-7, there are quite a few options for customizing a register report. The word Client appears in the Include Fields box of this illustration, because I have set up a classification with that name. Your own classification types will appear in this box. If you have set up no classifications, then none will be included in this field. Check the Memo, Account, Cleared Flag, or Category boxes, depending on what fields you want included in your register report.

The Date Range box is used to indicate the period you want the report to cover. The list of choices included in Dates are Year to Date, Month to Date, Current Year, Previous Year, Previous Month, Last 30 Days, Last 12 Months, or Custom Dates. If you type dates in the From and To boxes, the Dates choice defaults to Custom Dates. Use this feature to produce reports from previous periods, and to specify a future period when you want to print scheduled transactions from your Future Transactions window. You might want to extend the dates or choose Current Year or Last 12 Months when you want to print a corrected audit trail, after making changes to prior period transactions.

The Subtotal By list includes choices for None, Account, Category, Classification, Month, Payee, or Week. You would subtotal by Payee if you were printing a register of Accounts Payable transactions. Another use for the Subtotal By option is to produce a register that includes subtotals by category for the same period of an income statement that you've produced. In this way, you can see the detail that adds up to each category on a given income statement. For example, the $345.65 shown on the Travel line of an income statement could be broken into detailed transactions, if you customize a register report to be subtotaled by that category for the same period as the income statement. Choose the Display Splits option when you want the details of the split transactions to be shown.

Use the Include Transactions box to specify which accounts you want to include on your report, or to indicate that All Accounts should be included. The list that cascades below the From Account option will display all accounts that you have created thus far, plus a Multiple Accounts item. If you choose Multiple Accounts, another list will open up where you can select which accounts to include.

The Include Transactions box also lets you designate whether you want to include all transactions (the default) or select transactions. If you choose Select Transactions, another dialog box will open to let you select very specific criteria using a layout like the Custom View box shown in Fig. 6-4, and Category List in Fig. 6-5. Basically, anything that can be accomplished with the Custom View option can be printed using the Customize Report dialog box for the register report.

If you have customized the view to select a specific account and a selected set of transactions, the register report will revert to these same settings.

Customizing income & expense reports The process of customizing income and expense reports is very similar to what was discussed for register reports. Figure 6-8 displays the Customize Income & Expense Report dialog box. The Date Range and Include Transactions boxes are used in exactly the same way as they are for customizing a register report. The Row for Every option list includes choices for category or subcategory. An example of an income statement with subcategories was presented in Fig. 4-12, while one with only categories was presented in Fig. 4-13. The Column for Every option list includes choices for None, Week, Two Weeks, Half Month, Month, Quarter, and Year. In the business setting, historical analysis is often performed by comparing month to month and quarter to quarter. Specify columns for every month or quarter for this purpose. Once you've saved data for several years, you can choose the Year item in the Column for Every list and see the past few years side by side on the report.

```
┌─────────────────────────────────────────────────────────────────┐
│ ▬         Customize Income and Expense Report                    │
├─────────────────────────────────────────────────────────────────┤
│                                                                   │
│   Title: [INCOME AND EXPENSE REPORT        ]      ┌─────────┐    │
│                                                    │  View   │    │
│   Row for Every:   [Subcategory         ▼]        └─────────┘    │
│                                                    ┌─────────┐    │
│   Column for Every: [None                ▼]       │ Cancel  │    │
│                                                    └─────────┘    │
│   ┌─Date Range──────────┐  ┌─Include Transactions─┐ ┌────────┐   │
│   │ Dates               │  │ From Account:         │ │  Help  │  │
│   │                     │  │                       │ └────────┘   │
│   │ [Year to Date   ▼]  │  │ [All Accounts      ▼] │            │
│   │                     │  │                       │            │
│   │ From:  [1/1/91 ]    │  │ ◉ All Transactions    │            │
│   │ To:    [9/20/91]    │  │ ○ Select Transactions…│            │
│   └─────────────────────┘  └───────────────────────┘            │
│   ┌─Report Transfers by──────────────────────────────────────┐  │
│   │ ○ Income Statement   ◉ Expenditures    ○ Cash Flow       │  │
│   └──────────────────────────────────────────────────────────┘  │
└─────────────────────────────────────────────────────────────────┘
```

6-8 Customize Income and Expense Report dialog box

The Report Transfers By box includes three choices. Choose Income Statement to exclude transfer amounts from the report. Choose Expenditures if you want the report to include a separate section, labelled *transfers*, treated as expenditures (deducted from Income). Choose Cash Flow to include transfers that represent an inflow or outflow of cash in an income or expense category. Transfers are not included unless they affect income or expense categories.

Customizing summary reports The Customize Summary Report dialog box is exactly the same as the Income & Expense Report dialog box shown in Fig. 6-8. The only difference is that the Row for Every list and the Column for Every list are more comprehensive on a summary report.

The Row for Every list includes choices for Payee (which is the default), Account, Category, Subcategory, Project, Week, and Month. The Column for Every list presents choices for None (which is the default), Account, Payee, Category, Classification, Week, Two Weeks, Half Month, Month, Quarter, or Year. Chapter 9 describes how these options can be used to produce a payroll report. Chapter 10 suggests using these options to produce a schedule of accounts payable or receivable. If you use the Include Transactions box to customize a summary report, you can restrict the report to any one (or group of) transaction types, payees, categories, classifications, or accounts. A business example of this would be a summary report restricted to Payment transaction type, with a row for every Payee and a Date Range of the last 6 months to get a look at the magnitude of dollars being spent with each payee. Ask the payees with the largest dollar amounts for a trade discount.

Customizing tax reports   The Tax Reports feature is not needed by businesses because the Income & Expense report serves as the tax report because all categories are tax related. If you are using the Business & Home Categories provided by Money, some of your categories are tax related and some are not. Look for the tax flag on the category list.

The Customize Tax Report dialog box looks exactly like the Customize Income & Expense Report box shown in Fig. 6-8, with one exception. For a Tax report, you can choose to see a Summary of the results, which shows the total amount in each category, or you can choose to see Transactions, which will provide a detailed list of transactions for each category, subtotalled by category. Both of these forms of the tax report are presented in the format of an income and expense report.

Customizing budget reports   An entire chapter of this book is devoted to the budgeting process and budget reports. Customizing budget reports is covered in chapter 7.

Fonts and Widths   The Fonts option in the Report dialog box is used to choose a font style to be used on the report. The fonts that will be available to you depend on the printer you have chosen. You'll have to experiment with this option to see what works with your setup. The Width option allows you to change column widths on both the screen and the printed output. Be warned that when you specify the Narrow width, you sometimes cannot see all the data in a field, but this is a good way to fit a wide register report on one page.

Customizing other settings

There is a Settings choice on the Options menu item that allows you to have further control over how Money works. You can change some screen colors, fonts and sizes, date formats, data entry formats, and how Money warns you about transac-

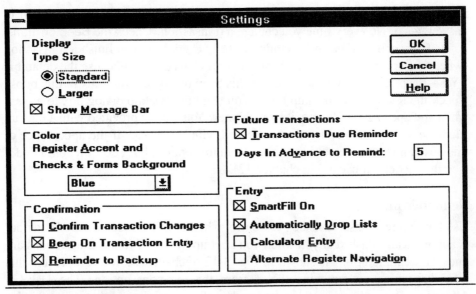

6-9 Settings options dialogue box

tion changes and backups. Figure 6-9 illustrates the options available in the Settings dialog box.

Changing screen attributes

The Display box invites you to change the size of forms and characters on your screen from Standard (the default which you've been seeing), to Larger, which is about 120% of standard. This is a big help for users of laptops or palmtop computers, whose screens are very tiny. The Display box also provides an option button that allows you to Show Message Bar at the bottom of your Money window, or to suppress this bar. This refers to the prompt line noted in the tour of the Money Window that was presented in Fig. 1-1.

The Color box presents a list of colors available on your monitor type that can be used as the accent behind some of the lines in the account book, and as the background of the Checks & Forms Window. The default color (i.e., Blue) is seen in the list box. Activate this list and select a color you'd like to try. When you choose Ok to return to the account book, you can see the color change.

Confirming actions

Use the Confirmation box to control how Money warns you about transaction entry and changes, and about making a backup copy of your file. Check the Confirm Transaction Changes option if you want to be asked for confirmation each time you change any part of a transaction. The default here is not to ask for confirmation. If you check this box, a Confirmation box will appear requiring you to answer Yes or No every time you change a transaction. Check the Beep on Transaction Entry option to make the computer beep every time you finish a transaction (whether an original entry or a change to a previous entry). Because the default is "Yes—Beep Me," we've been hearing this beep during the tutorials in this book. Check the Reminder to Backup box if you want the Backup dialog box to appear when you open a new file or exit from Money. You will be provided with a backup filename and location and you can proceed with Yes or No. If the appearance of this box annoys you, remove the check from this option, but I don't recommend it (see the section on backup in chapter 12).

Reminder message

Use the Future Transactions box to control whether a Transactions Due Reminder is automatically flashed at you when you start up Money if future transactions are due. An example of this is shown in Fig. 3-12 of chapter 3. You can prevent this from happening by removing the X from the reminder option. The Days in Advance to Remind box contains the number of days in advance that this reminder message will appear. The default number of days is 5, but you can change this to anything from 1 to 254.

Data entry style

The Entry box is used to choose the style of data entry that suits your personal preference. Turn the SmartFill option on or off, depending on whether you want the payee, amounts, and category fields automatically filled by Money as soon as a few recognizable characters are entered. Leave the Automatically Drop Lists option checked to have lists drop from the payee, category, and classifications fields during data entry. If you prefer not to have these lists drop down, remove the check from this box; you would still be able to activate the lists by pressing the Alt—Down Arrow keys. Check the Calculator Entry box if you want to be able to enter dollar amounts in the form you use with most calculators. For example, if you press 123 and Tab in an amount field, the amount entered is $1.23. Leave the Calculator Entry box unchecked if you want 123 to be entered as $123.

Lastly, check the Alternative Register Navigation box so you can press Enter between each of the fields in a transaction, rather than having to press Tab. With this method, you must press Ctrl—Enter to complete a transaction.

Dates and amount formats

The formats used for dates and amounts are controlled by the control panel of your Windows installation. Changes in these formats apply to all Windows applications, not just Money. Select the International icon on the control panel, and then select the Change button in the Date Format box or the Currency Format box to see all the possibilities for setting these two formats. When you return to Money, your changes will be in effect.

Summary

This chapter has presented the many options that Money provides for customizing how your screen looks, how reports are produced, how you enter data, and how you are reminded about important changes. We have covered the procedures for using the View box in the Money window, and how this affects what transactions are included in your account book or Checks and Forms windows. We have further explored how to use the Customize option of the Reports menu to get what you want from Money reports. We also have been introduced to the settings changes you can make to mold the screen and some activities to your own personal preferences (like entering dollar amounts).

A custom job tutorial

This tutorial builds on the concepts learned in chapters 1 through 5, and assumes that you have completed the chapter 4 and 5 tutorials. Even if you skipped the chapter 2 tutorial, this exercise assumes that you are familiar with Windows terminology. Access Money from the Program Manager window of Windows 3.0.

Part A

This first section encourages you to experiment with changing the order in which transactions appear in the Money window. We will use only the account book, but the activities practiced here apply to the Checks & Forms window and the Future Transactions window as well.

- ☐ Select File and Open, then select sample.mny
- ☐ Select Window then Account Book
- ☐ Activate the Account box then Business Checking

Note The above steps simply ensure that we are all at the same beginning point.

- ☐ Activate the View box, then select All by Num
- ☐ Notice how the view has changed to order by number
- ☐ Select the Top Line View tool from the toolbar (or you can select Options then Top Line View)
- ☐ Now it is easier to see that the book is in order by number
- ☐ Activate the View box, then select Other
- ☐ The Other View box appears
- ☐ Activate the Sort By list box, and select Payee

- ☐ Choose Ok
- ☐ Note how the view has changed to order by payee
- ☐ Scroll to the first transaction (Ctrl−Home)
- ☐ Note how some of the transactions have an R in the C field
- ☐ Select View, Unreconciled by Date
- ☐ Note how the R's have disappeared; only the unreconciled transactions are in the view, in order by date
- ☐ Select View, then All by Date
- ☐ Select the Entire Transaction View from the toolbar (or select Options, then Entire Transaction View)
- ☐ This returns you to the default view

Part B

You also can restrict the view in the Money window to a select set of transactions. Whatever view is displayed in the window controls the content and in what order a register report will print. We will practice these two activities in this part.

- ☐ Select Account then All Accounts
- ☐ Scroll up through the lines in the account book
- ☐ Note how the view now includes transactions from Cash on Hand, Equipment and others
- ☐ The name of the account appears in the Num—Date field
- ☐ Select View then Other
- ☐ Activate the Category list box
- ☐ Select the Select Multiple Categories item from the list
- ☐ A Select Category box appears
- ☐ Choose the Select None button to remove all highlighting
- ☐ Scroll the list and select Revenue
- ☐ Scroll the list and select Office Expenses
- ☐ Scroll the list and select Training Materials
- ☐ Choose Ok twice to examine the view that results
- ☐ Scroll through the account book
- ☐ Transactions from all accounts for revenue, office expenses and training materials are in the view
- ☐ Select Report then Register Report

Note This report includes only the transactions that are currently in the window view. You might have to customize to specify a To date of 12/31.

- ☐ Choose Customize and note that the Customize Dialog box has the Select Transactions option already checked
- ☐ Select the Select Transactions option and the Select Transactions dialog box appears
- ☐ Note that the Category list box has Select Multiple Categories as the setting
- ☐ Activate the Select Multiple Categories list box
- ☐ Select the Select Multiple Categories item on this list
- ☐ Note that the Select Category dialog box already has some categories highlighted
- ☐ Scroll to see that Revenue, Office Expenses and Training Materials are highlighted

Note Whatever is being displayed in the window view will be reported when you choose Register Report from the Reports menu.

- ☐ Choose Ok twice, then View to return to the report
- ☐ Choose Close to return to the account book
- ☐ Select Account then Business Checking
- ☐ Select View, All by Date to return to the default view

Part C

In this section we will print a few reports by concentrating on the capabilities of the Customize option. First we need to enter a few more transactions. Then we'll customize an Income & Expense report and produce a Register report to match.

- ☐ Enter a new transaction in Business Checking as follows: Num of Print, Date of 12/17, Payee of Microsoft Press, Payment of 186, Memo of DOS Books, Category of Training Materials (no project)
- ☐ Enter another transaction as follows: Num of Dep, Date of 12/18, Payee of Little Guy Bros, Deposit of 50, Memo of Planning DOS Course, Category of Revenue, Subcategory of Training, Project of Little Guy-DOS
- ☐ Select Reports, then Income & Expense
- ☐ Choose Customize
- ☐ In the From date box, enter 12/1
- ☐ In the To date box, enter 12/31

- ☐ Verify that All Accounts is specified
- ☐ Choose View
- ☐ Choose Print, then Ok
- ☐ Circle the Training Revenue and Training Materials amounts on the printed report
- ☐ Choose Close to return to the Account Book
- ☐ Select Report, then Register Report
- ☐ Choose Customize
- ☐ Check the Memo option in the Include Fields box
- ☐ In the From date box, enter 12/1
- ☐ In the To date box, enter 12/31
- ☐ In the Subtotal By list box, select Subcategory
- ☐ Choose View
- ☐ Note that this Register report directly relates to the amounts on your Income & Expense report
- ☐ Scroll to the Training Revenue Amount column of the report
- ☐ There should be three transactions totalling to the amount you see on your printed Income & Expense report
- ☐ Scroll to the Training Materials Amount column of the report
- ☐ There should be three transactions with a total matched to the Income & Expense report

Part D

Don't erase the register report we created in Part C. Let's experiment with the Fonts and Width options of the Customize Report dialog box.

- ☐ Be sure the Register Report dialog box is still in the window
- ☐ Choose the Width option button
- ☐ Check the Narrow option in the Report Column Width dialog box
- ☐ Choose Ok
- ☐ Note that some of the columns are now narrower, but some characters get truncated
- ☐ Choose the Fonts option button
- ☐ In the Select Fonts dialog box, select Pica Compressed from the Font list box

Note If you don't have Pica Compressed on your fonts list, choose a font with 17

CPI in it, or scroll to find a font that shows a Size of 9 or less. We want to choose something that will produce very small characters, so the whole register report will fit across a page.

- ☐ Choose Ok to view the changed font
- ☐ Choose Print then Ok to print the report
- ☐ Choose Close to return to the account book

Part E

There's one other trick for getting a wide report to fit on a page. In the Print Setup option of the File menu, you can ask that the report be printed sideways on a page. This is referred to as landscape orientation. Let's try it.

- ☐ Select File then Print Setup from the menu
- ☐ Check the Report Printing option next to Setup For
- ☐ In the Orientation box, check the Landscape option

Note Some printers might not allow the landscape setting, or you might need to go to the *Windows* control panel to select another printer

- ☐ Notice how the illustrated paper is now turned on its side
- ☐ Choose Ok
- ☐ Select Reports then Register Report
- ☐ Choose Customize
- ☐ Check the Memo option in the Include Fields box
- ☐ Type 12/1 and 12/31 as the From and To dates, then View
- ☐ This is the Register report in order by date (not subtotalled)
- ☐ Choose Fonts, then Tms Rmn or Courier from the list
- ☐ Type 8 in the Size box, then Ok

Note The fonts that are available to you depend on the printers that you have installed with Windows. If Tms Rmn doesn't show on your fonts list, pick any font with a small Size. You might have to experiment a bit.

- ☐ Choose Print then Ok
- ☐ Be patient; it takes time for Money to figure out how to reorient the report into a sideways print, but it's worth it
- ☐ Choose Close to return to the account book
- ☐ Select File then Print Setup
- ☐ In the Orientation box, check Portrait then Ok

Part F

Now let's customize a summary report for the express purpose of viewing only those payees with whom we've had big money dealings.

- ☐ Select Report, then Summary Report
- ☐ Choose Customize
- ☐ Type the title Big Money Payees
- ☐ Verify that the Row for Every list box names Payee
- ☐ In the To date box, enter 12/31
- ☐ Select Business Checking in the From Account box
- ☐ Check the Select Transactions option
- ☐ You now see the Select Transactions dialog box
- ☐ In the Amount box, type 500
- ☐ Choose Ok then View
- ☐ This summary lists only payees with over $500 in activity
- ☐ Notice that the fonts and width settings remain in place for all subsequent reports
- ☐ Choose Fonts, and select Pica or Courier, then Ok

Note The font options depend on your printer setup.

- ☐ Choose Width, and select Wide, then Ok
- ☐ Choose Print, then Ok
- ☐ Choose Close to return to the account book

Part G

In this section we will experiment with changing the screen size and colors, and you can decide if you want confirmation warnings when you enter or change transactions.

- ☐ Select Options then Settings from the menu
- ☐ Notice the message on the prompt bar at the bottom of the window: Set User preferences for display, reminders, etc.
- ☐ Check Larger in the Type Size list at the upper left
- ☐ Remove the check from the Show Message Bar option
- ☐ Choose Ok to see the effect of these changes
- ☐ The message bar is gone, and the screen contents are larger
- ☐ Select Options, then Settings from the menu

- ☐ Check the Standard option in the Display box
- ☐ Check the Show Message Bar option
- ☐ Activate the Color List in the Color box
- ☐ Select a color of your own liking
- ☐ Choose Ok and see how you like the color change
- ☐ Select Options then Settings
- ☐ Try another color
- ☐ Check the Confirm Transaction Changes option in the Confirmation box
- ☐ Choose Ok
- ☐ Select the 12/18 Little Guy transaction
- ☐ Select the Memo field, and edit it to read Materials for DOS Course
- ☐ Press Enter to record the changes
- ☐ A Confirmation box will appear
- ☐ Choose Yes, and you will hear the beep indicating completion

Part H

In this section we will experience data entry without some of the Money helping hands; SmartFill and drop down lists. Because these features are so helpful, we'll turn them back on before we leave.

- ☐ Remember the data entry routine?
- ☐ Select a new transaction line
- ☐ Type p, 12/19, West S, then 22
- ☐ SmartFill supplies all the rest of the data
- ☐ Press Enter to complete the transaction
- ☐ Type Dep, 12/19, then Baldwin Inc
- ☐ Type 40 in Deposit, and Sold Books in Memo
- ☐ Tab to the Category field and a list drops down
- ☐ Select Other Income and press Tab twice
- ☐ Another drop down list appears for the Project
- ☐ No project is involved, so press Enter to finish
- ☐ What would it be like without SmartFill and drop down lists?
- ☐ Select Options then Settings
- ☐ Remove the check from the SmartFill On option in the Entry box
- ☐ Remove the check from the Automatically Drop Lists option of the Entry box

- □ Remove the check from the Confirm Transaction Changes box
- □ Choose Ok
- □ Type p, 12/20, West Side Mobil, then 18
- □ In the Memo field, type Gas Fill Up
- □ Tab to the Category field
- □ Notice that no Category List drops down from this field
- □ Type Automobile in the Category field
- □ Tab to the Subcategory field
- □ No list drops down from this field either
- □ Press Alt−Down Arrow, or click on the Down Arrow button at the right edge of the Category field
- □ Now you can select Gasoline from this list
- □ Press Enter to complete this transaction
- □ Transaction entry takes more time this way
- □ Select Options, then Settings
- □ Check the SmartFill On option in the Entry box
- □ Check the Automatically Drop Lists option
- □ Choose Ok

Step I
Back up your work and exit.

- □ Select File then Exit
- □ Insert your backup disk
- □ Answer Yes in the Backup dialog box
- □ Confirm the Overwrite box if asked
- □ See you soon

7
CHAPTER

Budgeting

This chapter presents the techniques of budgeting as they apply to personal home use and, especially, to small business use. The budget process starts with an analysis of historical data to determine the amounts that are reasonable budget goals for each category. Budget figures for some future period are then entered into categories in your Money file. Effective budgeting relies on reports that present the budget data for a quarter or whole year, as well as reports that compare actual revenue and spending figures to a planned budget for any time period you want to specify. All of these budgeting techniques are covered in this chapter.

Management control

The purpose of budgeting in the business setting is to accomplish the important management responsibility of control. Controlling business finances includes planning for business operations, comparing results to the plans, and adjusting for change. Budgeting is the key ingredient in this process. Money provides a Budget dialog box within the Category List window for entering, editing, and reviewing budget data. This means that you can enter budget figures on an annual or monthly basis for all categories and subcategories. At this time, Money does not provide for budgeting at the account level; in general, you cannot assign budget data to assets and liability accounts.

You can probably better understand how budgeting is used as a control tool by studying Fig. 7-1. This Budget report from Money summarizes the activity of my small business for the third quarter of a year. An individual or small business person uses this kind of report to take a look at how things are going financially—identifying the trouble spots and noting intentions for correction in weak areas.

Money allows you to enter budget data for monthly or annual periods. Some categories can be assigned monthly budgets, while others are assigned annual

BUDGET REPORT
12/1/91 Through 12/31/91

Category	Actual	Total Budget	Difference
INCOME CATEGORIES			
Interest Income		20.00	(20.00)
Revenue	4,800.00	4,500.00	300.00
TOTAL INCOME CATEGORIES	4,800.00	4,520.00	280.00
EXPENSE CATEGORIES			
Advertising	720.00	800.00	(80.00)
Automobile/Truck	108.00	60.00	48.00 *Trouble*
Bank Charges	30.70	20.00	10.70
Entertainment	41.50	30.00	11.50
Insurance	640.00	640.00	0.00
Miscellaneous	16.50	10.00	6.50
Office Expenses	73.00	30.00	43.00
Professional Fees	112.00	0.00	112.00
Training Material	120.00	60.00	60.00
Travel	645.00	200.00	445.00 *why?*
TOTAL EXPENSE CATEGORIE	2,506.70	1,850.00	656.70
GRAND TOTAL	2,293.30	2,670.00	(376.70)

Check on these . . . *unacceptable*

7-1 Management analysis of a budget

ones. You also can specify custom budgets where you assign different amounts each month. The really nice aspect of this is that when you ask for a budget report that covers a period of two months, for example, Money displays a two month budget figure by multiplying monthly budgets by two, or multiplying annual budgets by 2/12 (1/6). You can specify any period you want for your report, and Money will prorate the budget for that period, even down to one day.

The planning stage

The preliminary step to budgeting involves taking a look at your financial history to determine what amounts in each category would be reasonable goals. Get out your old tax returns, any summary work sheets you might have prepared, or a summary of your Income & Expense report data for last year or for the last few months. If you've been using Money for a few months, you can print out the Income & Expense report with columns for every month that you've recorded thus far. This report, a sample of which is shown in Fig. 7-2, provides you with a good picture of your spending habits. You could use the monthly spending figure

INCOME AND EXPENSE REPORT
10/1/91 Through 12/31/91

Category	10/1/91 – 10/31/91	11/1/91 – 11/30/91	12/1/91 – 12/31/91	Total
INCOME				
Interest Incom	12.00	18.50		30.50
Other Income	14.50	32.00	40.00	86.50
Revenue	3,850.00	4,175.00	4,850.00	12,875.00
TOTAL INCOME	3,876.50	4,225.50	4,890.00	12,992.00
EXPENSES				
Advertising	720.00	780.00	720.00	2,220.00
Automobile/Tru	54.00	88.00	182.00	324.00
Bank Charges	22.50	22.50	30.70	75.70
Computer Suppl	42.00	18.75		60.75
Entertainment	62.50	52.65	41.50	156.65
Insurance			640.00	640.00
Miscellaneous	42.00	44.00	16.50	102.50
Office Expense	88.50	75.88	42.00	206.38
Training Mater	52.35	88.00	306.00	446.35
TOTAL EXPENSES	1,083.85	1,169.78	1,978.70	4,232.33
INCOME LESS EXPENS	2,792.65	3,055.72	2,911.30	8,759.67

7-2 Historical data for budget planning

in any category, take a quarter and multiply by four for an annual figure, or adjust those figures up and down depending on your predictions of the future for the category in question.

For the business setting, you can check the local library reference section for booklets published annually that report the industry average percentages for expenditure categories based on gross revenue. These types of statistics are referred to as *Financial Ratios* and are published by Dun & Bradstreet, Robert Morris Associates, and Prentice Hall (Leo Troy, author). You can use the Money calculator to apply a percentage to your budgeted revenue figure.

Entering budget data

The Category List dialog box contains a Budget box where all budget data is entered. Figure 7-3 illustrates the lower half of the Category List dialog box so you can see that when a category or subcategory is highlighted, its associated budget data appears in the Budget box. In this illustration, we can see that the Training subcategory of the Revenue account has been assigned a $2500 per month budget.

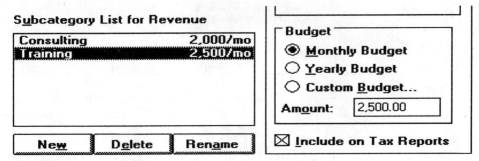

7-3 Budget dialog box from category list

Monthly and annual budget plans

To enter data in the budget box, select List then Category List from the menu. Scroll through the category list and select the category where you want to enter a budget. If you want to enter the budget at the subcategory level, scroll through the subcategory list to highlight the subcategory. The Monthly Budget option in the Budget box is checked as the default. If you want to enter a monthly budget, activate the Amount field (by clicking on it, or pressing Alt−O) and enter the budget amount. If you want to enter an annual amount, check the Annual Budget option first, then move to the Amount field to enter the amount. Return to the category or subcategory list and scroll to the next item and repeat the above procedure for each item.

Custom budgets

When it is inappropriate to schedule an equal budget amount for each month, you can use the Custom Budget option. Check the Custom Budget option and a Custom Budget dialog box will appear, as illustrated in Fig. 7-4. For example, let's assume that we use our automobile a lot less in the winter than in summer and want to budget automobile expenses accordingly. On the Custom Budget box, you can jump to any month by clicking there or pressing Tab. For our example, I typed 22, 30, and 38 in the boxes for the first three months. After typing 45 in the Apr box, I chose the Fill Down button and 45 appeared in all the rest of the months. I then tabbed to the Oct box and typed 30 and chose Fill Down again to repeat the 30 in Nov and Dec.

As you can see by this example, the Fill Down button is used to repeat the amount in the currently selected month to all months following that month. You can use the Fill Down button several times in the same category. Although at first April to December will be filled with 45's, you can override some of these by moving to any month and typing over the amount.

```
┌─────────────────────────────────────────────────────┐
│ ▭          Custom Budget                              │
├─────────────────────────────────────────────────────┤
│  Category:      Automobile/Truck          ┌────────┐ │
│                                           │   OK   │ │
│                                           └────────┘ │
│                                           ┌────────┐ │
│  Annual Total:   $450.00                  │ Cancel │ │
│                                           └────────┘ │
│                                           ┌────────┐ │
│                                           │  Help  │ │
│                                           └────────┘ │
│   ┌──────────────────────┐   ┌──────────────────────┐│
│   Jan  │ 22       │         Jul  │ 45.00     │       │
│   Feb  │ 30       │         Aug  │ 45.00     │       │
│   Mar  │ 38       │         Sep  │ 45.00     │       │
│   Apr  │ 45.00    │         Oct  │ 30.00     │       │
│   May  │ 45.00    │         Nov  │ 30.00     │       │
│   Jun  │ 45.00    │         Dec  │ 30.00     │       │
│   └──────────────────────┘   └──────────────────────┘│
│   ┌───────────────────┐      ┌───────────────────────┐│
│   │    Fill Down      │      │  Total Subcategories  ││
│   └───────────────────┘      └───────────────────────┘│
└─────────────────────────────────────────────────────┘
```

7-4 Custom Budget dialog box

If you only wanted to budget an amount in a few of the months and leave the rest blank, simply move to the appropriate months and type the unique amount for that month. Note that the Annual Total line at the top of the month list provides you with a running total for the year. This will appear as the annual total on the category list when you return there.

The Total Subcategories button is used when you want Money to total the subcategories so that they appear as the total budget for the category. Normally you would select this option whenever you enter subcategory budgets. The Total Subcategories button is found only in the Custom Budget dialog box. You would choose not to select this button when you want to enter additional amounts assigned to the category, over and above the amounts assigned to the subcategories. The effect of this technique will only be shown on Budget reports that report subcategories. It is possible to customize so that only category totals show on this report. When you do this, all subcategory budgets are automatically totalled to the category level.

Printing your budget

You can print a complete copy of your budget in one of two formats. You can print a summary budget list, which shows only the data in the Budget box of the Category List dialog box, or you can print a detailed month-by-month budget for a twelve month period.

Summary budget reports

A quick summary budget list can be printed from the Category List dialog box at any time. You've selected List then Category List from the menu, and you entered budget figures. Choose the Report button while the category list is displayed and choose Customize. A Customize Category List dialog box will appear where you will see an option for Basic Budgets. If you choose this option, uncheck the Tax Flag and Shortcut options, and choose View, you will see a budget list similar to the one in Fig. 7-5. In this format, either a monthly or annual budget figure is listed for each category and subcategory. If a custom budget was entered for any item, only the annual total for the category is shown. It does not include the details of custom budgets. To print a hard copy of this budget list, choose Print when the budget list is on screen.

Detailed budget reports

The Detailed Budgets option in the Customize Category List dialog box is used to produce a 12 month widespread of budget details. Custom budgets will be seen

1992 BUDGET

Category	Budget	
INCOME CATEGORIES		
Interest Income	180.00	per year
Other Income	10.00	per month
Revenue	4,500.00	per month
Consulting	2,000.00	per month
Training	2,500.00	per month
EXPENSE CATEGORIES		
Advertising	800.00	per month
Automobile/Truck	840.00	per year
Gasoline	635.00	per year
Maintenance	205.00	per year
Bank Charges	20.00	per month
Computer Supplies	20.00	per month
Entertainment	50.00	per month
Meals	50.00	per month
Other	0.00	per month
Insurance	1,280.00	per year
Automobile	480.00	per year
Liability	800.00	per year
Miscellaneous	30.00	per month
Office Expenses	90.00	per month
Rent	0.00	per month
Repairs	600.00	per year
Supplies	40.00	per month
Training Material	50.00	per month

7-5 Summary budget report

across the twelve months exactly as you specified in the Budget box. To print a hard copy of this type of budget list, choose Print when the budget list is on screen. I recommend changing the Print Setup to Landscape orientation when printing wide reports of this nature.

A partial example of the detailed budget list is shown in Fig. 7-6. Unfortunately this format does not allow you to customize further to view and print only specified months; and existing categories with no budget are included in the report. Microsoft might add these features in its next upgrade.

Matching expenditures against budget

Select Reports then Budget Report from the menu when you want to produce reports that compare a budget to actuality. Budget reports are displayed and printed in income & expense format because only categories have budgets. You won't see your Checking account or other assets and liabilities on a budget report.

At the simplest level, you could compare budget to actual for just the current month, but you can specify any period in your reports. Eventually you will want to print a budget report that covers a whole year.

Budget versus actual for one month

After selecting Reports then Budget Report from the menu, you will see that the default format is for the entire current year up to the current date, with a set of three columns for each month. To see the budget versus actual for just the current month, choose the Customize option and specify a date range of the beginning and ending month date. On the Customize screen, you can select None in the Column for Every list box in order to see only the current month without an added year to date total column. Figure 7-7 provides an example of this type of Budget report for just one month.

If you want to suppress the subcategories and show only categories, you can specify Category in the Row for Every list box of the Customize screen. There is also an option to Display Empty Categories, which allows you to display or suppress categories that have budget amounts but no actual. For business purposes, you would always want to leave this check box marked to display empty categories (which is how it is marked at default).

The data presented for each month in each category includes the actual amount spent or received in the month, the budget for that month and the difference between budget and actual. If the amount of actual expenditures or revenue exceeds the budget amount, the difference is shown as a positive number (you are over budget). If the actual amount is less than the budget amount, the difference is shown as a negative number (you are under budget).

1992 BUDGET

Category	January	February	March	April	May
INCOME CATEGORIES					
Interest Income	15.00	15.00	15.00	15.00	15.00
Other Income	10.00	10.00	10.00	10.00	10.00
Revenue	4,500.00	4,500.00	4,500.00	4,500.00	4,500.00
Consulting	2,000.00	2,000.00	2,000.00	2,000.00	2,000.00
Training	2,500.00	2,500.00	2,500.00	2,500.00	2,500.00
EXPENSE CATEGORIES					
Advertising	800.00	800.00	800.00	800.00	800.00
Automobile/Truck	50.00	50.00	75.00	75.00	75.00
Gasoline	40.00	40.00	55.00	55.00	55.00
Maintenance	10.00	10.00	20.00	20.00	20.00
Bank Charges	20.00	20.00	20.00	20.00	20.00
Computer Supplies	20.00	20.00	20.00	20.00	20.00
Entertainment	50.00	50.00	50.00	50.00	50.00
Meals	50.00	50.00	50.00	50.00	50.00
Other	0.00	0.00	0.00	0.00	0.00
Insurance	0.00	0.00	0.00	0.00	0.00
Automobile	0.00	0.00	0.00	0.00	0.00
Liability	0.00	0.00	0.00	0.00	0.00
Miscellaneous	30.00	30.00	30.00	30.00	30.00
Office Expenses	90.00	90.00	90.00	90.00	90.00
Rent	0.00	0.00	0.00	0.00	0.00
Repairs	50.00	50.00	50.00	50.00	50.00
Supplies	40.00	40.00	40.00	40.00	40.00
Training Material	50.00	50.00	50.00	50.00	50.00

7-6 Detailed budget report

```
                    DECEMBER BUDGET ANALYSIS
                    12/1/91 Through 12/31/91


                                          Total
    Category                 Actual       Budget     Difference

    INCOME CATEGORIES

    Interest Income                        15.00       (15.00)
    Other Income              40.00        10.00        30.00
    Revenue                4,850.00     4,500.00       350.00

    TOTAL INCOME CATEGORIES  4,890.00     4,525.00      365.00

    EXPENSE CATEGORIES

    Advertising              720.00       800.00       (80.00)
    Automobile/Truck         182.00        65.00       117.00
    Bank Charges              30.70        20.00        10.70
    Computer Supplies                      20.00       (20.00)
    Entertainment             41.50        50.00        (8.50)
    Insurance                640.00       640.00         0.00
    Miscellaneous             16.50        30.00       (13.50)
    Office Expenses           42.00        90.00       (48.00)
    Training Material        306.00        50.00       256.00

    TOTAL EXPENSE CATEGORIE 1,978.70     1,765.00      213.70

    GRAND TOTAL             2,911.30     2,760.00      151.30
```

7-7 Budget versus Actual report

Budget versus actual for a quarter or a year

When you want to see several months (even up to 12 months) side by side for comparison purposes, you must still select Month in the Column for Every list box of the Customize screen, but specify a date range that you want broken down into months. For example, specify a date range of 10/1/92 through 12/31/92 to see a month by month comparison for the third quarter of the year. Figure 7-8 provides an example of this type of budget report, additionally customized to show only categories and not subcategories. I recommend changing your Print Setup to Landscape orientation when printing a wide report like this so you can keep the comparison data flowing across the width of a row.

When printing budget reports, you should be careful to use exact month-ending dates (6/30, 7/31, 8/31 or 9/30, etc.), because if you choose anything less than a month, Money will automatically prorate the monthly budget data by day. For example, if you mistakenly enter a date of 7/30 for a July month ending date, the monthly budget amounts will be multiplied by 30/31; thus, the budgets you see on the report will represent 30 days out of the 31 in the month of July.

BUDGET REPORT
11/1/91 Through 12/31/91

Category	11/1/91 Actual	Through Budget	11/30/91 Difference	12/1/91 Actual	Through Budget	12/31/91 Difference	Actual	Total Budget	Difference
INCOME CATEGORIES									
Interest Incom	18.50	15.00	3.50		15.00	(15.00)	18.50	30.00	(11.50)
Other Income	32.00	10.00	22.00	40.00	10.00	30.00	72.00	20.00	52.00
Revenue	4,175.00	4,500.00	(325.00)	4,850.00	4,500.00	350.00	9,025.00	9,000.00	25.00
TOTAL INCOME CATEG	4,225.50	4,525.00	(299.50)	4,890.00	4,525.00	365.00	9,115.50	9,050.00	65.50
EXPENSE CATEGORIES									
Advertising	780.00	800.00	(20.00)	720.00	800.00	(80.00)	1,500.00	1,600.00	(100.00)
Automobile/Tru	88.00	65.00	23.00	182.00	65.00	117.00	270.00	130.00	140.00
Bank Charges	22.50	20.00	2.50	30.70	20.00	10.70	53.20	40.00	13.20
Computer Suppl	18.75	20.00	(1.25)		20.00	(20.00)	18.75	40.00	(21.25)
Entertainment	52.65	50.00	2.65	41.50	50.00	(8.50)	94.15	100.00	(5.85)
Insurance				640.00	640.00	0.00	640.00	640.00	0.00
Miscellaneous	44.00	30.00	14.00	16.50	30.00	(13.50)	60.50	60.00	0.50
Office Expense	75.88	90.00	(14.12)	42.00	90.00	(48.00)	117.88	180.00	(62.12)
Training Mater	88.00	50.00	38.00	306.00	50.00	256.00	394.00	100.00	294.00
TOTAL EXPENSE CATE	1,169.78	1,125.00	44.78	1,978.70	1,765.00	213.70	3,148.48	2,890.00	258.48
GRAND TOTAL	3,055.72	3,400.00	(344.28)	2,911.30	2,760.00	151.30	5,967.02	6,160.00	(192.98)

7-8   Budget report for multiple months

Comparing this year to last year

You can compare this year's results with last year by specifying a date range of greater than a year. I wouldn't recommend doing this with columns for every month, or you'll be waiting until next year for the printout to finish. If you have all the data for two years stored in your Money file, you can specify a date range of 1/1/91 through 12/31/92 and select Year in the Column for Every list box. Your report will list the two years side by side. You also could customize to display columns for every quarter if you want a further breakdown. Just one note of caution: because you can only store one budget year's data at a time, Money assumes the same budget amount for this year as well as last year. The budget figures you see in a two year report would be the budget data associated with the current category list. The actual amounts will be the actual dollars spent or received in the date range you specified.

Setting up next year's budget

The budget data you enter for Jan, Feb, Mar, etc., is year independent. The budget data is stored as part of your category list, not as part of your transactions. When you delete last year's data from your file, you are not deleting the budgeted amounts. To update your budget for the upcoming year, print out a detailed budget list using the process described earlier in this chapter and review the figures compared to actual versus budget reports. Make notations on the items you want to change and then edit each category or subcategory using the Category List dialog box as described at the beginning of this chapter.

Summary

Now that you have completed this chapter, you can start using the tools that help you gain better control over your spending habits because of your understanding of the budget process. Planning for the budget process, entering budgets, and comparing actual results against the budget were all covered in this chapter. Using budget reports enables you to identify weak spots in both receipts and expenditures in order to initiate action to correct these problems.

Spending control tutorial

This tutorial builds on the concepts learned in chapters 1 through 5. If you have not completed the tutorials at the end of chapters 3 − 6, some transaction data will be missing from your file and you might not have some of the categories referred to in this tutorial. You probably can get by without these, if you ad lib a little through some of the steps below. You're probably familiar enough with Money by now to handle that. Access Money from the Program Manager window of Windows 3.0.

Part A

This section leads you through the process of producing some historical reports to help you get ready to set budget goals. We will print income statements in several formats.

- ☐ If you don't have the sample file on screen, select File then Open from the menu. Select the sample.mny file, then Ok. Choose Yes if you want to back up the current file
- ☐ Select the Account box, and select Business Checking
- ☐ Select Window then Account Book
- ☐ Select Reports then Income & Expense Report
- ☐ Choose Customize and enter a Title of Budget Plan
- ☐ Enter a Date Range of 12/1 to 12/31
- ☐ Look around the Customize Report dialog box
- ☐ Verify that settings are in place for
  Row for Every - Subcategory
  Column for Every - None
  All Accounts
  All Transactions
  Report Transfers By - Income Statement
- ☐ Choose View to see the report on screen
- ☐ Choose Print then Ok to get a paper copy
- ☐ Do not close the report window!

Note In previous tutorials we have only entered one month's worth of data, as you see in the income statement we have just printed. In a real-life setting, we would have more historical data to rely on, and it would be better to base your budget plan on three or more months of data. We'll set up to print a quarterly income statement by month just for practice.

- ☐ Choose Customize again
- ☐ Enter a From date of 10/1
- ☐ Select Month in the Column for Every list box
- ☐ Choose View to see the report
- ☐ This would be better for budget planning
- ☐ Choose Close to return to the account book

Part B

Now we are ready to enter budget figures by accessing the category list and focusing on the Budget box in the bottom right corner of the window. In this part, we'll enter simple monthly or annual budgets for Interest Income, Miscellaneous, and Training Materials. I assume that you have already entered the following budgets during the chapter 1 tutorial:

Revenue	4500	per month
Advertising	800	per month
Bank Charges	20	per month
Insurance	1280	per year
Automobile	480	per year
Liability	800	per year

☐ Select List then Category from the menu

☐ Select the Interest Income category

☐ Check the Yearly Budget option in the Budget box (Alt−Y)

☐ You can Tab to the Amount box or click there

☐ Enter 180 in the Amount box

☐ Select the Miscellaneous Expense category (you can scroll and click there, or Alt−L then use the arrow keys)

☐ Note that the Monthly Budget option is already checked

☐ Move to the Amount field (Alt−O) and type 30

☐ Enter a 500 monthly budget for Training Materials

☐ Don't choose Close, we'll enter more budgets below

Part C

Entering budgets in subcategories and getting them to total to the category level is a little trickier. In this part, we'll enter budgets for Entertainment: Meals, Office Expenses: Repairs, and Office Expenses: Supplies.

☐ Select the Entertainment category

☐ Move to the Subcategory list (Alt−U) and choose Meals

☐ Be sure the Monthly Budget option is checked

☐ Select the Amount box and type 50

☐ Move back to the Category list and select Entertainment

- ☐ Notice that these items show no budget
- ☐ Select the Custom Budget option (Alt−B)
- ☐ The Custom Budget dialog box appears
- ☐ Choose the Total Subcategories button (Alt−S)
- ☐ Notice that the Entertainment category now holds the Meals budget as its budget—this is the total of all the subcategories under Entertainment
- ☐ Choose Ok then select the Office Expense category
- ☐ Move to the Subcategory list (Alt−U) and choose Repairs
- ☐ Select the Yearly Budget option in the Budget box
- ☐ Tab to the Amount box and type 600
- ☐ Select the Supplies subcategory under Office Expenses
- ☐ Note that the Monthly Budget option is already checked
- ☐ Move to the Amount field (Alt−O) and type 40
- ☐ Return to the category list and scroll up a few categories
- ☐ Notice that the Office Expense category shows no budget, even though we just entered budgets in its subcategories
- ☐ Select the Office Expense category again
- ☐ Select the Custom Budget option (Alt−B)
- ☐ Choose the Total Subcategories button (Alt−S)
- ☐ Note that the monthly amounts fill with the total of the monthly amounts for Repairs and Supplies (90 per month)
- ☐ Choose Ok to return to the Category List dialog box
- ☐ Return to the category list and scroll one line
- ☐ Note that the Office Expenses category now has a budget
- ☐ Don't close the Category List window, there are more budgets

Part D

In this section we will practice using the custom budget option in order to enter unequal amounts per month in the Automobile Expense category. In the two sub-categories of this category, we want to budget for lower amounts in winter months and higher amounts in summer.

- ☐ Select Automobile/Truck on the category list
- ☐ Select the Gasoline subcategory
- ☐ Choose the Custom Budget option from the Budget box
- ☐ Type 40 in the Jan box and choose Fill Down (Alt−F)

- ☐ Although this places 40 in all months, we can change that
- ☐ Tab to the Mar box, type 55, and choose Fill Down
- ☐ Tab to the Jun box, type 60, and choose Fill Down
- ☐ Tab to the Oct box, type 50, and choose Fill Down
- ☐ Notice that the Annual Total is now $635
- ☐ Choose Ok
- ☐ Select the Maintenance subcategory
- ☐ Choose the Custom Budget option from the Budget box
- ☐ Type 10 in the Jan box and choose Fill Down (Alt−F)
- ☐ Tab to the Mar box, type 20 and choose Fill Down
- ☐ Tab to the Oct box, type 15, and choose Fill Down
- ☐ Notice that the Annual Total is now $205
- ☐ Choose Ok
- ☐ Select the Advertising category
- ☐ Notice that the Automobile category has no total budget
- ☐ Select the Automobile category
- ☐ Choose the Custom Budget option from the Budget box
- ☐ Choose the Total Subcategories button
- ☐ Notice that the months fill with totals from the subcategories
- ☐ Choose Ok
- ☐ Scroll up the Category list a few lines
- ☐ Notice that the Automobile category now has an $840 budget
- ☐ Stay in the Category List dialog box for the next part

Part E

This section demonstrates the steps for printing both a summary format budget and a detailed budget.

- ☐ With the Category List dialog box on screen, choose Report
- ☐ Choose Customize
- ☐ Check the Basic Budgets option
- ☐ Uncheck the Shortcut and Tax Flag options
- ☐ Choose View
- ☐ Scroll down to view each category and subcategory
- ☐ Choose Print, then Ok if you want this on paper

- [ ] Choose Customize again
- [ ] Check the Detailed Budgets option
- [ ] Choose View to see the month by month spread
- [ ] Scroll to the right to see the Feb through Dec and Annual budgets
- [ ] Choose Close twice to return to the account book

Part F

To print the detailed budget, we want to adjust the print setup to print sideways on the paper and change to the smallest font we can find. Let's try it.

- [ ] Select File then Print Setup from the menu
- [ ] In the Print Setup dialog box, check Report Printing
- [ ] Check the Landscape option in the Orientation box

Note The Landscape option might not be available, depending on your printer type.

- [ ] Choose Ok
- [ ] Select List then Category List
- [ ] Choose the Report option, then Customize
- [ ] Check the Detailed Budgets option
- [ ] Uncheck the Shortcut and Tax Flag options
- [ ] Choose View and scroll around a bit—same budget?
- [ ] Choose Fonts and scroll through the fonts list box
- [ ] Select a compressed or elite font (smallest size), then Ok
- [ ] Choose Print, then Ok
- [ ] Go get yourself a hot cup of coffee and relax while your full year budget prints out
- [ ] Choose Close twice to return to the account book
- [ ] Select File then Print Setup
- [ ] Check the Report Printing option
- [ ] Check the Portrait orientation option
- [ ] Choose Ok to return to the account book

Part G

The most helpful budget report is the one that compares budget to actual. Because we only have one month's worth of transactions, we'll print the December budget report—but you can print any period you'd like.

- [ ] Select Reports then Budget Report from the menu
- [ ] Note that the report defaults to current year to date
- [ ] You probably can't see December
- [ ] Choose Customize
- [ ] Select None in the Column for Every list box
- [ ] Enter a Date Range of 12/1 to 12/31
- [ ] Choose View to see the result
- [ ] Choose Print, then Ok
- [ ] Choose Close to return to the account book

Part H

When you need to edit budget items that were previously entered, follow procedures similar to Parts B and C. When we first entered the Revenue budget of $4500 per month, we had not established subcategories. We now have Consulting and Training subcategories where we want to split the budget. The following list walks you through the procedure.

- [ ] Select List then Category List
- [ ] Select the Revenue category
- [ ] Select the Consulting subcategory
- [ ] Enter 2500 in the Amount field of the Budget box (this is a monthly budget)
- [ ] Select the Training subcategory
- [ ] Enter 2000 in the Amount field of the Budget box
- [ ] Select the Revenue category again
- [ ] Select the Custom Budget option
- [ ] The Custom Budget dialog box appears
- [ ] Choose the Total Subcategories button
- [ ] Note that the subcategories are totalled in Jan through Dec
- [ ] Choose the Ok button and scroll up the category list
- [ ] Notice how the Revenue budget is now $4500 again
- [ ] Choose Close to return to the account book
- [ ] Select File then Exit and make a backup of your work

8

CHAPTER

Managing credit cards

Buying and selling on credit is so popular today that most individuals and businesses could no longer continue their day to day affairs without it. When you buy anything on credit, the transaction should be categorized in Money so that it is included on your financial reports. Whenever you make a payment to your credit card company, this should be recorded in your Checking account and deducted from your checking balance. This chapter presents all the procedures necessary for recording these credit transactions, and also provides suggestions for reconciling credit card statements with your Money accounts.

Two possible approaches

You can either handle all credit card transactions from within the Checking account that you will make payments from, or you might set up separate "accounts" for each of your credit cards. If you have only a few credit card transactions each month and/or you pay the full balance owed each month, it is probably better to stay within your Checking account. If you use your credit cards often or if you do not pay that full balance each month, it is probably better to set up separate accounts in your Money file.

With the first and simpler approach (staying within your Checking account) enter a split transaction in your Checking account when you pay the credit card bill. With a split transaction, you can use over 100 lines to categorize individual items from your statement. The only drawback to this is that with SuperSmartFill in action, each successive payment will automatically call up the last payment's split data, so you won't have much help with data entry. In a split transaction that has already been filled by SuperSmartFill, you must type over each line of old data with new data and delete specific fields with the Del key. Future transaction entry is simplified when you keep a separate Credit Card account.

The second approach (creating a separate Credit Card account) requires setting up a new account within your Money file, for example, American Express. With this new account, you can enter each purchase transaction at the time of purchase or when you receive your monthly statement. When you make a payment on account, you would enter the payment in the American Express account but transfer the transaction to your Checking account where a check can be printed. After these purchase and payment transactions are entered once, SuperSmartFill makes entering future transactions a snap, because most of the data is provided to you from the last transaction. When you receive a credit card statement, you can use Money's "Balance Account" feature to review your transactions and make adjustments if necessary.

Handling credit cards in your Checking account

If you intend to handle your credit card transactions within your Checking account, simply wait until you receive your credit card statement and then enter a payment transaction that is categorized for the many items that appear on your statement. For example, let's assume you have just received the VISA statement shown in Fig. 8-1. We want to write a check for $227.24, the current balance owed.

In the Account Book or Checks & Forms window for your Checking account, you would enter Print, 9/4, VISA-Key Bank, and $227.24 in the payment column. Then click the Split Transaction icon, or press Ctrl−S to access the Split Transaction window. In this window, you would enter a separate line for each of the charges and adjustments on your credit card statement. If any items are credits from previous months, they should be entered as minuses in the split transaction and categorized the same as the original transaction that caused the credit. If you are paying an interest charge, this can be categorized as Interest Expense. If you are paying the monthly or annual credit card usage fee, this can be categorized as Bank Charges or Miscellaneous Expense (or you could set up a special category for it). If there are small amount items that you don't want to enter individually, you could lump some items together to be charged to Miscellaneous Expense. Figure 8-2 illustrates the completed Split Transaction window for this example transaction.

If your Credit Card account includes check writing privileges and cash advances, these transactions should be recorded as part of the split transaction when you receive your statement. If you maintain a Cash On Hand account, and have taken a cash advance from your credit card to fatten your cash on hand, the split transaction should show the cash advance as a Transfer to Cash on Hand. Then the categorization of this cash can be made in the Cash on Hand account.

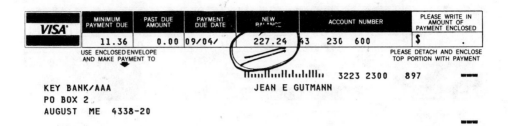

VISA®	MINIMUM PAYMENT DUE	PAST DUE AMOUNT	PAYMENT DUE DATE	NEW BALANCE	ACCOUNT NUMBER	PLEASE WRITE IN AMOUNT OF PAYMENT ENCLOSED
	11.36	0.00	09/04/	227.24	43 230 600	$.

USE ENCLOSED ENVELOPE
AND MAKE PAYMENT TO

PLEASE DETACH AND ENCLOSE
TOP PORTION WITH PAYMENT

ıllıııllıııllıdııldllıı 3223 2300 897

KEY BANK/AAA
PO BOX 2
AUGUST ME 4338-20

JEAN E GUTMANN

CUSTOMER INFORMATION
(See reverse side for billing rights summary) 800-452-8779 5594

ACCOUNT NUMBER	CREDIT LIMIT	AVAILABLE CREDIT	DAYS IN BILLING CYCLE	BILLING CYCLE CLOSING DATE	PAYMENT DUE DATE	MINIMUM PAYMENT DUE
332 23 6009	3400	2994	30	08/10/	09/04/	11.36

DATE OF TRANS.	POST	REFERENCE NUMBER	CHARGES, PAYMENTS AND CREDITS SINCE LAST STATEMENT		AMOUNT
0713	0716	7441800JJ5M2B69S0	R C STEELE SPENCERPORT NY		77.86
0713	0717	7431903JMW1TVB667	SPORTS STEP INC MARIETTA GA		66.95
0721	0723	7440851JVMXAFB5ET	NEW BALANCE SKOWHEGAN ME		35.67
0727	0727	7461651K0WGW3A1NY	FRAME CENTER PORTLAND ME		57.86
0727	0806	7416800KAS8LG1EMA	MAINE SPORT ROCKPORT ME		28.30
0808	0808	7433223KDX2QLBJPE	PAYMENT - THANK YOU		605.55-
0808	0809	7441800KQ6DGA1S0T	R C STEELE SPENCERPORT NY	CREDIT	39.40-

PREVIOUS BALANCE	PAYMENTS	CREDITS	CASH ADVANCES	MERCHANT ADVANCES	DEBIT ADJUSTMENTS		NEW BALANCE
605.55	605.55	39.40	0.00	266.64	0.00	0.00	227.24

8-1 Sample VISA statement

Managing a separate Credit Card account

A Credit Card account is set up by selecting the List and Account List items from the menu. Indicate that you want to set up a New account and fill in the title box (something like VISA-Fleet Bank, or AmExp). On the Create New Account screen, you must check the type of account you want. There is an option for Credit Card Account. After choosing this option, you are asked for the beginning balance.

The beginning balance should be based on your last credit card statement. You could use the ending balance from that statement, but take into consideration whether you want to individually categorize the items that make up the balance. If

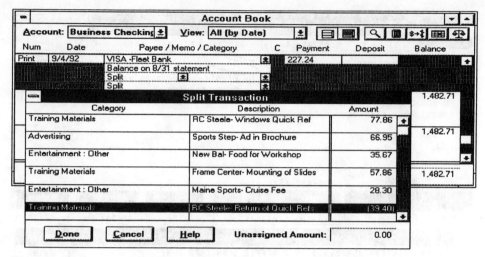

8-2 Split transaction window for VISA payment

you do want to categorize, then it might be better to start with a beginning balance of zero and enter individual unpaid items in the new account, each assigned to a category.

Once you enter the beginning balance, you should Close the Category List window. Select the Account box in the Checking Account window and you will see the new Credit Card account on your cascading list of accounts. Select this Credit Card account to begin entering transactions.

Recording purchases on account

Whether you choose to enter credit card transactions as they occur and you bring home the source document (your receipt), or whether you enter them when you receive your monthly statement, the Money process is the same. Enter purchases or interest as Charges, and enter payments or returns as Credits.

A credit purchase is recorded in much the same manner as any payment transaction in your Checking account. Enter a Num (optional), the date of the purchase, the vendor (payee), charge amount, a description, and a category/subcategory. A sample credit card purchase is shown in Fig. 8-3. If the charge

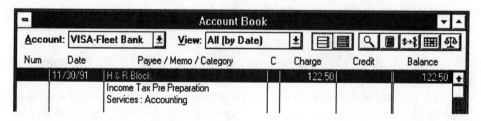

8-3 Credit card purchase in a Credit Card account

covers several items, you can switch to the Split Transaction window and charge the total to several individual categories.

If the charge involves amounts that would not be categorized as Expenses, they might need to be categorized as Transfers to asset accounts. For example, let's say that you bought a new computer printer and some paper using your VISA. The printer should be charged as a transfer to an asset account (e.g., Computer Equipment), while the paper should be charged to Office Expenses, Supplies. This transaction is illustrated in Fig. 8-4.

Whether you are maintaining personal records or business records, building (home) improvements should be categorized as Transfers to your asset accounts (e.g., Building, or Home).

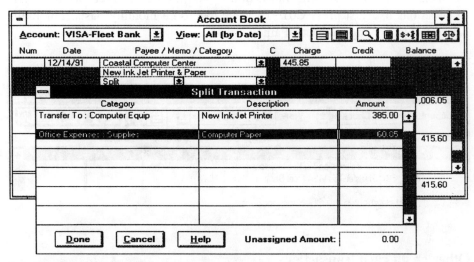

8-4 Purchase of an asset with a credit card

Recording payments on the Credit Card account

Although you could record payments on your credit card in either your Checking account or in your credit card account, it will be easier to record them in the Credit Card account. If you do this, you have a picture in front of you that provides you with the balance owed. If you are making a partial payment, it really doesn't matter which account you record the payment in.

When you record the payment in the Credit Card account, you should categorize it as a Transfer to your Business Checking account. See Fig. 8-5 for an example of a payment (credit) recorded in the sample VISA-Fleet account.

Once the transaction is recorded in the Credit Card account, you should switch to the Checking account view and verify that the payment has been transferred there. Put a Print indicator in the Num field of the credit card payment in

8-5 Payment in a Credit Card account

the Checking account, then request that a check be printed. Figure 8-6 illustrates the credit card payment in the Checking account.

This credit card payment transaction should then be entered on the Future Transactions list (just press Ctrl−E) to be paid on a monthly basis. For future payments, just change the actual amount paid.

8-6 Credit card payment in the Checking account

Other credit card transactions

Returns of merchandise purchased with your credit card are credits to your account. These are recorded in the same fashion as the payments with one big exception: they should be categorized in the same category you used when you recorded the purchase. For example, let's assume we had to return half of the computer paper purchased in the example shown in Fig. 8-4. When the transaction is entered in the Credit Card account, the amount is entered in the credit column, and categorized as Office Expenses, Supplies. The effect of this credit to the Supplies subcategory is a decrease in the overall total spent on supplies. A small portion of a customized register report is shown in Fig. 8-7.

When you receive your credit card statement, you might be assessed interest on your account. This transaction would be recorded in the Credit Card account as a Charge and categorized as Interest Expense. If you are charged a user fee, this also would be recorded in your Money Credit Card account as a Charge, and probably categorized as Bank Charges, or Miscellaneous Expense.

```
                    REGISTER REPORT FOR OFFICE EXPENSES
                          12/1/91 Through 12/31/91


   Num         Date    Payee                Memo                        Amount

EXPENSE CATEGORIES

Office Expenses

   Supplies
              12/3/91   Loring Short Printing   Stationery & Cards          (53.16)
              12/11/91  VISA-Fleet Bank         C & R Printing - Station   (122.00)
              12/14/91  Coastal Computer Center Computer Paper              (60.85)
              12/16/91  Coastal Computer Center Return 1/2 of Computer P      30.25
                                                                          (205.76)

      Total Office Expenses                                               (205.76)

TOTAL EXPENSE CATEGORIES                                                  (205.76)

GRAND TOTAL                                                               (205.76)
```

8-7 Register report showing a return of supplies

Credit card reports

Probably the only credit card report you'll ever need is a register report that lists
all the transactions in your Credit Card account for a specific period. Most likely,
you would want a list of transactions for the same period of time that is covered by
your card statement. A sample Credit Card Transaction list is shown in Fig. 8-8.
This is obtained by customizing a register report to include the memo and category fields restricted to the month of December, with no subtotals, to display
splits, include only a specific Credit Card account, and include all transactions in
that account. You might prefer to subtotal your credit card transaction list by payee
or category.

```
                        VISA TRANSACTION LIST FOR
                          12/1/91 Through 12/31/91


   Num         Date    Payee                Category                     Amount
              12/2/91   HuShang Restaurant      Entertainment : Meals       (88.90)

              12/3/91   AmTrak                  Travel : Ground Transpor   (132.89)

              12/3/91   Loring Short Printing   Office Expenses : Suppli    (53.16)

              12/5/91   Holly House             Travel : Lodging           (142.50)

              12/12/91  Interest Paid           Interest Expense            (12.00)

              12/14/91  Coastal Computer Center Split                      (445.85)
                                                   Transfer To : Comput    (385.00)
                                                   Office Expenses : Su     (60.85)

              12/16/91  Coastal Computer Center Office Expenses : Suppli     30.25

              12/22/91  VISA-Fleet Bank         Transfer From : Business    590.45


GRAND TOTAL                                                               (254.60)
```

8-8 Credit card transaction list

Although you probably won't need to print a separate summary of ending balances in your Credit Card accounts, you will see the ending balances in these accounts when you print a summary report of all accounts or a net worth report. Balances owed on your credit cards are a liability of a business. Figure 8-9 shows how several Credit Card accounts would appear on a net worth report.

```
                    NET WORTH REPORT
                    As of 12/31/91


ASSETS                            Total


Bank and Cash Accounts
Business Checking                 1,709.95
Cash on Hand                        122.00
        Total Bank and Cash Accounts  1,831.95


Other Assets
Computer Equip                      385.00
        Total Other Assets          385.00

TOTAL ASSETS                      2,216.95


LIABILITIES                       Total


Credit Cards
American Express                    602.80
Discovery Card                       35.50
VISA-Fleet Bank                     415.60
        Total Credit Cards        1,053.90

TOTAL LIABILITIES                 1,053.90


NET WORTH                         1,163.05
```

8-9 Net worth report with credit card balances

Balancing a Credit Card account

The process of balancing a Credit Card account is pretty much the same as balancing a Checking account. Balancing a Checking account is covered in chapter 12. The general procedure for balancing a Credit Card account follows.

When you receive a credit card statement, select the Options then Balance Account menu items to reconcile your Money records against the statement. You will need to enter a beginning and ending balance from the statement and any interest or fee charges found on the statement. Then you are presented with a list of all the transactions in the Money account, so that you can scroll through them and mark items that appear on the statement as Cleared.

A status report of total items cleared and total items from the statement appears at the bottom of the Balance Account window. When the status area reports a Difference of zero, you have balanced the account. If a Difference amount is showing, you need to review your transactions and your card statement to determine what's missing in one place or the other. Select the Finish option if you get frustrated, because Money has a hidden treat on the next screen that helps you find the difference in the account. This hidden treat is called the Account Didn't Balance Window, and offers you a selection of Use SmartReconcile to help find the error. Select this option, and Money will identify transactions that fit the dollar amount of the Difference. Refer to chapter 12 for illustrations of the screen boxes during the Balance Account procedure.

Summary

This chapter has presented the procedures to be followed to manage the transactions that flow through a Credit Card account. Managing a credit card from within your regular Checking account was discussed along with how to set up separate Credit Card accounts. Also included were details on how to enter purchases, adjustments, and payments in a Credit Card account, how to produce useful reports on these transactions, and how to reconcile a Credit Card account.

Charging it tutorial

This tutorial builds on the concepts learned in chapters 1 through 5. Although it assumes that you have practiced the concepts in the chapter 4 and 5 tutorials, you do not need any of the data from those chapters. Access Money from the Program Manager window of Windows 3.0.

Part A

This first section leads you through the simple process of recording a credit card payment in the Checking account, assuming that you do not want to set up a separate account. You have just received your VISA statement with a balance due of $423.60, made up of various items that you want to categorize as expenditures and one asset.

- ☐ Select File then Open, and choose the sample.mny file
- ☐ Open the Account Book window
- ☐ Select the next available transaction line
- ☐ Enter p, 12/19, VISA-CitiBank, then 423.60
- ☐ Access the split transaction window (Ctrl − S)
- ☐ Fill in the split as follows:
    Automobile, Gasoline, Irving-Fill Up, 24
    Computer Supplies, (no sub), Ace-Disks & Cleaner, 46.50
    Entertainment, Meals, Rock Road-Lunch w/Mid, 43.35,

Project, Middle Co-Spreadsheets
Office Expense, Repairs, Canon-Copier Repair, 35
Transfer, to Equipment, Locke-Office Chair/Pad, 274.75

☐ Press Alt−D (Done) when amount totals 0

☐ Press Enter to complete transaction

☐ Select File, then Print Checks from the menu

Note If there are several checks you haven't printed, the Print Checks dialog box will let you know that. If you want to print only this check, mark the Select Checks option and select this specific check.

☐ Choose Ok

☐ If you've chosen voucher style checks, the details of this transaction appear on the check stub

☐ Choose Continue to return to the account book

Part B

In this section we have decided that we want to set up a separate account for our credit card transactions and not pay the full balance each month. Then we will record credit card purchases as they occur, a few at a time.

☐ Select List, then Account List from the menu

☐ Choose the New option

☐ Type VISA-CitiBank and check the Credit Card Account option (you can press Alt−C for this)

☐ Choose Ok

☐ Enter an opening balance of 0 and choose Ok

☐ Choose Close to return to the Checking account book

☐ Select the Account list box, and select VISA-CitiBank

☐ You are now in the new credit card account

☐ Tab to the Date field and type 12/19

☐ Type West and Tab to the amount field (SmartFill provides data from a recent transaction for West Side Mobil)

☐ Type 17.60 in the Charge field

☐ Type Oil Change in the Memo field

☐ Select Automobile/Truck in the Category field

☐ Select Maintenance in the Subcategory field

- [ ] Press Enter to record this transaction
- [ ] Enter the next transaction as follows:
  Date: 12/20, Payee: Boston Hyatt, Charge: 144.58
  Memo: WP Conference, Category: Travel
  Subcategory: Lodging
- [ ] Enter one more transaction as follows:
  Date: 12/21, Payee: Boston Computer Society,
  Charge: 50, Memo: WP Conference Materials,
  Category: Training Materials

Part C

We have received our VISA statement and we want to pay $100 towards the total outstanding balance. The statement also includes $7.85 in interest charges.

- [ ] Type 12/22 in the Date field
- [ ] Type VISA in the Payee field
- [ ] When you Tab to the Charge field, the last VISA amount appears
- [ ] Press Del to remove the old amount
- [ ] Tab to the Credit field and type 100
- [ ] Type Partial Payment on Account in the Memo field
- [ ] Select or type Transfer in the Category field
- [ ] A warning message appears about deleting the old Split amount
- [ ] Choose Ok to delete the old Split
- [ ] Select or type Business Checking in the Subcategory field
- [ ] Press Enter to record
- [ ] Select Account, then Business Checking
- [ ] Scroll to the Dec 22 area of the account book
- [ ] Verify that the VISA $100 payment was transferred here
- [ ] Enter a p in the Num column of this $100 VISA transaction
- [ ] Press Enter to complete the transaction
- [ ] Select File, Print Checks, then Ok, then Continue
- [ ] The VISA payment will be recorded, and check # displayed
- [ ] Our VISA statement includes $7.85 in interest charges
- [ ] Select Account, then VISA to return to the VISA account
- [ ] Enter a transaction for interest as follows:
  Date: 12/22, Payee: VISA-Interest, Charge: 7.85

Memo: Interest on Charge Card,
Category: Interest Expense

☐ Press Enter to record

Note   Now that this payee name includes the word *Interest*, the next time we enter this payee, SuperSmartFill will provide the details of the last interest transaction.

Part D

The other type of credit card transaction that sometimes needs recording is the return of goods for credit against the credit card. Let's assume we returned some of the computer supplies recorded in Part A, and a credit for this appears on our latest VISA statement.

☐ Be sure you are in the VISA-CitiBank account

☐ Select the next available transaction line

☐ Enter a transaction for this credit as follows:
   Date: 12/23, **Payee:** Ace Computer Inc., **Credit:** 8.50
   Memo: Return of Bad Disks, **Category:** Computer Supplies

☐ Press Enter to complete the transaction

☐ Notice that this amount is deducted from the balance

☐ Let's see how this affects the Computer Supplies category

☐ Select Report, Register Report

☐ Choose Customize

☐ Check the Memo field in the Include Fields box

☐ Enter From and To dates of 12/1 and 12/31

☐ Select All Accounts in the Include Transactions From box

☐ Check the Select Transactions option at the bottom right

☐ Activate the Category list box

☐ Select the Computer Supplies category from the category list

☐ Choose Ok, then View

☐ Notice how the credit from the VISA account is shown as a deduction in this category. Normally expenses are minuses, so this credit is shown here as a plus

☐ Choose Close to return to the account book

Part E

Credit card management requires only one basic report; the Register of Transactions that corresponds to the period of the credit card statement billing period.

Balancing of the account to this statement is covered in chapter 12. In this section we will print the transaction register for the period of our latest VISA statement.

- ☐ Be sure you are still in the VISA-CitiBank account
- ☐ Select Report, then Register Report from the menu
- ☐ Choose Customize
- ☐ Type a Title of VISA Transaction Register
- ☐ Check the Memo field in the Include Fields box
- ☐ Enter From and To dates of 12/19 and 12/23 (this was a short statement period, just an example)
- ☐ Be sure the Include Transactions From box specifies VISA
- ☐ Choose View to see the report
- ☐ Choose Print, then Ok
- ☐ Choose Close to return to the account book

Part F

Lastly we want to see the effect this account has on our overall records. The VISA-CitiBank account appears as a liability on the balance sheet.

- ☐ Select Report, then Net Worth Report from the menu
- ☐ Choose Customize
- ☐ Enter a Date of 12/23
- ☐ Choose View
- ☐ Scroll to see the liability section of this report
- ☐ The VISA account balance appears as a liability
- ☐ Print this report if you would like
- ☐ Choose Close

Part G

Make a backup copy and exit from Money.

- ☐ Select File then Exit
- ☐ Insert a diskette and choose Yes
- ☐ Choose Yes to confirm the overwrite
- ☐ Well done!

9
CHAPTER

Small business payroll

When you employ individuals in your business, you have to manage a payroll. Although Money does not calculate the amounts for withholding taxes on your payroll, it can help you prepare the payroll checks automatically each pay period, keep track of payroll tax obligations to the government, and even remind you to send payroll taxes to the taxing authorities on the correct dates. This chapter presents techniques to help you manage all necessary payroll records.

Basic steps of payroll management

The task of maintaining payroll records has three basic parts: calculating and paying the periodic payroll to employees, recording this payroll with associated payroll taxes owed by the employer, and making payments to taxing authorities periodically. Integrated with all of these is the preparation of necessary payroll reports. We'll discuss each of these steps in detail after a brief introduction to the accounts and categories that are needed to record payroll transactions.

Payroll accounts and categories

You can either write payroll checks from your regular Business Checking account or set up a separate Payroll Checking account. The following procedures can be applied in either of these situations.

When you write a payroll check, the gross pay dollar amount would be categorized as Salaries & Wages, but the amounts withheld from wages as taxes and employee contributions to insurance or retirement plans must be recorded in liability accounts. Only the net pay is deducted from your Checking account. In Money these tax liabilities and contributions will be recorded as negative transfers from your Checking account to various liability accounts.

In other words, your payroll records must include several accounts for the liabilities that result from a payroll. For example, when you deduct Federal Income Tax Withholding from your employees' wages, it must be set aside in an account called Federal Withholding Tax Payable. The *Payable* here means payable to the Federal government. For most companies, it will probably be sufficient to set up three or four of the following liability accounts:

- ☐ FICA Tax Payable
- ☐ Federal Withholding Tax Payable
- ☐ State Withholding Tax Payable
- ☐ Employee Retirement Contributions Payable
- ☐ Employee Medical Insurance Contributions Payable
- ☐ Other Withholding Plans Payable

In addition to the taxes deducted from employee wages, the employer incurs some liability for payroll taxes at the time the payroll is written. The employer's portion of FICA taxes should be recorded in the FICA Tax Payable account listed above, and unemployment taxes (these are not paid by the employee) must be recorded in liability accounts that might be titled: Federal Unemployment Tax Payable, or State Unemployment Tax Payable.

It is possible to record a zero amount transaction in Money in order to categorize a noncash expenditure. We will employ this technique for recording these employer taxes.

Getting ready for the first payroll

Before you write your first paycheck, you should select the List menu and the Account List option to display your current account list. Then you must select the New option button and type the name of your first new liability account (e.g., FICA Taxes Payable), select the account type of Liability and indicate a zero beginning balance. Do this for each of the payroll liability accounts listed in the previous section that would be needed for your particular situation. You also might invent a shortcut code, enter a bank name and account number to be associated with this account, and use the comment field for a brief explanation of what amounts will be charged to this account. A sample updated Account List is shown in Fig. 9-1.

Customizing categories

The Money business categories list includes subcategories within the Payroll category for Federal W/H, FICA W/H and State W/H, which you will not need because you are going to maintain tax records as liabilities. Access the category list, high-

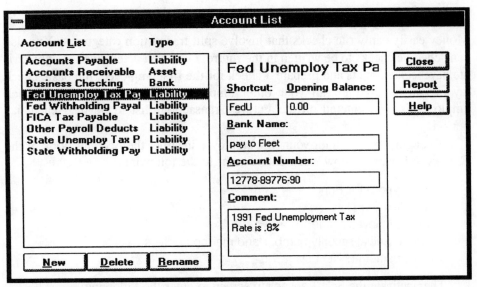

9-1 Account list with payroll accounts

light the three W/H subcategories within Payroll, and delete each of them. If you do not pay commissions or bonuses, you also might want to delete these subcategories from within the Payroll category. You will need a Taxes subcategory within the Payroll category, so while you are editing the Category list, choose the New button and add this subcategory. Your Category list for the Payroll category would then be similar to Fig. 9-2.

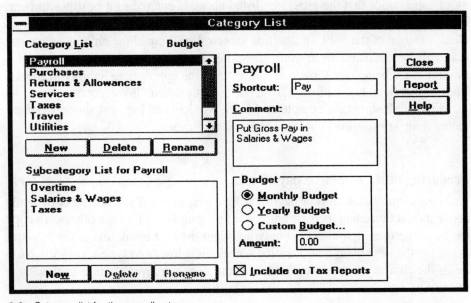

9-2 Category list for the payroll category

Producing payroll checks

Money easily can write checks that involve split transaction categories. You also can schedule checks to be written in the future. Once you determine the appropriate paycheck amounts and prepare a check for the first employee, the basic check layout can be used for all your other employees. The payroll data for each employee is then entered on the Future Transactions list to be paid each pay period.

To begin, enter data for your first employee in either the Account Book or the Checks & Forms window using data similar to the following:

Num: Type p for Print
Date: Next Pay Date
Payee: Employee Name
Address: Social security number and mailing address
Payment amount: Net pay

Then activate the Split Transaction screen to enter the following:

Line:	Category:	Subcategory:	Amount:
1	Payroll	Salaries & Wages	Gross Pay Amt
2	Transfer	FICA Tax Payable	−FICA Tax Amt
3	Transfer	Fed Withhold Tax	−Fed Income Tax
4	Transfer	State Withhold Tax	−State Income Tax
5	Transfer	Other Withhold Payable	−Other Deducts

Please notice that the gross pay listed above is entered as a positive amount, but all other amounts are entered as negatives. When these five lines are complete, the total of the Split Transaction screen should equal the amount of net pay that will be deducted from your Checking account. Also notice that lines 2 through 5 are being categorized as Transfers to the appropriate liability accounts. They will appear automatically as increases in those liability accounts.

Figure 9-3 shows the completed Check Window and Fig. 9-4 shows the completed Split Transaction Window for a real employee.

Preparing other employee pay checks

Successive employees on your payroll will be easy to pay if you enter a copy of the above transaction using the first employee as a template for all the others. To copy the first employee's paycheck, simply highlight the next blank line in the Account Book (or the next blank check in the Checks window) and type a p in the Num field, the paydate in the Date field, and the first employee's name in the Payee

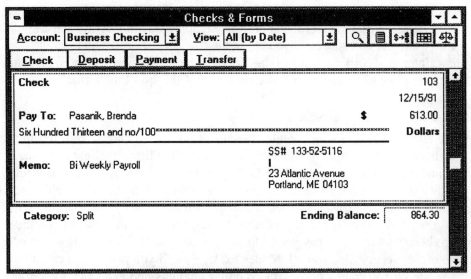

9-3 Paycheck in the Checks and Forms window

Category	Description	Amount
Payroll : Salaries & Wages	Gross Pay	1,000.00
Transfer From : FICA Tax Payable	FICA Taxes Payable	(75.00)
Transfer From : Fed Withholding Payable	Fed Income Tax Withheld	(210.00)
Transfer From : State Withholding Payable	State Income Tax Withheld	(82.00)
Transfer From : Other Payroll Deducts Pay	Family Medical Ins Premium	(20.00)

Split Transaction

Done   Cancel   Help   Unassigned Amount: 0.00

9-4 Split transaction for a paycheck

field. When you Tab to the Amount field, SuperSmartFill will fill in the rest of the fields with the data for that first employee.

You should then edit the data to suit the second employee. Overtype the proper net pay for the second employee in the Amount field. Press Ctrl−S or select the Split Transaction icon to access the Split Transaction window. Adjust the gross pay and each tax line for the second employee. Be sure the Split window totals zero, return to the pay check, and press Shift−Tab to select Payee (or click on the Payee field) and enter the appropriate employee name. Also enter a social security number and address if you are in the Checks & Forms window, and then press Enter to record the transaction. This technique relieves you from retyping the dates, categories, and memos for each part of the split transaction.

Scheduling future payrolls

Once all of your employee's regular paychecks have been entered the first time, you should place all of them on the Future Transaction list. Highlight each one in turn and press Ctrl−E, or select the Schedule in Future tool. You then can specify whether your payroll is to be paid weekly, biweekly, semimonthly, monthly, etc., and specify the next pay date. Then you might want to switch to the Future Transaction window to verify the paychecks scheduled there. If the amounts on these payroll checks vary from pay period to pay period, you will have a chance to edit each of them every time you ask Money to Pay Bills. If you prefer, you could save the future payroll transactions with no dollar amounts and enter the appropriate amounts at each pay period.

Printing payroll checks

What we just did was the footwork; actually meeting the payroll each period will be very easy. All you need to do is verify that there is a Print indicator in the Num field of each of the transactions for payroll. Then select File and Print Checks from the menu. After aligning the checks in the printer, specifying the starting check number, and selecting specific checks, if necessary, just tell the printer to get going; Ok. I highly recommend voucher checks for this purpose. As you can see in Fig. 9-5, a voucher check will provide your employees with all the current payroll deduction data they might need.

Maintaining tax records

The employer (company) incurs a liability to pay FICA taxes, federal and state unemployment taxes, and other taxes depending on your location. These taxes can be recorded at the same time as the payroll checks by entering a transaction in either the Checking account or the liability account. I recommend entering individual transactions for each employee, and entering them in the account book of your Checking account. This way all the data for payroll can be found on continuous lines in your account book, and a register report can be printed from those lines.

For example, let's assume that the FICA tax rate is 7.5% for both employee and employer, the Federal unemployment tax rate is 3%, and the State unemployment tax rate is .7%. For the Brenda Pasanik paycheck illustrated in Figs. 9-3 and 9-4, the employer payroll tax transaction would be recorded as in Fig. 9-6. In this

JEAN E. GUTMANN

FLEET/NORSTAR
STRATTON, MAINE 04902
52-36-112

1306

12/15/91

PAY TO THE
ORDER OF   Pasanik, Brenda _____ $ *****613.00

Six Hundred Thirteen and no/100***********************************____ DOLLARS

SS# 133-52-5116

23 Atlantic Avenue
Portland, ME 04103

MEMO___ Bi Weekly Payroll _____   _____

⑈OO1306⑈ ⑈O11 003 5⑈ 0090 66 30⑈

JEAN E. GUTMANN   12/15/91

Pasanik, Brenda   **1306**

Payroll : Salaries & Wages   Gross Pay   1,000.00
Transfer From : FICA Tax Payab   FICA Taxes Payable   (75.00)
Transfer From : Fed Withholdin   Fed Income Tax Withheld (210.00)
Transfer From : State Withhold   State Income Tax Withheld (82.00)
Transfer From : Other Payroll   Family Medical Ins Premium (20.00)

Business Checking Bi Weekly Payroll   *****613.00

9-5   Voucher style paycheck

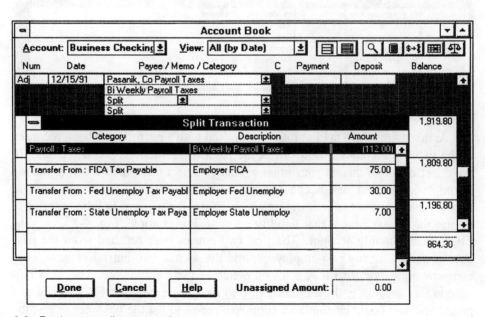

9-6   Employer payroll tax transaction

case, we are transferring $75, $30 and $7 to the appropriate liability accounts and charging the total $112 to the Payroll Taxes category. Because the total of the transaction is zero, the balance of your Checking account is unaffected.

Once the tax liability for the first employee is recorded, it can be copied back into the account book window by repeating the first employee name in the Payee field. Then you can edit the first employee transaction with the tax data for subsequent employees. See the section on preparing other employees' paychecks for the details of editing a split payroll transaction.

After tax entries have been made for the first payroll of all employees, then the tax transactions for all employees can be scheduled on the Future Transaction list as described previously for the paychecks themselves. If the first payroll was paid on December 15, and employees are paid biweekly, the Future Transaction list would appear similar to Fig. 9-7 for the two employees on my payroll.

Future Transactions					
View: All (by Date)					
Date	Freq. / Acct.	Num	Payee / Memo / Category	Payment	Deposit
1/12/92	BiWeekly Business Checking		Pasanik, Brenda Bi Weekly Payroll Split Split	613.00	
1/12/92	BiWeekly Business Checking		Goodman, George Bi Weekly Payroll Split Split	332.50	
1/12/92	BiWeekly Business Checking		Pasanik, Co Payroll Taxes Bi Weekly Payroll Taxes Split Split		0.00
1/12/92	BiWeekly Business Checking		Goodman, Co Payroll Taxes Bi Weekly Payroll Taxes Split Split		0.00

9-7 Scheduled future payroll

At this point all the tax liabilities associated with a payroll have been recorded in the liability accounts as a result of the payroll transactions just discussed. To see the effect of all this on your other accounts, select the Account box at the top of the Account Book or Checks & Forms window. A list of your accounts will appear. Select one of the tax Payable accounts and the window will be redrawn to display the transactions in that liability account. For example, Fig. 9-8 shows the FICA Taxes Payable account. The first two entries here resulted from the paychecks written for my two employees, and the second two entries represent my company obligation for FICA taxes on behalf of these employees. The $225 balance in this account is the amount I owe to the government for FICA tax at this point. You also could customize a summary report to list the balances in just the tax liability accounts.

9-8 Tax liability in the FICA Tax Payable account

Paying future payrolls

If you have activated the Reminder option of Money, you will be reminded about checks that must be written when you first access the Money window. Select Options then Pay Bills from the Menu (or click the Pay Bills icon) and follow the prompts on screen to specify which future transactions to pay. Each transaction that is scheduled within the date you specify will be brought to the window where you can indicate that you want to Enter or Don't Enter it, and modify the date if necessary. Then you should switch to the Account Book window, review the amounts of these transactions, and edit them if necessary. Be sure the Num column contains the Print indicator for any paychecks that must be written. All future payrolls will be as easy as that.

Paying payroll taxes

The balances in the payroll tax liability accounts represent the amount that you owe to taxing authorities at any point in time. For example, after one month of business (two payroll periods) the balances in my liability accounts would be as they are shown in Fig. 9-9. At the end of a month or quarter, I would be obligated to write a check to the depository for tax collection (usually a local bank) for the accumulated amount of taxes.

Let's assume that at the end of the first month we wanted to pay the amount of Federal Income Tax Withheld, the FICA taxes, and the Federal Unemployment taxes. We would enter the payment transaction in our checking account, as illustrated in Fig. 9-10, indicating a transfer to the three tax liability accounts using the Split Transaction window. A check would be printed for the total tax liability, and

```
        TAX LIABILITY SUMMARY AS OF
          12/1/91 Through 12/31/91


Account                          Total

Other Liability Accounts
Fed Unemploy Tax Payable          90.00
Fed Withholding Payable          604.00      9-9   Summary of tax liability for one month
FICA Tax Payable                 450.00
Other Payroll Deducts Payable     40.00
State Unemploy Tax Payable        21.00
State Withholding Payable        240.00
    Total Other Liability Accoun 1,445.00

GRAND TOTAL                   (1,445.00)
```

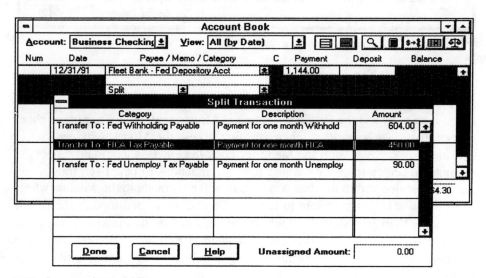

9-10 Payment of a tax liability

the liability accounts would hold a zero balance as a result of the payment. Figure 9-11 shows how the FICA Taxes Payable is affected.

Producing payroll reports

The most basic payroll report would be the Payroll Register, which presents the detailed data for each payroll date broken down by employee. Some businesses would require a summary report also, which presents the total amounts transferred between accounts.

The Payroll Register is produced by customizing a Register Report to include only the Memo field, a Date Range of the specific pay date (e.g., 12/15 to 12/15), subtotaled by Payee, checked to Display Splits, and Include Transactions only

9-11 FICA Tax Payable account after tax payment

from the Business Checking account. If you had entered other transactions in your checking account on the Payroll date, other than Payroll, you could filter out these other transactions by specifying that only Select Transaction be included from Multiple Categories and then highlight only the Payroll category with its associated subcategories.

A Payroll Register for the two sample employees for December 15 is shown in Fig. 9-12.

PAYROLL REGISTER REPORT
12/15/91 Through 12/15/91

Num	Date	Payee	Memo	Amount
Goodman, George				
104	12/15/91	Goodman, George	Bi Weekly Payroll	(332.50)
			Gross Pay	(500.00)
			FICA Taxes Payable	37.50
			Fed Income Tax Withh	92.00
			State Income Tax Wit	38.00
				0.00
	Total Goodman, George			(332.50)
Pasanik, Brenda				
103	12/15/91	Pasanik, Brenda	Bi Weekly Payroll	(613.00)
			Gross Pay	(1,000.00)
			FICA Taxes Payable	75.00
			Fed Income Tax Withh	210.00
			State Income Tax Wit	82.00
			Family Medical Ins P	20.00
	Total Pasanik, Brenda			(613.00)
GRAND TOTAL				(945.50)

9-12 Payroll register for one pay period

Tax reports

By customizing a summary report to include only the Tax Liability accounts and specifying a date range of the payroll date, you can produce a report to show the amounts that were transferred from Business Checking to the tax Liability accounts for one specific payroll. This is the same report that was used in Fig. 9-9 to determine tax liability over a particular period, but the Paydate Tax Liability report is restricted to a specific date. To do this, you should customize a summary report to include a Row for Every Account, a Date Range of the payroll date, and you should include Select Transactions from Multiple Accounts, then highlight only the Tax Liability accounts. See Fig. 9-13 for the result.

You also could customize a summary report to present the quarterly data for a 941 Tax Form, or to determine the year end amounts for W-2 forms. The key to this report is that you must restrict one printout to the transactions for a specific payee (just one employee), and specify a date range of the quarter or year you want to report on the tax form. In other words, you need to produce a separate report for each employee.

```
          TAX LIABILITY FOR PAYROLL DATE
          12/15/91 Through 12/15/91


Account                                 Total

Other Liability Accounts
Fed Unemploy Tax Payable                 45.00
Fed Withholding Payable                 302.00
FICA Tax Payable                        225.00
Other Payroll Deducts Payable            20.00
State Unemploy Tax Payable               10.50
State Withholding Payable               120.00
     Total Other Liability Accoun       722.50

GRAND TOTAL                            (722.50)
```

9-13 Tax liability summary report

Other reports where payroll is used

One final note on payroll; the real results of all this can be clearly seen on an income and expense report and the net worth report. Payroll, salaries/wages, and taxes will be reported as expenses on the income and expense report. The balances in your Tax Liability accounts will appear on the net worth report, along with other Liabilities.

Summary

In this chapter you have been introduced to the techniques for recording and managing payroll. The steps for preparing individual payroll checks, recording the associated tax liability, and scheduling both of these for future periodic payment were presented in detail. The chapter also provided general instructions for producing payroll reports, and some hints concerning accumulation of data for quarterly and annual tax forms.

Setting up a payroll tutorial

This tutorial builds on the tutorial of chapter 5; it assumes that you have the knowledge gained in chapters 1 through 5. If you have completed chapters 6 through 8 you will have more data in your Money file than might be assumed by this tutorial, but this should not interfere in any way.

Part A

Setting up accounts and categories for payroll is the first step necessary before you can actually produce a payroll check. These first few steps will lead you through the activity of setting up payroll tax liability accounts.

- ☐ Bring Money to the window and be sure that the Account Book for the sample Business Checking account is displayed

Note If you were working with your own file, rather than the sample one associated with this book, you might have to select the File then Open, menu items and select the sample.mny file.

- ☐ Select List then Account List from the menu
- ☐ Choose the New button and type FICA Taxes Payable
- ☐ Check the Liability Account option button and choose OK
- ☐ Type 0 (zero) as the Opening Balance and choose OK
- ☐ Repeat the previous 3 steps for each of the following new accounts:
  Federal Withhold Tax Payable
  State Withhold Tax Payable
  Federal Unemploy Tax Payable
  State Unemploy Tax Payable
  Other Employee Withhold Payable
- ☐ Choose the Close button

Part B

The next few steps are needed to customize the category list to handle payroll transactions.

- ☐ Select List then Category List from the menu
- ☐ Scroll to the Payroll category
- ☐ Select Federal W/H in the subcategory list
- ☐ Choose the Delete button
- ☐ Notice that the Federal W/H subcategory is now deleted
- ☐ Repeat the previous 3 steps to delete FICA W/H
- ☐ Repeat again to delete State W/H
- ☐ Choose the New button within the Subcategory box
- ☐ Type Payroll Taxes and choose Ok
- ☐ Choose the Close button

Part C

We are now ready to prepare the first payroll check. You can enter payroll transactions in either the account book or on a check form. In this section we'll enter the first employee on a check form so that we can include her social security number and her address.

- ☐ Select Window then Checks & Forms
- ☐ Choose the Check button
- ☐ This calls up a Check form
- ☐ Type a p in the # field
- ☐ Type 12/15 in the Date field
- ☐ Type Gutmann, Jean in the Pay To field
- ☐ Tab to the $ amount field
- ☐ Press Ctrl−S to display the Split Transaction window (or click on the Split Transaction tool)
- ☐ Under the Category field, select Payroll
- ☐ As Subcategory, select Salaries & Wages
- ☐ Under Description, type Gross Pay
- ☐ Under Amount type 800

Note If you've completed all of the chapter tutorials, you will have a Classification field on the next line. Press Tab again to leave this field blank.

□ In the next section of the Split Transaction:
Select Transfer
Select FICA Tax Payable
Type FICA Taxes Withheld
Type − 60
If needed, press Tab past the Classification field

□ In the next section:
Select Transfer
Select Federal Withhold Tax Payable
Type Federal Income Tax Withheld
Type − 180
If needed, press Tab past the Classification field

□ In the next section:
Select Transfer
Select State Withhold Tax Payable
Type State Income Tax Withheld
Type − 25
If needed, press Tab past the Classification field

□ Verify that the Total at the bottom is now 535.00.

Note You can press Shift−Tab to return to previous lines and fields to correct any discrepancies.

□ Press Esc to remove the Category list, and select Done
□ Read the Spend or Receive? box and select OK
□ Press Tab to move to the Memo field
□ Type Semimonthly Payroll and press Tab
□ Type SS#123-45-6789 and press Enter
□ Type 122 Maine Street and press Enter
□ Type Portland, ME 04189 and press Enter
□ Press Enter three times to record this transaction in your file

Part D

We can now copy this transaction onto another check form and edit it to pay a second employee.

□ Begin to enter another transaction by pressing Tab twice
□ Enter Gutmann as the payee and Tab to the Amount field
□ SuperSmartFill fills in the data for another Gutmann paycheck

- [ ] Type 695 in the Amount field; this is the net pay for the second employee
- [ ] Access the Split Transaction window
- [ ] Move to the Amount column of the first line
- [ ] Type 1000 and press Tab
- [ ] Move to the Amount column of the second section
- [ ] Type −75 and press Tab
- [ ] Move to the Amount column of the third section
- [ ] Type −202 and press Tab
- [ ] Move to the Amount column of the fourth section
- [ ] Type −28 and press Tab
- [ ] Press Alt−D (or choose the Done button)

Note If you make a mistake, you can return to the Split window with Ctrl−S, then Shift−Tab and Tab around to make needed changes. Press Alt−D to return to the Check form

- [ ] Press Shift−Tab to move to the Pay To box, or click there
- [ ] Type Money User and Tab to the Address field
- [ ] Type SS#100-10-1000 and press Enter
- [ ] Type your own street address, Enter
- [ ] Type your city and zipcode, Enter
- [ ] Press Enter three times to record this transaction in your file
- [ ] Select Window then Account Book

Part E

Now that the second employee is completely entered in the account book, we should copy these transactions to the Future Transactions list. If you have completed all the chapter tutorials, the 12/15 transactions might be quite a ways back in your account book. Press the Up Arrow or scroll up to find the 12/15 Gutmann paycheck.

- [ ] Select the Gutmann paycheck
- [ ] Press Ctrl−E or click the Schedule in Future icon to schedule this transaction in the Future
- [ ] Select a Frequency of SemiMonthly
- [ ] In the Next Date box, type 12/30
- [ ] Choose Ok

- [ ] Select the Money User paycheck
- [ ] Press Ctrl−E, or click the Schedule in Future icon, to schedule this transaction in the Future
- [ ] In the Next Date box, type 12/30
- [ ] Choose Ok
- [ ] Select Window then Future Transactions
- [ ] Notice that the two employee payroll transactions are now scheduled to be paid at the next pay date—December 30
- [ ] Select Window then Account Book

Part F

Finally! We can actually write the paychecks for December 15. Don't worry, it'll be much easier the next time.

- [ ] Be sure there is a Print indicator on the two paychecks
- [ ] Select the File then Print Setup menu items
- [ ] Check the Check Printing option button
- [ ] Select the Voucher option in the Check Types list box

Note The Check Types options depend on your printer type; if you don't have a Voucher option, then Standard will do.

- [ ] Choose OK
- [ ] Select File then Print Checks
- [ ] Read the screen (plain paper in the printer will do)
- [ ] Choose OK
- [ ] After the checks are printed, choose Continue

Note If you had problems with the printing refer to the Money or Windows User Guide for printer troubleshooting hints.

Part G

The next few parts describe the procedure for entering a transaction for each employee to recognize the employer's obligation for payroll taxes. First we will enter a tax transaction for Jean Gutmann.

- [ ] Be sure you are in the Account Book window of Business Checking
- [ ] Select the next available blank transaction line
- [ ] Type Tax in the Num field

- ☐ Type 12/15 as the Date
- ☐ Type Gutmann Payroll Taxes as the Payee
- ☐ Type Company Portion of Payroll Taxes as a description
- ☐ Press Ctrl–S to access the Split Transaction window
- ☐ Select Payroll from the category list
- ☐ Select Payroll Taxes from the subcategory list
- ☐ Type Company Taxes on Gutmann Salary in the Memo field
- ☐ Type 89.60 in the Amount field
- ☐ If a classification list appears, press Tab to skip to next line
- ☐ Select Transfer from the drop down list
- ☐ Select FICA Tax Payable as the subcategory
- ☐ Type Company FICA on Gutmann as the Memo
- ☐ Type –60 and Tab to the next line
- ☐ If a classification list appears, press Tab again
- ☐ Select Transfer as the next category
- ☐ Select State Unemployment Tax Payable as the subcategory
- ☐ Type Unemploy Taxes on Gutmann as the Memo
- ☐ Type –24 in the Amount field
- ☐ If a classification list appears, press Tab again
- ☐ Select Transfer as the next category
- ☐ Select Federal Unemployment Tax Payable as the subcategory
- ☐ Type a " in the Memo field
- ☐ Type –5.60 as the Amount and press Tab
- ☐ If a classification list appears, press Tab again
- ☐ Note that the total of this transaction is now 0.00
- ☐ Press Alt–D or choose Done
- ☐ Press Enter to enter this transaction in your file

Part H

Now we can copy this employer tax liability transaction to use for other employees, and edit it for the second employee.

- ☐ On a new transaction line, press Tab twice to Payee
- ☐ This causes the Num & Date of previous transaction to be reused
- ☐ Enter Gutmann Pay and press Tab

- [ ] SmartFill supplies data in all the fields
- [ ] Press Ctrl–S to edit the Split Transaction
- [ ] Tab to the Description field
- [ ] Use the Left Arrow and Del to remove the name Gutmann and type in User
- [ ] Tab to the Amount field and type – 112
- [ ] Tab to the Description field of the next section
- [ ] Edit the description again with the name User
- [ ] Tab to the Amount field and type 75
- [ ] Tab to the Description field of the next section
- [ ] Edit the description again with the name User
- [ ] Tab to the Amount field and type 30
- [ ] Tab to the Description field of the next section
- [ ] Edit the description again with the name User
- [ ] Tab to the Amount field and type 7
- [ ] Press Alt–D or click Done
- [ ] Select the Payee field in the account book (Shift–Tab)
- [ ] Type Money User Payroll Taxes over Gutmann Payroll Taxes
- [ ] Press Enter to complete the Money User tax transaction
- [ ] Scroll up the Account Book to Dec 15 so you can view the payroll transactions

Part I

After setting up the transactions for payroll tax liability once, you should schedule these transactions on the Future Transactions list just as we did for the payroll checks.

- [ ] Select the Gutmann Payroll Taxes transaction
- [ ] Press Ctrl–E, or click the Schedule in Future icon to schedule this transaction in the future
- [ ] Select a Frequency of SemiMonthly
- [ ] In the Next Date box, type 12/30
- [ ] Choose Ok
- [ ] Select the Money User Payroll Taxes transaction
- [ ] Press Ctrl–E, or click the Schedule in Future icon, to schedule this transaction in the future

- [ ] In the Next Date box, type 12/30
- [ ] Choose Ok
- [ ] Select Window then Future Transactions
- [ ] Notice that all four payroll transactions are now scheduled to be entered at the next pay date—December 30
- [ ] Select Window then Account Book

Part J

In this section I am encouraging you to recognize the effect of payroll transactions on the liability accounts by viewing these accounts and printing a summary of them.

- [ ] Select Account then select the FICA Tax Payable account
- [ ] You are now in the FICA Tax Payable Account, Account Book
- [ ] Notice that the December 15 payroll results in four entries in this account: two for taxes withheld, and two for the company FICA tax obligation. You might have to scroll up to see all four transactions
- [ ] A total of $270 in FICA taxes are owed to the government as a result of this payroll
- [ ] Select Account and scroll to the State Unemployment Tax Payable account to select and view that account
- [ ] We now owe the State $54 in unemployment taxes
- [ ] Select Account and select Business Checking to redisplay the account book for the Checking account

Part K

Various reports can be produced to provide detail or summary data about payroll transactions. The most basic of these is the payroll register for each pay date. Here's how you produce a payroll register.

- [ ] Select Report then Register Report from the menu
- [ ] Choose Customize and type Payroll Register
- [ ] On the Customize Report window:
  Check the Memo field
  Uncheck all other fields in the Include Fields box
  Subtotal by: scroll to Payee
  Check the Display Splits box
  Type 12/15 in the From Date box

Type 12/15 in the To Date box
Include Transactions From: Business Checking
Check the Select Transactions button
In the Type box, scroll to and select Payments
Choose OK

☐ Choose View and scroll to view the payroll register

☐ Choose Print then OK to print the report on paper

☐ Choose Close to return to the account book

Part L

The following steps are necessary for producing a Payroll Tax Liability report each pay period.

☐ Select Report then Summary Report

☐ Choose Customize and type Payroll Tax Liability For

☐ On the Customize Report window:
Select Account in the Row for Every list box
Type 12/15 in the From box
Type 12/15 in the To box
In the From Account box, select Multiple Accounts
Choose Select None to clear the List
Select each of the Tax Payable accounts
In other words, highlight the FICA, Federal Withholding, Federal Unemployment, State Unemployment and State Withholding Tax Payable accounts
Choose OK and then View

☐ Review the Payroll Tax Liability report for December 15

☐ Choose Width and check the Extra Wide option, then Ok

☐ Choose Print and Ok to print a copy of this

☐ Choose Close to return to the account book

Part M

I'll admit that the initial setup for paychecks takes some time, but it will all be worth it at the next payroll date. This section describes the few simple steps you'll execute on each payday in the future.

☐ Select Options then Pay Bills (Ctrl–P)

☐ Type 12/30 in the Record Due Transactions box

☐ Choose OK

Note We've entered 12/30 here because it is the next pay date after 12/15 in a semimonthly pay cycle

- [ ] Review the transaction presented
- [ ] Note that it is a payroll tax transaction dated 12/30
- [ ] Choose Enter and review the next transaction
- [ ] This is the second tax transaction
- [ ] Choose Enter and review the next transaction
- [ ] This is the first employee paycheck, note the pay date
- [ ] Select the Date box and enter 12/30
- [ ] Choose Enter and review the next transaction
- [ ] Select the Date box and enter 12/30
- [ ] Choose Enter
- [ ] Notice that the Future Transactions screen has been updated to schedule the next pay date on 1/15
- [ ] Select Window then Account Book
- [ ] Notice that the four payroll transactions for 12/30 have been entered in the account book
- [ ] Select File then Print Checks and choose Ok
- [ ] When the paychecks have been printed, choose Continue
- [ ] That's all there is to it. The semimonthly payroll has been paid and recorded in all the appropriate categories and accounts

Part N

Let's take a look at the tax liabilities now that a full month of payroll has been recorded.

- [ ] Select Account and then the FICA Tax Payable account
- [ ] Browse through the entries in this account
- [ ] We now owe the government a total of $540 for the two payroll periods
- [ ] Browse around some of the other tax liability accounts to view the transfers made to them

Part O

The overall effect of a Payroll on the bottom line is seen on the income statement. Follow the next few steps to view the Income & Expense report.

- ☐ Select Account and then Business Checking
- ☐ Select Report then Income & Expense Report
- ☐ Choose Customize and type 12/31 in the To date box
- ☐ Choose View and scroll down the income report to view the payroll expense lines
- ☐ Salaries & Wages (gross pay) should amount to $3600
- ☐ Print the report if you'd like
- ☐ Choose Close to return to the account book
- ☐ Select File then Exit and make a backup of your work

10
CHAPTER

Managing payables and receivables

Although this topic comes late in the book, it might be the most important one to you. If you sell goods or services on credit, then the collection of the amount owed to you is probably foremost in your mind. Just about any business must sell on credit these days in order to compete. The money that is owed to you as a result of selling or providing a service on credit is your *receivables*. In order to keep the cash flowing in, you must have good control over these receivables.

On the other hand, when you buy needed goods on credit a *payable* comes into existence. All businesses also must have good control over what is payable to their creditors. You don't want to pay too much, too early, or, heaven forbid, pay the same bill twice. Money can help you manage payables and prevent any of these problems.

This chapter presents the procedures you can use with Money to manage these two important aspects of credit. Start with Accounts Payable or Accounts Receivable depending on what's most important for your business.

Accounts payable

You've already learned a lot about liability accounts in the previous chapter on payroll and in the chapter 4 discussion of loans. Accounts payable is another type of liability. These are the amounts that you owe to creditors, and if you need detailed records of how much you owe to each creditor, Money can do the trick with an Accounts Payable account. Maintaining accounts payable records is a four part process. You must establish a liability account titled Accounts Payable, then you must record purchases and adjustments in this account, you will later make payments on account, and periodically you will want to produce reports focused on payables.

If you have very few items that are payables, it might be easier to schedule them as Future Transactions in your checking account and not establish a separate liability account for accounts payable. This process is fully explained in the Money User Guide. The rest of this section is presented for those of you who need more detailed records of accounts payable.

Setting up Accounts Payable

Select the List menu and the Account List option to display your current Account List. You must then select the New option button and type Accounts Payable as the account name. Select the account type of Liability and indicate a zero beginning balance. If you haven't previously kept an accounts payable record, then zero is actually your beginning balance. If you've previously maintained an accounts payable record, you will know the specific creditors and amounts that comprise your beginning balance figure, and you can enter each creditor as a transaction in the next step.

Entering purchases and adjustments

When you make a purchase on account, the transaction should be entered in your new Accounts Payable account as an Increase. An example of a purchase transaction is shown in Fig. 10-1. An important ingredient here is that the transaction is categorized to an expense account, or as a transfer to an asset or other liability account.

Num	Date	Payee / Memo / Category	C	Increase	Decrease	Balance
23678	12/12/91	Locke Office Supply		110.00		110.00
		Folders, Notepads & Desk Supplie				
		Office Expenses : Supplies				

10-1   Credit purchase transaction in accounts payable

If you need to make an adjustment on any invoice in your Accounts Payable account, I recommend that you return to the original purchase transaction and edit it. If you want to retain the original amount as well as the adjustment, you can use the Split Transaction window to show the original purchase amount on one line and the adjustment amount on a second line (this might need to be a minus amount).

Scheduling payments on account

At the same time that you enter the purchase or adjustment transaction described above, you should schedule the appropriate future payment of the invoice. With the purchase transaction highlighted in the Accounts Payable account, select the Edit then Schedule in Future menu item (Ctrl – E or click on the Schedule in Future icon of the Toolbar). Specify a Frequency of Only Once and the appropriate payment due date in the Next Date field.

If you do not see the Future Transactions window, select this as the current window and look for the payment that you just entered there. If the Future Transaction window is only showing one line for each transaction, switch to the Entire Transaction View with Ctrl – T (or select Options, then Entire Transaction from the Menu). Now we need to edit this future transaction so that it is charged against Accounts Payable when paid, rather than being charged to the expense category of the original purchase.

The "payment" described in the previous two paragraphs was scheduled in your Accounts Payable account. When we actually make the payment, we want to pay it from our business checking account and categorize it as a transfer to Accounts Payable. Here's how it works.

While still in the Future Transaction window, change the Account field so the payment will be written from the Business Checking account. Change the Category field so this payment will be a Transfer to the Accounts Payable account. After editing the Future Transactions window, my sample transaction is shown in Fig. 10-2.

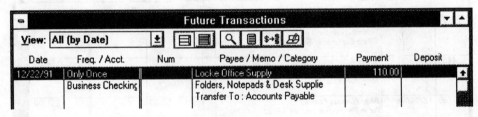

10-2 Future scheduled payment for credit purchase

Paying your creditors

Display the account book for the business checking account. Select the Options then Pay Bills menu items (Ctrl – P). You'll be able to see the dates of your scheduled transactions on the Future Transactions window, and must specify a date for which you wish to include payments. Specify the date on which you are making your payments and verify that the payment is marked as Enter In: Business Checking, then choose Enter to proceed. Take a look at the account book and you will see that this payment is made from your checking account and is charged to Accounts Payable. The checking account payment for my sample transaction is shown in Fig. 10-3.

Num	Date	Payee / Memo / Category	C	Payment	Deposit	Balance
Print	12/22/91	Locke Office Supply		110.00		2,843.80
		Folders, Notepads & Desk Supplie				
		Transfer To : Accounts Payable				

10-3 Payment to creditor in Checking account

The last step is to mark Print in the Num column of the account book and then select the File and Print Checks menu items to print the actual check. Take a look at the account book in Fig. 10-4 for the Accounts Payable account. Look for the payment that has automatically been entered there as a decrease (payment on account) because of the Transfer from business checking that was shown in Fig. 10-3. When you make a payment on account in your checking account and categorize it as a transfer to Accounts Payable, the transaction is automatically recorded as a decrease in Accounts Payable.

Num	Date	Payee / Memo / Category	C	Increase	Decrease	Balance
23678	12/12/91	Locke Office Supply		110.00		110.00
		Folders, Notepads & Desk Supplie				
		Office Expenses : Supplies				
4456	12/13/91	Jones Accessories, Inc		86.00		196.00
		Books				
		Miscellaneous				
7a9	12/14/91	Allen Avenue Agency		55.00		251.00
		Ad in Pennywise Jouranl 12/23				
		Advertising				
	12/22/91	Locke Office Supply			110.00	141.00
		Folders, Notepads & Desk Supplie				
		Transfer From : Business Checking				

Ending Balance: 217.00

10-4 Payment to creditor in Accounts Payable account

Accounts payable reports

The discussion of reports that follows deals specifically with Accounts Payable reports. If the Accounts Payable account is the one currently being displayed in your window, then it will be this account that is selected in the Customize Report dialog box to be included in any report. Therefore, it is assumed for the following procedures that you already have the Accounts Payable account displayed in your Money window.

Checking on a payee's balance   For a quick look at a specific creditor's account balance, select the Account Book window for your Accounts Payable account. Remember the View Box at the top of the Account Book window that is usually set at View All by Date? Select A Payee in this View box and then select the specific payee that you want to view. Notice in Fig. 10-5 for my sample creditor (Locke Office Supply) that the current balance owed to this creditor is $76 after two purchases and the $110 payment. If you wanted a printed copy of this Register view, select the Reports then Register Report menu items and customize for the appropriate date. Be sure to return the screen view to All by Date.

Account:	Accounts Payable ±	View:	Locke Office Supp ±				
Num	Date	Payee / Memo / Category	C	Increase	Decrease	Balance	
23678	12/12/91	Locke Office Supply Folders, Notepads & Desk Supplie Office Expenses : Supplies		110.00		110.00	
23689	12/14/91	Locke Office Supply Bookcases Office Expenses : Equipment		76.00		186.00	
	12/22/91	Locke Office Supply Folders, Notepads & Desk Supplie Transfer From : Business Checking			110.00	76.00	
					Total:	76.00	

10-5   Restricted view of one payee in accounts payable

The schedule of accounts payable   A Schedule of Accounts Payable lists the current ending balance owed to each creditor (payee). Produce this with Money by selecting Report then Summary Report from the Menu. Customize this summary report with an appropriate title, a Row for Every Payee, Date Range of the current date, and in the From Account box, specify only your Accounts Payable account. This report shows all balances as minuses (credits) because all Accounts Payable amounts are minuses against Asset accounts like Cash on Hand or your Business Checking account. A sample Schedule of Accounts Payable is shown in Fig. 10-6.

Accounts Payable Transaction Register   As long as the View in your Accounts Payable account book is set for All by Date, you can produce a register report of all

```
       SCHEDULE OF ACCOUNTS PAYABLE
          1/1/91 Through 12/31/91


    Payee                          Total

    Allen Avenue Agency            (55.00)      10-6   Schedule of accounts payable
    Jones Accessories, Inc         (86.00)
    Locke Office Supply            (76.00)

    GRAND TOTAL                   (217.00)
```

transactions for any specified period. Select Report then Register Report from the menu. Customize the register report with an appropriate title, the fields you want to print, a date range of your choice, and Subtotal By Payee. Be sure that Include Transactions is set for only the Accounts Payable account. You could print this report each month, or print year-to-date reports from the beginning of the year.

Cash needs analysis   You can get a quick idea of how much cash you'll need to cover upcoming payments if you display the Future Transactions window and then produce a customized register report that includes only Payment transactions. You can further customize this report to include Future Transactions for just the upcoming week (or any specific time period) to determine your cash needs for any period.

Accounts receivable

The management of Accounts Receivable is very similar to the management of Accounts Payable. Accounts Receivables are assets and are increased when a sale is made on credit, or decreased when payment is received. When payments are received a deposit is made in your business checking account. This deposit can be accomplished with a future transaction that causes a transfer between Accounts Receivable and Business Checking.

Again, if you have very few items that are receivable, it might be easier to schedule them as future transactions in your account book and not establish a separate asset account for Accounts Receivable. This process is fully explained in the Money User Guide. The rest of this section is presented for those of you who need more detailed records of Accounts Receivable transactions.

Setting up Accounts Receivable

Select the List menu and the Account List option to display your current Account List. You must then select the New option button and type Accounts Receivable as the account name. Select the account type of Asset and indicate a zero beginning balance. If you haven't previously kept an Accounts Receivable record, then zero is actually your beginning balance. If you've previously maintained an Accounts

Receivable record, you will know the specific customers and amounts that comprise your beginning balance figure, and you can enter each customer beginning balance as a transaction in the next step.

Entering sales and adjustments

When you make a sale on account, the transaction should be entered in your Accounts Receivable account as an Increase. An example of a credit sale transaction is shown in Fig. 10-7. If you need to make an adjustment on any invoice in your Accounts Receivable account, I recommend that you return to the original sale transaction and edit it. If you want to retain the original amount as well as the adjustment, you can use the Split Transaction window to show the original sale amount on one line and the adjustment amount on a second line (this might need to be a minus amount).

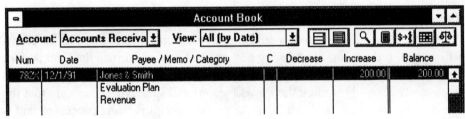

10-7 Credit sale transaction in accounts receivable

Scheduling receipts on account

At the same time that you enter the sale or adjustment transaction described above, you should schedule the appropriate future receipt of cash from your customer. With the sale transaction highlighted in the Accounts Receivable Account Book window, execute the Edit then Schedule in Future menu item (Ctrl−E or click the Schedule in Future icon). Specify a Frequency of Only Once and then indicate the due date for this receipt in the Next Date field.

If you do not see the Future Transactions window, select this as the current window and look for the receipt that you just entered there. If the Future Transactions window is only showing one line for each transaction, switch to the Entire Transaction View with Ctrl−T (or click the Entire Transaction icon on the Toolbar).

Now we need to edit this future transaction so that it is charged against Accounts Receivable when received, rather than being charged to the revenue category of the original sale. The *receipt* described in the previous two paragraphs was scheduled in the Accounts Receivable account. When we actually receive this payment, we want to deposit it in our business checking account and categorize it as a transfer from Accounts Receivable. To do this, select the receipt transaction in the Future Transactions window, change the Account field so the receipt will be recorded in the Business Checking account, and change the Category field so this receipt will be a Transfer to the Accounts Receivable account. After editing the Future Transactions window, the sample transaction we have been working with is shown in Fig. 10-8.

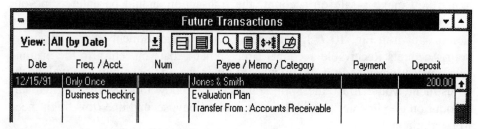

10-8 Future scheduled receipt of credit sale

Recording receipts from your customers

When you receive money from a customer on account, display the Future Transactions list for the business checking account and browse (or use the Find option) to identify the scheduled receipt on this list. Execute the Options then Pay Bills menu items (Ctrl−P or click the Pay Bills icon) and specify the due date that the receipt was scheduled for. Verify that the proper receipt is being processed and is marked as Enter In: Business Checking, then press Enter to proceed. You might have to indicate Don't Enter for some other scheduled transactions that you don't want to process at this time.

Now change to the account book of your Business Checking account, and you will see that this receipt is recorded in your checking account and is charged to Accounts Receivable. You might want to change the date to the actual date of the receipt if the money was not received on the due date. The checking account transaction for my sample receipt is shown in Fig. 10-9.

When you look at the account book for the Accounts Receivable account, at this point you would see that the receipt has automatically been entered there as a decrease (payment on account) and noted as a Transfer from Business Checking.

10-9 Deposit transaction for accounts receivable

Accounts Receivable reports

The discussion of reports that follows deals specifically with Accounts Receivable reports. If the Accounts Receivable account is the one currently being displayed in your window, then it will be this account that is selected in the Customize Report dialog box to be included in any report. Therefore, it is assumed for the following procedures that you already have the Accounts Receivable account displayed in your Money window.

Checking on a customer's balance   For a quick look at a specific customer's account balance, select the Account Book window for your Accounts Receivable account. Change the View box to A Payee and then select the specific payee that you want to view. Refer to the previous discussion of Accounts Payable for a sample of this (Fig. 10-5). If you need a printed copy of this Register view, select the Reports then Register Report menu items and customize for the appropriate date. Be sure to return the screen view to All by Date.

The Schedule of Accounts Receivable   A Schedule of Accounts Receivable lists the current ending balance owed to you by each customer (Money still refers to these as *payee*). Produce this with Money by selecting Report then Summary Report from the menu. Customize this summary report with an appropriate title, a Row For Every payee, date range of the current date, and in the From Account box, specify only your Accounts Receivable account. A sample Schedule of Accounts Receivable is shown in Fig. 10-10.

SCHEDULE OF ACCOUNTS RECEIVABLE
1/1/91 Through 12/31/91

Payee	Total
Bigtime Corporation	800.00
Jones & Smith	0.00
Middle Company	1,200.00
Zaner, Inc.	185.00
GRAND TOTAL	2,185.00

10-10   Schedule of accounts receivable

Accounts Receivable Transaction Register   As long as the View in your Accounts Receivable account book is set for All by Date you can produce a register report of all transactions for any specified period. Select Report then Register Report from the menu. Customize the register report with an appropriate title, the fields you want to print, a date range of your choice, and Subtotal By payee. Be sure that Include Transactions is set for only the Accounts Receivable account. You could print this report each month, or print year-to-date reports from the beginning of the year.

Cash flow projections   You can get a quick idea of how much cash you'll have coming in if your customers pay on time by displaying the Future Transactions window and then producing a customized Register report that includes only Deposit transactions. You can customize this report further to include future transactions for just the upcoming week (or any specific time period) to determine expected cash inflow for any period.

Summary

Controlling the necessary business activity of using credit was covered in this chapter. The management of accounts payable and accounts receivable will be easier now that you have Money to help. In this chapter, we have explored the techniques for setting up accounts for payables and receivables, recording purchases, sales and adjustments in these accounts, scheduling receipts and payments on account in the future, and producing useful reports for these activities.

Small business credit management tutorial

This tutorial builds on the tutorial of chapter 5; it assumes that you have the knowledge gained in chapters 1 through 5. If you have completed chapters 6 through 9, you will have more data in your Money file than might be assumed by this tutorial, but this should not interfere in any way.

In Parts A through M, we will set up and use Accounts Payable.

Part A

First we must set up a new Liability account for Accounts Payable.

- ☐ Select the List then Account List menu items
- ☐ Choose New
- ☐ Type Accounts Payable and press Alt−L (for Liability)
- ☐ Choose Ok and type 0 for Opening Balance, then Ok
- ☐ Choose Close to exit from the Account list

Part B

With the account book for Accounts Payable displayed in the window, we can now enter our first transaction for a purchase on credit.

- ☐ Select Account, then Accounts Payable
- ☐ Type 5677 in the Num field (invoice number) and press Tab

- ☐ Type 12/13 and press Tab
- ☐ Type Ace Supply Company and press Tab
- ☐ Type 420 in the Increase column and press Tab twice
- ☐ Type Purch Computer Supplies and press Tab
- ☐ Select Office Expenses as the category
- ☐ Select Supplies as the subcategory
- ☐ Press Enter to complete this transaction

Part C

Let's enter a second purchase on account as follows.

- ☐ Num: 78b
- ☐ Date: 12/14 (or you can press + to increment the date)
- ☐ Payee: Smith Photo Products
- ☐ Increase: 50
- ☐ Memo: Public Relations Photos
- ☐ Category: Advertising

Part D

Enter a third purchase on account as follows.

- ☐ Num: 111
- ☐ Date: 12/15 (or press + to increment the date)
- ☐ Payee: Mobil Portland, Inc
- ☐ Increase: 82
- ☐ Memo: Tune up
- ☐ Category: Automobile
- ☐ Subcategory: Maintenance

Part E

To schedule these three transactions for payment we need to enter them on the Future Transactions list.

- ☐ Highlight the Ace Supply transaction
- ☐ Press Ctrl−E or click the Schedule in Future icon
- ☐ Select Only Once in the Frequency box

- ☐ Type 12/23 in the Next Date box and Choose Ok
- ☐ Highlight the Smith Photo Products transaction
- ☐ Press Ctrl−E or click the Schedule In Future icon
- ☐ Only Once should appear in the Frequency box
- ☐ Type 1/14 in the Next Date box and choose Ok
- ☐ Highlight the Mobil Portland transaction
- ☐ Press Ctrl−E or click the Schedule in Future icon
- ☐ Only Once should appear in the Frequency box
- ☐ Type 1/15 in the Next Date box and choose Ok
- ☐ Select Window then Future Transactions and verify that the Ace, Smith and Mobil transactions are on this list
- ☐ If the Future Transaction window is only showing Top Line View select the Entire Transaction View icon on the Toolbar (or select Options, Entire Transaction View)

Part F

We need to edit these transactions slightly so that when they are paid, they are categorized as transfers to Accounts Payable and paid from the checking account.

- ☐ Highlight the Ace Supply transaction in the Future window
- ☐ Tab to the Num field and type a p
- ☐ Tab to the Account field in the Freq/Acct column
- ☐ Select Business Checking from the pull down list
- ☐ Tab to the Category field and type Transfer
- ☐ Tab to the Subcategory field and type Acc (The Accounts Payable account should then be displayed in the Subcategory field)
- ☐ Press Enter to record the changes in your file
- ☐ Now edit the Smith Photo future transaction so it contains the following:
  enter a Num of p
  change the Account to Business Checking
  select Transfer in the Category field
  select Accounts Payable as the Subcategory
  press Enter to record the changes
- ☐ Lastly, edit the Mobil Portland future transaction so it contains the following:
  enter a Num of p
  change the Account to Business Checking

type Trans in Category
type Accounts Payable in Subcategory
press Enter to record the changes

Part G

Let's assume that it is now December 23 and we want to pay the Ace Agency bill.

☐ Select Window then Account Book
☐ Select Account then Business Checking
☐ Select Options then Pay Bills (or press Ctrl−P)
☐ Type 12/23 in the Date box and choose Ok
☐ Type 12/23 again in the Date box of the Enter Scheduled Transactions dialog box

Note The default date shown in the Enter Scheduled Transactions dialog box is your current system date. If that is the date on which you want to make this payment, you would leave it as is. In this tutorial, we need to change it because we are working in December, but the current date that you are reading this is probably not December.

☐ Choose Enter to enter the Ace Supply payment
☐ Select Window then Account Book
☐ Note that the scheduled transaction has been entered as a payment in the business checking account
☐ Select File, Print Checks, and then choose Ok

Part H

We can verify that this payment was also recorded in the Accounts Payable account by displaying that account in the window.

☐ Activate the Account box
☐ Select Accounts Payable

Note Observe that the payment entered in the checking account is also shown in the Accounts Payable account, because it was categorized as a Transfer. The check payment is a decrease in Accounts Payable.

Part I

Smith Photo called to say they were allowing a $7 credit on our account because of poor quality photos. We need to enter this adjustment in the Accounts Payable account, and adjust the amount of the scheduled future payment.

- ☐ Select the Smith Photo transaction in the Accounts Payable account and Tab to the amount field
- ☐ Press Ctrl−S and you will see the original $50 transaction
- ☐ Press Enter to get to the next available transaction line
- ☐ Select Advertising in the Category field
- ☐ Type Allowance for Poor Quality in the Description field
- ☐ Type −7 as the amount and press Alt−D to complete the split
- ☐ Check the Adjust Total option button and choose Ok
- ☐ Press Enter to complete the transaction
- ☐ Notice that the transaction amount for Smith is now $43
- ☐ Select Window then Future Trans
- ☐ We must now edit the future payment
- ☐ Select the Smith Photo transaction and select the Payment field
- ☐ Type 43 and press Enter
- ☐ Select Window then Account Book

Part J

Accounts Payable reports provide a long term record of your credit purchases and creditor records. The most basic report is a Schedule of Accounts Payable, which lists the ending balance owed to each creditor. To produce a Schedule of Accounts Payable, follow these steps.

- ☐ Select Reports then Summary Report
- ☐ Select Customize
- ☐ Type Schedule of Accounts Payable in the Title box
- ☐ Select Payee in the Row for Every box
- ☐ Type 12/31 in the To: date box
- ☐ Select Accounts Payable in the From Account box
- ☐ Choose View to display the report
- ☐ Choose Print and Ok if you want a paper copy
- ☐ Choose Close to return to the account book

Part K

To produce a report of all the transactions entered into your Accounts Payable account for a specified period, perform the following steps.

☐ Select Reports then Register Report

☐ Select Customize

☐ Type Accounts Payable Transactions in the Title box

☐ Check Memo in the Include Fields box

☐ Check Category in the Include Fields box

☐ Select Payee in the Subtotal By list box

☐ Check the Display Splits option box

☐ Tab to the From box under Date Range

☐ Type 12/1 in the From box under Date Range

☐ Type 12/31 in the To box under Date Range

☐ Be sure Accounts Payable is selected as the From Account

☐ Choose View to display the report

☐ Scroll to browse through the Amount column and report Totals

☐ Choose Print and Ok if you want a paper copy

☐ Choose Close to return to the account book

Part L

When you want to check on the balance owed to one of your creditors without customizing a report, you simply need to change the "view" within the Accounts Payable Account Book. This will allow you to see all the transactions in your current file that led up to the current balance for one payee.

☐ Select the View box just below the Account Book title

☐ Scroll to select A Payee from the View list

☐ Select Ace Supply Company from the Payee list

☐ The window now displays only the Ace Supply transactions

☐ The ending balance for this creditor is zero

Note You could print a register report at this time, customizing for a title and a To date of 12/31 to print the activity for this one creditor.

☐ Select View then All by Date to see all creditors

Part M

To determine the amount of cash you would need to cover upcoming payments from your checking account, you can view and print the Future Transactions report at any time.

- ☐ Select Window then Future Transactions
- ☐ All future transactions are shown, including the payroll and any deposits or adjustments that are scheduled
- ☐ Select Report then Register Report
- ☐ Select Customize
- ☐ Check the Payments option and select View
- ☐ Now the report displays only funds needed for payments
- ☐ Print the report if you would like
- ☐ Choose Close
- ☐ Return to the Account Book window

In the remaining parts of this tutorial, we will set up and use Accounts Receivable

Part N

The process of using an Accounts Receivable account is the same as that for using Accounts Payable except that the former is an asset account. When a sale is made on credit it is an increase in Accounts Receivable, categorized as Revenue or Sales. When a payment is received on account it is an increase in your Checking account, categorized as a transfer to Accounts Receivable. This becomes a decrease in your Accounts Receivable account. I'll get you started with setting up the account; I think you can do the rest.

- ☐ Select the List then Account List menu items
- ☐ Choose New
- ☐ Type Accounts Receivable and press Alt−A
- ☐ Choose Ok and type 0 for Opening Balance, then Ok
- ☐ Choose Close to exit from the account list

Part O

Select Account then Accounts Receivable to display the new Accounts Receivable account in the window. You can now enter transactions for sales on credit, adjustments to customer balances and payments received on account. Try it by referring to parts B through M in the Accounts Payable section of this tutorial.

11
CHAPTER

Small business assets, liabilities, and net worth

As you have worked your way through this book you have created assets and liabilities in your Money file. Your Checking account is an example of an asset; your Loans Payable account is an example of a liability. Assets are things of value that you own, and liabilities are amounts that you owe. A business can determine its net worth (otherwise called *Owner's Equity*) by subtracting the total of its liabilities from the total of its assets. This chapter presents several transactions that belong in various asset and liability accounts, that were not covered previously. It describes how to handle depreciation of assets and record taxes payable, and concludes with a more in depth look at the concept of net worth (equity).

Assets

Businesses and individuals acquire assets as they purchase equipment, major tools, clothing, property, real estate, and other costly items that they plan on using over a long period of time. For example, your wardrobe is an asset. In the business setting, a restaurant that owns uniforms for employee use would classify these uniforms as an asset. Usually the largest value asset that any of us owns is our real estate. If a business owns a building and land, the cost of these should be recorded in asset accounts. Chapter 4 presented a basic list of accounts that might be needed for small business use. Figure 11-1 shows a complete business account list in the Money window.

11-1 Sample business account list

When an asset is purchased by writing a check, using a credit card, or borrowing money, it should be categorized in Money as a Transfer to an asset account. This is the method used to be sure that every transaction is assigned to a category and establishes the appropriate cost values in asset accounts. The basic concept of using transfers was introduced in chapters 3 and 4 (see the sections on "Transfers between accounts" and "Sample transactions" in those two chapters respectively).

Property, plant, and equipment

We'll follow through with the example of purchasing a fax machine in this chapter. Figure 11-2 illustrates the record of this transaction in the Business Checking account assuming that the price of the machine was $1210, with a down payment of $210 and the balance to be paid over 2 years at 14% interest to the seller. Notice in this figure that the cost of the machine is categorized as Office Equipment, while the borrowed amount is categorized as Equipment Loans Payable. This causes the net amount (the down payment) to be deducted from the Checking account. The Office Equipment account is an asset account.

The procedure for setting up new accounts was detailed in chapter 5. Here's a quick review: set up an account for office equipment by selecting the List then Account List menu items, choose New and type in the account name, an account type, and opening balance. Alternatively you can set up a new account on the fly as you enter this transaction. Select Transfer in the Category field and type Office Equipment in the Subcategory field. When Money does not find an existing

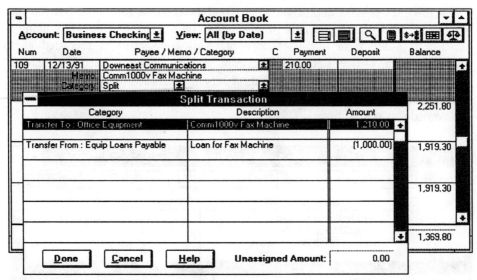

11-2 Purchase of a long term asset in the Checking account

account in the file named Office Equipment, it will ask if you want to set up the account, and you can specify the type (asset) and its opening balance.

Although the example transaction shown in Fig. 11-2 was recorded in the Checking account because of the $210 down payment, the Transfer category caused an offsetting entry in the Office Equipment account. Figure 11-3 shows how the transaction appears in the Office Equipment account. A full discussion of Loans Payable and the repayment of loans can be found in chapter 4 in the section on sample transactions.

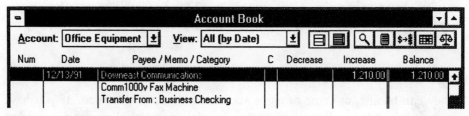

11-3 Purchase of a long term asset in the Equipment account

Depreciation of assets

A logical question might be coming to mind about this fax machine. If it is recorded in an asset account how will its cost ever show up as an expense on the income statement? This happens by applying depreciation against the asset and charging it to an expense category titled Depreciation Expense.

A full discussion of depreciation is beyond the scope of this book, but you can see in Fig. 11-4 that Depreciation Expense can be allocated periodically using a noncash transaction in the asset account. This transaction is recorded as a decrease in the Office Equipment account and is categorized as Depreciation Expense. Because there is no depreciation expense included in the Business Categories provided with Money, you will be adding this to your category list when you record this transaction.

Num	Date	Payee / Memo / Category	C	Decrease	Increase	Balance
	12/13/91	Downeast Communications Comm1000v Fax Machine Transfer From : Business Checking			1,210.00	1,210.00
	12/31/91	Depreciation on Fax Machine Month Estimated-Fax Depreciation : Office Equipment		217.80		992.20

11-4 Depreciation expense transaction

Schedule the depreciation expense transaction on the Future Transaction list with a monthly frequency, and you will be reminded to record this transaction at the end of each month.

The important result of this estimated transaction is seen on the income statement later in this chapter (Fig. 11-9). The net income is now more realistic, because it includes this additional cost of doing business; that is the Depreciation Expense.

Your accountant can advise you on the appropriate amount to depreciate in any year; then you can divide that amount by 12 for a monthly transaction. If you want to estimate depreciation yourself, use the depreciation tables provided by the IRS for tax purposes.

Other assets

Money can handle any type of asset account that you might need. If you have excess cash invested in the money market, bonds, or stocks, these are recorded as assets when you buy them. The purchase of common stock is illustrated in Fig. 11-5. The transaction is recorded in the Checking account, because a check is written to pay the stock broker and is categorized as a transfer to an asset account titled Investments. When the investments are sold, the transaction also will be recorded in the Checking account, because the receipts from the sale are deposited in this account. At that time, the transaction is categorized again as a transfer to the asset account, Investments, for the original cost of the investment and might

11-5 Purchase of stock as an investment

require a split transaction where the excess is categorized as Other Income or Loss on Sale of Investments.

In accordance with sound accounting principles, some small businesses record purchases of supplies as a transfer to an asset account titled Supplies. Then as the supplies are used up, a decrease transaction is recorded in the Supplies account, categorized as Office Expenses: Supplies. Various methods can be employed to determine the amount of supplies used up. You might keep an inventory list and record deductions there; or you could simply take a physical inventory once in a while and place an estimated value on what you have left.

Cash on Hand (or Petty Cash) is also an asset account and the procedures for handling this were detailed in chapter 3.

Liabilities

When you buy anything on credit or when you borrow money, you are accepting the liability to pay the amount back. A liability like loans payable is recorded by entering a deposit transaction in the Checking account and categorizing this as a transfer to a Notes Payable or Loans Payable account. The procedures for recording loans and mortgages were covered in chapters 3 and 4.

When the payroll is paid by a business, an associated liability for payroll taxes must be recorded. This was covered in chapter 9. The procedures for managing Accounts Payable, another type of liability, were covered in detail in chapter 10.

Taxes payable

In order to get an accurate picture of net income, all tax liabilities associated with the period of the income statement should be shown for that period. In other words, when you produce a monthly income statement, you would want to include that month's taxes. For example, you might pay property taxes only once a year, but those taxes are an expense of doing business every day. An easy method of handling this in Money is to record an estimated monthly portion of taxes in a Property Taxes Payable account. When the property tax bill is received, record the actual payment in the Checking account as a transfer to Property Taxes Payable.

This is similar to recording the cost of an asset when you buy it, then allocating a monthly amount to depreciation.

The transaction to record the monthly estimated property tax is shown in Fig. 11-6. This transaction causes an increase in the Property Tax Expense that is reported on the monthly income statement. Look for this on the income statement later in this chapter (Fig. 11-9). The monthly estimated property taxes should be entered on the Future Transactions list so you will be reminded to record it at the end of each month and won't have to type the data again.

11-6   Monthly estimated property tax transaction

When the actual payment of property taxes occurs, it can be recorded in the Checking account and categorized as a transfer to Property Taxes Payable as shown in Fig. 11-7. This transaction will then appear in the Property Tax Payable account as a decrease. If the actual tax payment is not the same as the figure you used for estimating at the beginning of the year, you should make an adjusting entry in Property Taxes Payable so the end of year balance comes to zero in this account.

11-7   Payment of property taxes

Other liabilities

I hope you can see from the previous section that other liabilities like income taxes payable, major interest payments on loans, the liability for a legal judgment, and other unique payable situations could all be handled in this manner. Set up a Payable account and record increases in it for the estimated monthly amount of these obligations. When the payment of the liability occurs, record it in your Checking account as a transfer to the Payable account.

Your net worth

A Net Worth report summarizes what you own and what you owe; your assets and liabilities. When a business applies for a bank loan, they will be required to produce such a report and will need to show the banker one periodically while the loan is outstanding. This is a good reason for attempting to get all actual assets and liabilities in your Money file as described in the last few chapters and the current one.

The "other" bottom line

The bottom line of the New Worth report is calculated by Money for you. Net worth refers to the excess of your total assets over total liabilities. In a sense this is the current value of the owner's investment in the business. Many lending institutions watch this figure as a percentage of total assets to determine how it sizes up in relation to your liabilities.

Take a close look at the net worth report in Fig. 11-8. If you are recording depreciation in your Office Equipment account, the balance shown on the net worth report is the *net value* of these assets; that is, the original cost reduced by accumulated depreciation over time. Also note that in the month that property taxes are paid, the Taxes Payable account will show a zero balance. As you record more estimated taxes, the balance in this account represents the accumulated amount payable towards the next year's tax bill.

The income statement bottom line

Because much of the presentation in this chapter was directed toward the execution of an accurate net income, let's take another look at the income statement. Figure 11-9 shows an income statement produced for the sample business for one month. Please note the Depreciation Expense and Taxes Expense that are listed on this report. These are the result of the estimated monthly entries presented in the examples shown in this chapter. You might find other expenses (and revenue) that should be included in your accurate picture of net income that can be handled in a manner similar to depreciation or taxes payable.

Summary

This chapter explained the definition and use of assets and liabilities. Procedures for recording estimated depreciation and taxes on a monthly basis were covered so that you can produce a more accurate income statement. The net worth report was revisited to see how these additional accounts will be reported.

```
                    NET WORTH REPORT
                     As of 12/31/91


    ASSETS                                    Total

    Bank and Cash Accounts
    Business Checking                        479.00
    Petty Cash                               123.00
          Total Bank and Cash Accounts       602.00

    Other Assets
    Accounts Receivable                    2,000.00
    Building                             122,000.00
    Computer Equipment                     2,528.50
    Investments                            1,234.80
    Office Equipment                         992.20
          Total Other Assets             128,755.50

    TOTAL ASSETS                         129,357.50


    LIABILITIES                              Total

    Credit Cards
    VISA-Key Bank                            456.70
          Total Credit Cards                 456.70

    Other Liabilities
    Accounts Payable                         217.00
    Equip Loans Payable                    2,802.00
    Fed Unemploy Tax Payable                  90.00
    Fed Withholding Payable                  604.00
    FICA Tax Payable                         450.00
    Mortgage Payable                      87,256.40
    Other Payroll Deducts Payable             40.00
    Property Tax Payable                     300.00
    State Unemploy Tax Payable                21.00
    State Withholding Payable                240.00
          Total Other Liabilities         92,020.40

    TOTAL LIABILITIES                      92,477.10


    NET WORTH                              36,880.40
```

11-8 Net worth with depreciation and property taxes

A tutorial on the balance sheet accounts

This tutorial builds on the tutorials of chapters 9 and 10; it assumes that you have the knowledge gained in chapters 1 through 10, although with some business experience this tutorial will be easily understood even if you have little Money experience. It is assumed that you have all the data in your file that was entered in the tutorials of earlier chapters. If you have not completed all chapters, go ahead with this tutorial understanding that the resulting reports will not be totally complete.

Sample Company - Income Statement
12/1/91 Through 12/31/91

Subcategory	Total
INCOME	
Revenue	7,750.00
TOTAL INCOME	7,750.00
EXPENSES	
Advertising	775.00
Bank Charges	30.70
Depreciation	
Computer	127.00
Office Equipment	217.80
Total Depreciation	344.80
Insurance	
Automobile	240.00
Liability	400.00
Total Insurance	640.00
Miscellaneous	86.00
Office Expenses	
Equipment	76.00
Supplies	110.00
Total Office Expenses	186.00
Payroll	
Salaries & Wages	3,000.00
Taxes	336.00
Total Payroll	3,336.00
Taxes	
Property & Use Taxes	100.00
Total Taxes	100.00
TOTAL EXPENSES	5,498.50
INCOME LESS EXPENSES	2,251.50

11-9 Comprehensive income statement

Part A

In earlier tutorials we set up new accounts using the List then Account List menu. In this first part we will set up a new account by entering it as part of a transaction. Let's begin with the purchase of a large piece of machinery for $8000 with a $1000 down payment. We'll set up a new account for Machinery to keep this separate from the equipment we purchased earlier.

☐ Access Money and select File then Open

☐ Select the sample.mny file used in previous tutorials

☐ Activate the account book of the Checking account

☐ Select the next available transaction line

☐ Type p in the Num field

☐ Type 12/14 in the Date field

☐ Type Gold Machinery Inc in the Payee field

☐ Type 1000 in the Payment Amount field

☐ Select the Split Transaction window (Ctrl−S or click the icon)

☐ Select Transfer in the Category field

☐ Type Machinery in the Subcategory field

☐ The Create New Account dialog box appears

☐ Note that the new account name is already filled in

☐ Select the Asset Account option then Ok

☐ Enter zero as the Opening Balance then Ok

☐ You are back in the Split Transaction window

☐ Type Ajax 5000D Presentation System in the Description field

☐ Type 8000 in the Amount field

☐ Move to the next split transaction entry section

☐ Select Transfer in the Category field

☐ Type Equip Loans Payable in the Subcategory field

Note   If you've completed all the previous tutorials, you will find that SmartFill locates this account and fills in its name. If not then you will see the Create New Account dialog box where you must indicate an account type of Liability Account and enter an Opening Balance of zero.

☐ Type a quote mark (") in the Memo field

☐ Note that the Amount field contains a negative 7000

☐ This is the amount of the equipment loan

☐ Select Done to return to the account book

☐ Press Enter to complete the transaction

☐ Select Machinery in the Account box

☐ You should now be in the account book for Machinery

☐ Note the 8000 transaction here resulting from the above entry

Part B

In this section we will set up the transaction for estimated depreciation that should be recorded in the Machinery account at the end of every month. Because we purchased this asset before the 15th of the month, we should depreciate it for the full month of December. A recent IRS publication indicates that a 18% annual depreciation rate would be appropriate for the first year of depreciation on this asset. We will divide this by 12 to arrive at an estimated monthly depreciation.

☐ Select the next available transaction line in the Machinery account
☐ Type Depre in the Num field
☐ Type 12/31 in the Date field
☐ Type Dep on Ajax 5000D in the Payee field
☐ Tab to the Decrease amount field
☐ Access the Calculator (Ctrl−K or click on Calculator icon)
☐ Enter 8000∗.18/12 and press Enter or =
☐ The result (120) is shown at the top of the calculator
☐ Press Ctrl−Ins to save the result in memory
☐ Press Alt−F4 to close the Calculator window
☐ With the cursor in the Decrease field, press Shift−Ins
☐ This pastes the result from the calculator
☐ Type Monthly Estimate in the Memo field
☐ Type Depreciation Expense in the Category field, then Tab
☐ The Create New Category dialog box appears
☐ Place a mark in the Include on Tax Reports box, then Ok
☐ Type Machinery in the Subcategory field, then Tab
☐ The Create New Subcategory box appears, choose Ok
☐ Press Enter to record this transaction
☐ Note the result of this transaction in the Machinery account

Part C

Let's take a look at the effect of this account on the net income. Depreciation expense will now appear on the Income & Expense report.

☐ Select Reports then Income & Expense
☐ Choose Customize

- ☐ Enter 12/1 in the From box for Date Range
- ☐ Enter 12/31 in the To box for Date Range
- ☐ Select Income Statement in the Report Transfers By box
- ☐ Choose View and scroll down to Depreciation Expense
- ☐ The amount we recorded in the Machinery account shows here
- ☐ Scroll down to Total Expenses
- ☐ Depreciation is included in this total
- ☐ Choose Close

Part D

After you've created the transaction for estimated monthly depreciation, you should schedule it on the Future Transactions list so that you can use it to "pay bills" at the end of every month. Although this isn't a "bill," the transactions can be automatically entered for you each month, and you'll even be reminded to do so.

- ☐ Select the Depreciation Expense transaction
- ☐ Schedule this on the Future Transactions list (by selecting Edit then Schedule in Future, by pressing Ctrl−E, or by clicking on the Schedule In Future icon)
- ☐ The Schedule Future Transaction box appears
- ☐ Select Monthly in the Frequency box
- ☐ Type 1/31/xx in the Next Date box (where xx = next year)
- ☐ Choose Ok
- ☐ Switch to the Future Transactions window by selecting Window then Future Transactions, by double-clicking on the Future Transaction icon, or by clicking on the Future Transaction window)
- ☐ Scroll to the bottom of the Future window
- ☐ The scheduled Depreciation transaction should be there
- ☐ Return to the Account Book window
- ☐ Return to the Business Checking account

Part E

In the next few sections we will set up an account for Property Taxes Payable and create an estimated tax entry for monthly property tax expense. Assume that your property tax bill is $1800 per year and is received and payable each June.

- ☐ Select List then Account List from the menu
- ☐ You should see the Account List dialog box
- ☐ Choose New
- ☐ Type Property Tax Payable
- ☐ Select Liabllity Account then Ok
- ☐ Enter 0 for Opening Balance, then Ok
- ☐ Choose the Report button to view all accounts you've created
- ☐ Choose Customize and select the Account Balances option
- ☐ Choose View
- ☐ Print the list on paper if you'd like
- ☐ Choose Close twice to return to the Account Book window

Part F

This part leads you through the creation of an estimated monthly property tax transaction in the Property Taxes Payable account.

- ☐ Select Account then Property Tax Payable
- ☐ Type Adj in the Num field
- ☐ Type 12/31 in the Date field
- ☐ Type Estimated Tax on Office in the Payee field
- ☐ Move to the Increase amount field and select the Calculator (you can press Ctrl−K or click on Toolbar)
- ☐ Enter 1800/12 and press Enter
- ☐ The result is shown at the top of the calculator
- ☐ Press Ctrl−Ins to save the result in memory
- ☐ Press Alt−F4 to close the Calculator window
- ☐ With the cursor in the Increase field, press Shift−Ins
- ☐ This pastes the result from the calculator memory
- ☐ Type Monthly Estimate in the Memo field
- ☐ Select Taxes in the Category field
- ☐ Select Property Tax in the Subcategory field
- ☐ Press Enter to complete the transaction
- ☐ Select Reports then Income & Expense
- ☐ Choose Customize

- ☐ Enter 12/1 in the From box for Date Range
- ☐ Enter 12/31 in the To box for Date Range
- ☐ Choose View and scroll down to Taxes Expense
- ☐ The amount we recorded in the Taxes Payable account shows here
- ☐ Choose Close

Part G

We should now schedule this transaction on the Future Transaction list so that it can easily be recorded in the account book each month. Let's try a new twist—we'll schedule the transaction for July 31 because we paid our last tax bill on June 30 of the current year. Then we'll use this scheduled transaction for each month, July through November of the current year, so that the December 31 Taxes Payable balance will reflect the six month period.

- ☐ Select the estimated tax entry in Property Tax Payable
- ☐ Select Schedule in Future (Ctrl−E or click on Toolbar)
- ☐ Select Monthly in the Frequency box
- ☐ Enter 7/31 in the Next Date box, then Ok
- ☐ Select the Future Transaction window to see this as scheduled

Note Because the 7/31 date is the earliest on this list, it should be at the top of the list. Now we can ask to pay bills up to 12/1 and all the tax transactions from July to Dec will be presented for payment.

- ☐ Select Pay Bills by pressing Ctrl−P or by selecting Options then Pay Bills (do not use the toolbar this time)
- ☐ Enter 12/1 in the Date box, then Ok
- ☐ Verify that the Enter Transaction box shows the 7/31 entry
- ☐ Choose Enter to record the 7/31 entry
- ☐ Notice that the 8/31 tax transaction is now presented
- ☐ Verify that the Enter Transaction box shows the 8/31 entry
- ☐ Choose Enter to record the 8/31 entry
- ☐ Verify that the Enter Transaction box shows the 9/30 entry
- ☐ Choose Enter to record the 9/30 entry
- ☐ Verify that the Enter Transaction box shows the 10/31 entry
- ☐ Choose Enter to record the 10/31 entry
- ☐ Verify that the Enter Transaction box shows the 11/30 entry
- ☐ Choose Enter to record the 11/30 entry

Note If you had experimented with other scheduled transactions, you might be presented with more "bills" to pay than just those itemized here. Choose Don't Enter for those transactions.

- ☐ When all transactions up to 12/1 are entered, you will be returned to the Future Transactions window
- ☐ Select the Account Book window for Property Tax Payable
- ☐ Notice that the ending balance in the account is $900
- ☐ This represents 1/2 of the year's property taxes
- ☐ Scroll through the account to view the past 6 months

Part H

Let's take a look at the overall effect of this on the net income for the year:

- ☐ Select Reports then Income & Expense
- ☐ Choose Customize
- ☐ Enter 6/1/xx in the From box for Date Range (replace xx with the current year)
- ☐ Enter 12/31 in the To box for Date Range
- ☐ Choose View and scroll down to Taxes Expense
- ☐ The total amount of estimated taxes now shows here
- ☐ Choose Close

Part I

Although we've been assuming it's December for purposes of recording sample transactions, let's skip ahead to June when the Property Tax bill arrives. The actual property taxes to be paid on June 25 are $1888.50. Here's how the payment should be handled.

- ☐ Select Account and select Business Checking
- ☐ Select the next available transaction line
- ☐ Type p in the Num field
- ☐ Type 6/25/xx in the Date field (xx = next year)
- ☐ Type City of Golden in the Payee field
- ☐ Type 1888.50 in the Payment field
- ☐ Select the Split Transaction window (Ctrl−S or click the icon)
- ☐ Select Transfer in the Category field
- ☐ Select Property Tax Payable in the Subcategory field

☐ Type Property Tax on Office in the Description field

☐ Type 1800 in the Amount field

☐ Move to the next split transaction entry section

☐ Select Taxes in the Category field

☐ Select Property Tax in the Subcategory field

☐ Type Adjustment for Excess in the Description field

☐ Note that the Amount field contains 88.50

☐ This is the amount of the excess over the $1800 we used to estimate the monthly tax portion

☐ Select Done to return to the account book

☐ Press Enter to complete the transaction

Part J

Lastly let's print and take a close look at the results of our work in this chapter as it relates to the financial statements. We will produce a net worth report.

☐ Select Report then Net Worth

☐ Choose Customize

☐ Enter Balance Sheet as the Title

☐ Enter 12/31 in the Date box

☐ Choose View and scroll through the report to observe the Machinery and Property Taxes Payable account

☐ Choose Print and Ok if you want a printed copy

☐ Choose Close

☐ Choose File then Exit and make a backup copy of your work

12
CHAPTER

Small business extras

This last chapter is a potpourri of additional features available in Money. The process of balancing a bank account is described in detail. The steps necessary for exporting reports to spreadsheet or word processor are explained. A review and some suggestions about backup routines will help you safeguard your data. Once your data is backed up, you might want to archive your file; put old transactions in a special file so they appear on the File, Open list, but so they do not appear in your current accounts. The procedure for archiving files is also included in this chapter.

Reconciling your bank statement

The bank reconciliation process consists of three simple steps: entering the balance and service charges from your bank statement, comparing items cleared by the bank with items you recorded in the Checking account, and ensuring the equality of the two forms. Sometimes this last step is tough, but Money and suggestions provided in this section can make this process easier every month. For purposes of example, we will assume that we have just received the bank statement shown in Fig. 12-1. Note the beginning and ending balances, and the service and interest items.

Entering bank data

First select the account you want to balance. This can be any kind of account that you receive a statement for and want to verify that everything you recorded in the account has been recognized by the institution who holds the account. The process of reconciling a credit card account was covered in chapter 8.

Access the account balancing routine by clicking on the Balance Account icon of the toolbar or by selecting Options then Balance Account from the menu.

219

```
Chase First Bank                    Account:        355-90-2345
Two Bank Plaza
Boston, MA 02110                    For Period:     11/30/92
                                                    12/31/92
```

Customer Service:	Account Name:
1-800-989-1111	
	Jean E. Gutmann
Your Branch:	P. O. Box 5300
Kingston, Rt 27	Kingston, ME 04876

Beginning Balance: 2000.00

Checks & Charges:

12/4	#101	-720.00	12/15	Svc Chg	-22.00
12/5	#102	-640.00	12/16	#106	-613.00
12/7	#104	-326.50	12/16	#107	-332.50
12/8	#103	-400.00	12/30	#110	-613.00
12/15	#105	-210.00			
	TOTAL CHECKS & CHARGES				-3877.00

Deposits & Credits:

12/12	3200.00	12/24		1450.00
12/15	200.00	12/31	Intr	4.65
	TOTAL DEPOSITS & CREDITS			4854.65

Ending Balance: 2977.65

12-1   Sample bank statement

Money then displays the Balance Account dialog box as shown in Fig. 12-2. If this is the first time you are balancing this account, you should enter both the Starting and Ending balance in the account as shown on your bank statement. If you have balanced the account previously, then Money provides the starting balance based on the original opening balance, plus or minus any reconciled transactions. The first time you balance an account, use the starting balance that you entered as the Opening Balance when you set up the account in Money. If that amount was other than zero, read the next section on getting the opening balance right.

Enter the amounts of any service charges, interest charges, or interest earned in the boxes for these within the Balance Account dialog box. Type the amount in the smaller box, and then select a category and subcategory to be charged in the

12-2 Balance Account dialog box

list boxes. Notice how the $22 service charge and the $4.65 interest earned are recorded in Fig. 12-2. Money will automatically create entries in your Checking account for these two transactions, and mark them as "cleared" by the bank. Choose Continue to proceed.

Getting the opening balance right

If there is a discrepancy between the starting balance you just entered and the last reconciled balance in this account, Money will display a Starting Balance Warning box with some hints on how to resolve the problem. This box is illustrated in Fig. 12-3. If you made an error when entering the opening balance in the Balance Account dialog box or when you created this account, choose Cancel and return to

12-3 Starting Balance Warning box

the previous dialog box to re-enter the amount. You also can choose Cancel again to abort the balancing process and select the Account List where you can change the Opening Balance in the account. This is the only circumstance where you should alter the opening balance in a checking account. Altering the opening balance after you've balanced the account will cause further problems during later months.

When you created the Checking account in Money and entered an opening balance, you might have taken that balance from your paper check register or from your last bank statement. In either case, you need to account for this opening balance during the reconciling process. For example, if you entered an opening balance of $200 from your bank statement and that amount consists of two outstanding checks for $110 and $90, you can make note of these two items on your bank statement, because they will not need to be cleared in your Money account book. If only one of these checks cleared during the current month ($90), the other amount of $110 could be entered in the account book so that it will appear as an uncleared item until a later month when it actually clears the bank. The Opening Balance in the Checking account should then be adjusted accordingly. As long as you give this $110 payment a date prior to the current month, you can prevent it from being included in reports that cover your current account activity.

If you are just starting to use Money to balance your checking account although you've entered previous month's transactions that have actually cleared the bank long ago, all of these previous transactions will appear as "uncleared" the first time you attempt to balance the account. To remove them from the uncleared list, simply click on the C column for each line as described below, or choose Cancel to return to the account book, and press Shift while clicking in the C column to mark each of the old transactions as R (reconciled).

Matching bank items to recorded items

This process is known as "clearing" transactions. Any item (payment or deposit) that has been recorded in your account and also has been cleared by the bank should be marked with a C in the C column of the account book to indicate that it has cleared. Money automatically redisplays your account book, changing the view to include only unreconciled transactions and in top line view format. Figure 12-4 illustrates this form. Notice that Money has automatically entered the service charge and interest shown in Fig. 12-3 and marked them as C for cleared.

You can mark a transaction as cleared by clicking on the C column of the transaction, or selecting the transactions with the Arrow keys and pressing the Spacebar. You might remove the C mark by clicking again or pressing the Spacebar again. So this step involves scrolling through the account book to mark any transactions that appear on the bank statement. Notice in Fig. 12-4 that the status area at the bottom of the Account Book window at this point provides a total of all the deposits cleared (including the interest income), and all the payments cleared

Num	Date	Payee / Memo / Category	C	Payment	Deposit	Balance
	12/31/91	Service Charge	C	22.00		(...00)
	12/31/91	Interest Earned	C		4.65	(17.35)
101	12/2/91	Cree Advertising Agency	C	720.00		(737.35)
102	12/4/91	Ritter Agency	C	640.00		(1,377.35)
103	12/6/91	Computerland	C	400.00		(1,777.35)
104	12/6/91	Haines Office Furnishings	C	362.50		(2,139.85)
105	12/13/91	Downeast Communications	C	210.00		(2,349.85)
106	12/15/91	Pasanik, Brenda	C	613.00		(2,962.85)
107	12/15/91	Goodman, George	C	332.50		(3,295.35)
108	12/21/91	Allen Avenue Agency		188.00		(3,483.35)

Account: Business Checking **View:** Unreconciled (by Nu

Starting Balance Difference: 0.00

Cleared Transactions

| 8 | Deposits | 4,854.65 |
| 9 | Checks & Payments | (3,913.00) |

Mark all transactions that appear on your statement as cleared.

Balance

Cleared Balance:	2,941.65
Statement Balance:	2,977.65
Difference:	(36.00)

Finish   Postpone   Help

12-4 Account book top line view for clearing transactions

(including service charges). You might be able to match these with totals that the bank provides on your statement. The status area also compares the total Cleared Balance with the Statement Balance that you entered to let you know how far off you are, or that the difference is zero. If the Difference is zero, the account is in balance.

Searching for differences

When you feel you are finished, choose Finish and you will either be returned to the account book or you will see the Account Didn't Balance dialog box (Fig. 12-5). Even if you can't get the Difference status to come to zero, go ahead and choose Finish, because Money provides some help in this next box. Notice the options in Fig. 12-5. You can go back to reconciling the account yourself, use SmartReconcile to help find the error, or you can ask Money to automatically adjust the balance to accommodate the error. Choose the first option if you think you know what's wrong. Then choose Postpone and return to the account book to enter a missing transaction or to delete a transaction that doesn't belong in the Checking account. When you choose Balance Account again, you'll be back in the balancing process exactly where you left off. I don't recommend entering a missing transaction from the Balance Account window, because the account book is in top line view and you won't be asked to enter a memo, category, or subcategory.

Choose the Use SmartReconcile option to have Money search for common errors like a misplaced decimal, transposed digits, or a missing item. For example, if you are off by $118 and there is a payment for $118, SmartReconcile will notice the payment in your account book and suggest that you neglected to clear it or that you cleared it too soon. In my example, check #104 was recorded in the

Account Didn't Balance

Your account doesn't balance with your statement. This is
probably for one of the following reasons:

- An incorrect amount was entered in a transaction. Check the amounts
  of cleared transactions against your statement to find the error.

- A transaction which is marked as cleared is not on your statement; or a
  transaction on your statement is not marked as cleared. Please check
  your statement to find the error.

You can:

○ **G**o back to reconciling the account
○ Use **S**martReconcile to help find the error
◉ Automatically **a**djust the account balance

Adjustment Amount: 36.00

Category:

OK Help

12-5 Account Didn't Balance dialog box

account book for $362.50, but the bank cleared it for $326.50. See Fig. 12-6 to
observe how Money might find and inform you of this. If you then choose Yes in
the Possible Error dialog box, Money will correct the specified payment for you
and let you know the account is now balanced.

Possible Error

Payee: **Haines Office Furnishings**
Amount: **362.50**
Type: **Payment**
Status: **Cleared**
Date: **12/6/91**
Category: **Transfer To : Computer**

**The amount of this transaction may be incorrect.
Changing the amount of this transaction to 326.50
would balance the account. Would you like to
change the amount of this transaction?**

Yes No Cancel Help

12-6 Possible error from SmartReconcile

If SmartReconcile can't find a possible error, it will let you know and you might want to choose the option to Automatically Adjust the Balance. If the amount of your difference is small and you don't want to bother trying to find the error, this is a good choice. Once you check this option the adjustment amount is displayed and you can then specify which category you want to apply the adjustment to. Notice the Adjustment amount and category boxes in Fig. 12-5.

If you want to postpone the balancing procedure, you can choose Go Back to Reconciling the Account and then choose the Postpone option. All work you've done on the reconciliation will be saved, but you can return to the present balancing status at any time.

Outstanding items

When the account balances properly, you will be congratulated on screen by Money and returned to the account book. Then you should notice that all transactions that were marked C have been changed to R, which means reconciled. If you'd like a list of outstanding items, you should produce a register report that is customized for the ending date of the statement and restricted to selected transactions—only those that are uncleared. This will be helpful when you start the next month's balancing process.

Exporting reports

Once you have customized a report to your liking in the Report window, you have the option of exporting that report to a file that can later be imported into a word processor or spreadsheet. The report is saved as a text file in tab-delimited form. This means that each field on the report is followed by a tab mark with a line feed at the end of each line.

Using Money reports for word processing

If you want to write a report or memo about some part of the data that is output by Money, you can choose the Export option from the Report window and then open the file in a word processing program. Further customization, like longer titles, elimination of a total column, placing page numbers or a footer at the bottom of all pages are examples of the reasons why you might want to export reports to be used later.

As an example, consider the two-month income statement produced in Money and shown in Fig. 12-7. Just after printing this, I chose the Export option and was asked to provide a file name for the exported file. I typed INC-TOWP (for Income Statement to Word Processor), and Money automatically saves this in the default disk directory with an extension of ".TXT." In other words, if you accepted the default setup when you first installed Money, the file will be stored in C: \ MSMONEY \ and be named INC-TOWP.TXT.

Nov and December Income Statement
11/1/91 Through 12/31/91

Category	11/1/91 – 11/30/91	12/1/91 – 12/31/91	Total
INCOME			
Revenue	3,600.00	4,800.00	8,400.00
TOTAL INCOME	3,600.00	4,800.00	8,400.00
EXPENSES			
Advertising	695.00	720.00	1,415.00
Automobile/Truck	92.50	108.00	200.50
Bank Charges	22.50	30.70	53.20
Entertainment	88.95	41.50	130.45
Insurance	102.00	640.00	742.00
Miscellaneous	12.13	16.50	28.63
Office Expenses	194.95	73.00	267.95
Professional Fees		112.00	112.00
Training Material	82.30	120.00	202.30
Travel		645.00	645.00
TOTAL EXPENSES	1,290.33	2,506.70	3,797.03
INCOME LESS EXPENSES	2,309.67	2,293.30	4,602.97

12-7 Two month income statement

You have a wonderful little word processor available to you with Windows 3.0 called Write. For purposes of example, let's explore how the Money INC-TOWP.TXT file can be used in Write. You don't have to exit from Money to use Write. Access the Program Manager (double-click on its icon if you can see it, or press Ctrl−Esc, and then select Program Manager from the task list). From the Program Manager, you can then double-click on the Write icon in the Accessories Group to access this word processor.

Within Write, you can use menus the same way you do in Money. Select File then Open from the menu line. Type c:\msmoney\inc-towp.txt in the Filename box and choose Ok. Select the option to Convert to Write Format, and you will see the Money report in the Write window as shown in Fig. 12-8. You'll need to set tab stops so the columns will be tabbed to your specifications. Do this by selecting Document then Tabs from the menu. You'll be presented with a Tab Settings dialog box where you can type 3, 4 and 5 in the Positions boxes and indicate decimal tabs. (Tab stops are indicated in inches from the left margin.) This is shown in Fig. 12-9.

In this example, I also wanted to focus only on the expenses from the income statement and write a brief memo to present them to colleagues. Select File then

```
━━                       Write - INCEXP.WRI                      ▼ ▲
 File  Edit  Search   Character   Paragraph  Document   Help
 INCOME AND EXPENSE REPORT                                          ⬆
 11/1/91 Through 12/31/91


       11/1/91 -    12/1/91 -
 Category11/30/9112/31/91Total

 INCOME

 Revenue3,600.004,800.008,400.00

 TOTAL INCOME3,600.004,800.008,400.00

 EXPENSES

 Advertising 695.00720.001,415.00
 Automobile/Truck92.50108.00200.50
 Bank Charges22.50 30.70 53.20
 Entertainment88.9541.50 130.45
 Insurance    102.00640.00742.00
 Miscellaneous12.1316.50 28.63
 Office Expenses194.9573.00267.95
 Professional Fees       112.00112.00
 Training Material 82.30 120.00202.30             ⬇
 Page 1            ◀ ▊                                    ➡
```

12-8 Income statement in Write window

```
━━                       Write - INC-TOWP.TXT                    ▼ ▲
 File  Edit  Search   Character   Paragraph  Document   Help
 INCOME AND EXPENSE REPORT                                          ⬆
 11/1/91 Through 12/31/91


       11/1/91 -    12/1/91 -
 Category11/30/9112/31/91Total

 INCOME

 Revenue3,600.004,800.008,400.00

 TOTAL  ┌──────────────────────── Tabs ────────────────────────┐
 EXPENS │ ━━                                                    │
        │ Positions:   3        4        5                      │
 Advert:│ Decimal:    ☒ .     ☒ .     ☒[] .    ☐ .    ☐ .   ☐ . │
 Automob│                                                       │
 Bank Cl│ Positions:                                            │
 Enterta│ Decimal:    ☐ .     ☐ .     ☐ .     ☐ .    ☐ .   ☐ . │
 Insura │                                                       │
 Miscel │                                                       │
 Office │ ┌──────────┐   ┌──────────┐   ┌──────────────┐        │
 Traini │ │   OK     │   │  Cancel  │   │  Clear All   │        │
 Page 1 └──────────────────────────────────────────────────────┘
```

12-9 Setting tabs in the Write window

Print in Write after you've entered your enhancements. The final outcome of my example is shown in Fig. 12-10.

Select File then Save As from the Write menu to save your document for later use, and select File then Exit to return to Money. Go ahead and explore the Write program; remember to press F1 or select Help from the menu to read on screen help information to assist you in accomplishing what you want.

```
TO:     Department Managers
FROM:   Jean Gutmann
DATE:   January 12
RE:     Expense Category Increases!


Expenditures have inreased dramatically over the past two months!  I would appreciate
your help in identifying weak areas.  Take a look at the following and let me know if
you have any insight into the causes of this:

EXPENSES                              NOV          DEC         TOTAL

Advertising                        695.00       720.00      1,415.00
Automobile/Truck                    92.50       108.00        200.50
Bank Charges                        22.50        30.70         53.20
Entertainment                       88.95        41.50        130.45
Insurance                          102.00       640.00        742.00
Miscellaneous                       12.13        16.50         28.63
Office Expenses                    194.95        73.00        267.95
Professional Fees                                112.00        112.00
Training Material                   82.30       120.00        202.30
Travel                                           645.00        645.00

TOTAL EXPENSES                   1,290.33     2,506.70      3,797.03

Call me at 780-8978..............THANKS !
```

12-10 Final printed result from Write

Exporting reports to spreadsheets

The same file that you create when choosing Export from the Report dialog box
can be used in some spreadsheet programs. You might want to export Money
reports into a spreadsheet so you can add columns for further calculations, or to
produce simple graphs from the data. Most Windows users have a version of
Microsoft Excel, a very popular spreadsheet program, so I will use that as an
example in this section. Let's assume we wanted to take the income statement presented in Fig. 12-7 into a spreadsheet, so that we could add a column to calculate
the percentage increase between the expenses for November and those for December.

The first step is to produce and customize the income statement as noted in
the previous section on word processing. Choose Export from the Report dialog
box and provide a filename like INC-TOSS.TXT (for income statement to spreadsheet). Switch to the Windows Program Manager and select the Excel icon. Once
in Excel the procedures for selecting items from menus is very similar to those in
Money. For example, you can click on the File then Open menu items, or type
Alt−F then O to open a file.

Select File then Open from the menu line. You will see a File Open dialog box
that is similar to the one you use in Money. Type c: \ msmoney \ inc-toss.txt in the
Filename box and choose Ok. You'll need to refer to the Excel user manual to
learn how to add columns and enter formulas to calculate differences and percentages but the outcome might look something like the example shown in Fig. 12-11.

Microsoft Excel — File Edit Formula Format Data Options Macro Window — Help

E3 — Percent

INC-TOSS.TXT

	A	B	C	D	E	F	G	H
1	INCOME AND EXPENSE REPORT			Nov-Dec 1992				
2								
3	Category	Nov	Dec	Increase	Percent			
4								
5	INCOME							
6	Revenue	3600	4800	1200	33%			
7								
8	EXPENSES							
9	Advertising	695	720	25	4%			
10	Automobile/Truck	92.5	108	15.5	17%			
11	Bank Charges	22.5	30.7	8.2	36%			
12	Entertainment	88.95	41.5	-47.45	-53%			
13	Insurance	102	640	538	527%			
14	Miscellaneous	12.13	16.5	4.37	36%			
15	Office Expenses	194.95	73	-121.95	-63%			
16	Professional Fees		112	112	na			
17	Training Material	82.3	120	37.7	46%			
18	Travel		645	645	na			
19								

Ready

12-11 Excel Window with Money report exported

I have added two columns to the income statement. One column (Column D) is used to calculate the increase in expenses between November and December; and the other (Column E) is used to calculate the percent of the increase.

Select File then Save As from the Excel menu to save your document for later use, and select File then Print to print a copy of your work. Select File then Exit to return to Money. Just to pique your interest, Fig. 12-12 includes a pie chart created from the December expense data using Excel charting features. Producing charts from financial data is a common task accomplished with spreadsheets.

This was just intended to give you some ideas. I'm sure you can think of a lot of things you'll want to do with your Money data once you learn a little about spreadsheets. Don't be afraid to try it on your own; there are very good help files available in Excel by pressing F1 or clicking on Help. Explore and have fun.

File import and export on the menu

You will find an Import and an Export option on the File menu within Money. These commands were included so that users of another money management package, called Quicken, can read their files into Money and export files later. When you select this option, you will see a dialog box that suggests that files with the ".QIF" extension will be imported or exported. At this time, these are the only types of files that can be translated. Watch for further news from Microsoft Corporation about additional types of files that can be handled by this option.

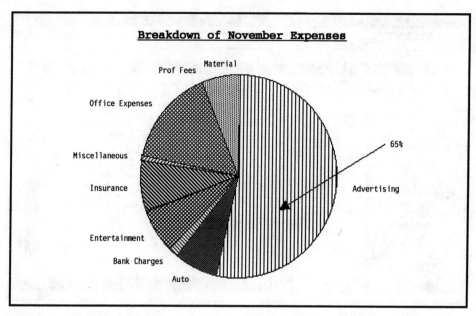

12-12 Pie chart of depreciation expense in Excel

Backup routines must be routine

You should make a backup copy of your Money files every time you use the accounts. I can't overemphasize the importance of this to guard against accidental loss of data. You have invested a lot of time in setting up Money and entering your transactions, so you don't want to take any chances on losing that important file. As long as you haven't altered the settings Money provides, you are faced with the Backup dialog box every time you exit from Money or ask to Open a file. Please don't ignore this question; choose Yes and let Money put an extra copy of the file on a diskette. If your hard disk should ever fail or crash, you can always pick up where you left off by using your backup copy.

Using automatic backup

Be sure that Money is set to remind you about backups. Do this by selecting the Options then Settings menu items and read the Settings dialog box. In the Confirmation box of this window, be sure there is an X in the Reminder to Backup box. You can see this in Fig. 6-9 of chapter 6.

Have two formatted diskettes ready to accept backup files; labelling them Money Backup 1 and Money Backup 2. The first time you do a backup, select File then Backup from the menu and insert Money Backup 1 in the disk drive. Money will suggest a backup file on disk drive A using the name of the original file with a ".BAK" extension. Accept this name by choosing Yes, or by typing a different disk drive followed by the name you want (e.g., B:BUSINESS.BAK). When you exit from Money, you will be presented with the Backup File To dialog box again. Insert the Money Backup 2 disk in the floppy drive and choose Yes to make the copy. The next time you make a backup, use only Money Backup 1. The next time, backup to Money Backup 2 and so forth. With this method, you'll have a reliable backup even if one of the disks becomes damaged.

As you reuse your backup disks, you will be asked if you want to overwrite an existing backup file. Choose Yes to indicate that you want to overwrite the earlier backup. You could hand mark dates on the disks and write over with a new date each time you make a backup. You also can use the Windows File Manager to take a look at the contents of your backup disks to see which one has the latest date.

Restoring records from a backup disk

It is my sincere wish for you that your hard disk never crash! If it does, however, you'll have to set up Money again within Windows and restore your Money data files from your backup disk as described in the next paragraph. This is when you'll be really glad you made all those backups. Sometimes you might be interrupted by a hard disk crash or you simply might make enough errors that you decide you want to restore yesterday's files instead of using the corrupted mess from today. Here's how you can restore the file from your backup disk.

Select File then Open from the menu. The following procedure assumes that you use the A: disk drive to store backups, which is where I recommend you store them. Figure 12-13 illustrates the familiar File Open dialog box; you should notice that in the bottom left corner there is a List Files of Type list box. Activate this box and select Backups (*.BAK). Insert your most recent backup disk in the

12-13 File Open dialog box for backup files

A: disk drive and in the Drives box, select A:. Choose the Ok button and Money will display a list of available backup files from drive A: in the Filename list box. Select the name of the file you want to restore and choose Ok again. At this point you will be asked if you want to back up the file that is in the window (which might be the corrupt file that you don't want to save). Answer No to the backup question this time, because you don't want to save the corrupt file. This would be especially important if the backup file you were trying to restore was named MS-MONEY.MNY, because this is the default file name that Money sets up for you the first time you start using the program. If you say Yes to back up a blank file named MSMONEY.MNY, the blank file will be placed over the good backup named MSMONEY.BAK that you need to restore. Say No to skip the dangerous backup at this point.

You will then see the Restore Backup dialog box as shown in Fig. 12-14. This informs you that Money will create a new file with the ".MNY" extension based on the name of the backup file. Either accept this name by choosing Ok, or type a new file name (it must still have the ".MNY" extension) and choose Ok. Money then creates this new file and displays it in the window for your use.

Restore Backup

You are trying to open a backup file. Microsoft Money cannot use a backup file directly. You must enter a filename to restore this file to; Microsoft Money will then open the restored file.

File **N**ame:
book12.mny

Directories:
c:\hj2

🗀 c:\
📁 hj2

Create Files of Type:
Microsoft Money Format

Dri**v**es:
💾 c: j-gutmann

OK
Cancel
Help

12-14   Restore Backup dialog box

Archiving old records

Archiving means to remove older, now unneeded, transactions from your current file and put them into cold storage. This storage place is a file on your hard disk or on a diskette that can be recalled to the window if you need it for reference. After you have many months of transactions in your file, it becomes harder to work with because you have so many lines in your account book, or forms behind your Checks & Forms window. The most likely candidates for archiving are last year's transactions, so the assumption here is that once you begin a new calendar year, you'll want to archive the previous year's transactions.

Getting ready to archive a file

When you ask Money to archive transactions, it will remove all reconciled transactions in a bank or credit card account, all cleared or reconciled transactions in an asset or liability account, and transactions up to a specified date in a cash account. At the same time, it makes a complete backup file of all transactions up to the date you specify. Your unreconciled transactions will remain in the current file, and starting balances in these accounts will be adjusted for archived transactions that have been removed.

An important point to understand here is that the transactions must be marked cleared or reconciled in order to be removed from your file. In accounts that you don't normally balance, like the asset and liability accounts, you should place an R in the C column for any transactions that you want removed into the archive file. Do this by scrolling through all of your accounts and holding the Shift key while clicking in the C column of the transactions you want to mark.

Creating an archive file

Select File then Archive from the menu, and the dialog box shown in Fig. 12-15 will appear. Leave the two options that are checked as is. You want a backup copy to be made, and you want to delete cleared or reconciled transactions from your file. Type the date up to which you want older transactions removed. When you choose Ok, you will have a chance to enter a filename for the archive file and to specify what disk drive is used to store the file. The year found in the transactions you are removing is used as the file name, and the file will be stored in c: \ msmoney, with an extension of ".MNY," unless you specify otherwise. For example, 1991 transactions will be stored in an archive file named "1991.MNY." The

12-15 Archive dialog box

name of this archived file will show up on your file list when you use the File, Open command. Once you choose Ok in this last dialog box, the archived file will be created and the old transactions will be removed from your current file.

Scroll through several of the accounts in the current file to see if old items were removed satisfactorily. If the correct transactions were not removed, you probably should restore the latest backup of your current file to try the procedure again. Even after you restore the latest backup, that backup file still exists on diskette, so you can do this archive attempt as many times as needed.

To review an archived file

It is assumed that you let the archive file be stored in C: \ MSMONEY. If you didn't, you might have to insert another disk and change the disk drive designation in the following procedure.

Select File then Open from the menu and scroll through the names in the File Name list box. You will see a file named with a year (1991 or 1992, etc.); this is your archive file. Select the archive file and choose Ok. You can work with the archived file in much the same way as any other file, but if you add transactions to it, the amount of these transactions won't be reflected in your current account balances. I recommend that you only use the archived file for inquiries about accounts and transactions, and for printing reports; do not enter transactions in the archive file.

To remove the archived file from the window and return to your current file, select File then Open again and select the file name of your current file.

Summary

This chapter has pulled together some of the helpful Money features that we could not devote an entire chapter to. We have explored the procedures for balancing accounts and learned of the many problems that might arise during this process. A brief introduction and example was presented for using exported Money report information in a word processing document or in a spreadsheet report. The requirements of making backup copies was further explored, and we close with a description of the process of archiving your old records.

A business bonus tutorial

This last tutorial is brief because you already practiced balancing an account in the first tutorial. We will, however, practice exporting a report and archiving old records. Access Money and use the File, Open routine to display the sample.mny file in the window.

Part A

Use the sample account now to experiment with the Balance Account procedure. Enter any approximate balance for the Statement Balance and December 31 for a statement date. Enter a bank charge as well as an interest charge just to see how Money handles this. Experiment with the process of marking checks as cleared, and editing some of the transaction data while you are still in the Balance Account form of the account book. Watch how the totals in the status area change as you mark or edit cleared items. Choose Finish while there is still an amount on the Difference line, so you can try out the SmartReconcile feature. When you want to exit from the balancing procedure, choose the option to have Money Automatically Adjust the Account. Money will make an entry for the difference between the bank statement balance you entered and the reconciled balance in the account. When you return to the account book, you can always delete this extra transaction if you want to.

Part B

In this section we will create a file based on an income and expense report, so we can use it in the Windows Write program. We will then write a simple memo in Write to present the data in the report to our banker.

- ☐ Select Reports then Income & Expense from the menu
- ☐ Choose Customize
- ☐ Select Category in the Row for Every box
- ☐ Enter a From date of 12/1
- ☐ Enter a To date of 12/31
- ☐ Select Income Statement in the Report Transfers By box
- ☐ Choose View to see the report
- ☐ Choose Print then Ok to print a copy
- ☐ Choose Export to create a text file on disk
- ☐ Enter a File Name of towrite and choose Ok

Note   The Export dialog box should contain notations indicating that the file will be saved on the c: drive, in c: \ msmoney, with an extension of ".TXT." Type c:msmoney in the filename box if necessary.

- ☐ Access the Program Manager by pressing Ctrl−Esc or double-clicking on the Program Manager icon if it is visible
- ☐ A task list will be displayed
- ☐ Select Program Manager from the task list

- ☐ Select the Switch To button
- ☐ The window then displays the Program Manager menu with icons
- ☐ Select the Write icon (it's the letter A with a pen point attached)
- ☐ You are now in the Write window
- ☐ Select File then Open from the menu
- ☐ Type c: \ msmoney \ towrite.txt in the Filename box, then Ok
- ☐ Choose Convert in the Convert to Write Format box
- ☐ Great! Here's the Income & Expense report ready to be used in a memo.

Part C

We will now use Write just a tiny bit to write a note to our banker, and save and print the document. For further information about how to use Write see your Windows documentation.

- ☐ Select Document then Tabs from the menu
- ☐ Type a 4 in the first Positions box at the upper left
- ☐ Press Tab and then the Spacebar to check the next box
- ☐ This indicates that the tab stop at 4 inches is a decimal tab
- ☐ Choose Ok to return to the document
- ☐ Now the income report is properly spaced
- ☐ The flashing line at the top left corner is the cursor

Note If the cursor on your screen is not in the top left corner, press Ctrl — Home to put it there (or you could click there).

- ☐ Type the following: (and don't worry about how the characters already on the screen jump around)
  January 5, 199x (press Enter twice to space down)
  Dear John, (press Enter twice to space down)
  Here are our December operating results. I am pleased to inform you that we've done quite well! Advertising Expenses are high now but they'll be declining in mid year.
- ☐ Press Enter twice to space down two lines
- ☐ Press Ctrl — End to get to the end of the document
- ☐ Press Enter twice to space down two lines
- ☐ Type Let me know what you think.
- ☐ Press Enter twice to space down two lines
- ☐ Type your own closing and name

☐ Select File then Print from the menu, then Ok

☐ Select File then Save from the menu

☐ Choose Ok to save the file with its original name

Note There are all sorts of other changes you can make. You could use the Del key to remove words or lines you don't want, change the heading dates to December, or whatever. Feel free to experiment.

☐ Select File then Exit to close the Write window

☐ Press Ctrl−Esc to see the task list

☐ Select Microsoft Money to return to the Money window

☐ Choose Close to return to the account book

Part D

Have you been making backup copies every time you are finished with Money? If not follow these steps to ensure that you'll always have a backup file to rely on.

☐ Select Options then Settings from the menu

☐ Place an X on the Reminder to Backup option (lower left)

☐ Choose Ok

☐ Select File then Exit from the menu

☐ The Backup reminder box appears

☐ Note the file name shown; change it if necessary

☐ Choose Yes to make the backup

☐ Choose Yes to indicate overwrite if asked

☐ Select the Program Manager icon if necessary

☐ Access Money again using the icon on the Program Manager menu

Part E

Lastly, we will archive all of the December transactions we've just finished, because we will be starting a new year soon. To do this we first need to "clear" all transactions in our nonchecking accounts.

☐ Select Equipment in the Account box

☐ Select the first transaction in the Equipment account

☐ Place the mouse pointer in the C column of this transaction

☐ Hold down the Shift key while clicking the mouse (or press Shift−Ctrl−M on the keyboard)

- ☐ Place the mouse pointer in the C column of the next transaction
- ☐ Hold down the Shift key while clicking the mouse
- ☐ Place the pointer in the C column of the next transaction
- ☐ Hold down the Shift key while clicking the mouse
- ☐ Do this for every December transaction
- ☐ You have to do this for all old transactions that you want to remove from your file
- ☐ Let's just do this for Equipment and Cash on Hand
- ☐ Switch to the Account Book for Cash on Hand
- ☐ Insert C in the C column for these December transactions
- ☐ Return to the account book of the Checking account
- ☐ Note that some transactions have an R and some don't; these are transactions you marked when balancing the account.
- ☐ Select the File then Archive items from the menu
- ☐ Type 12/31/x (where x is the current year) in the Remove Transactions box, and choose Ok
- ☐ Read the next dialog box and accept it by choosing Ok
- ☐ After a status message, you'll be back in the account book
- ☐ Scroll to the beginning of the book to see what's there and what's missing
- ☐ Select the Equipment account, and see what's left there
- ☐ Select the File then Open menu items
- ☐ There should be a file named 199x in the File List box
- ☐ Select this 199x file and choose No for backup
- ☐ You now have the archive file in the window
- ☐ Scroll around the archive file to see what's there
- ☐ Select other accounts within the archive file and explore
- ☐ Select File then Exit to end this session

A
APPENDIX

Keyboard reference for Microsoft Money

Quick keys for data entry:

PRESS:	TO:
F1	Get help on current topic
+	Increase the date or check number by one
−	Decrease the date or check number by one
"	Repeat the field from previous entry
Ctrl−S	Split transaction window
Ctrl−E	Enter transaction on future list
Ctrl−P	Pay future scheduled bills
Ctrl−F	Start the Find command
Ctrl−K	Access the Calculator
Ctrl−T	Switch between Top Line view and Entire Transaction View
Ctrl−O	Create a Custom view
Ctrl−D	Insert current date
Ctrl−M	Mark transaction as cleared
Ctrl−Z	Undo the current field entry
Shift−Ctrl−M	Mark transaction as reconciled
Alt	Activate the Menu bar
Alt−(a letter)	Activate a menu choice
Alt−Down Arrow	Reveal a Drop Down list in a field
Ctrl−Ins	Copy calculator results to memory
Shift−Ins	Paste calculator results into field

Quick keys for editing

PRESS:	TO:
Del	Delete the contents of a field or the entire selected transaction
Backspace	Delete the Contents of a Field
Alt – Backspace	Cancel the last change
Tab	Move to next field
Enter	Record the current transaction
Esc	Leave current transaction without recording
Ctrl – Ins	Copy the field to the clipboard
Shift – Ins	Insert field contents from clipboard

Use within dialog boxes

PRESS:	TO:
Tab	Move from option to option
Shift – Tab	Move backwards from option to option
Arrow keys	Move cursor within a field
Alt – (a letter)	Move to option with that underlined letter
Home	Move to first item or character in a list
End	Move to last item or character in a list
PgUp	Scroll a list up one window
PgDn	Scroll a list down one window
Spacebar	Select or cancel a selection in a list
Shift – Arrow key	Extends the selection through a list
Esc	Close the dialog box without completing it

Getting around windows

PRESS:	TO:
Alt – F4	Close the active window
Alt – Spacebar	Click the Control menu button on Title bar
Alt – Esc	Switch to next running application or minimized icon without closing Money
Ctrl – Esc	Switch to application of your choice without closing Money (task list comes up)
Ctrl – W	Cascade the currently active windows

B
APPENDIX

Menu map for Microsoft Money

File
-New
-Open
-Import
-Export
-Backup
-Archive
-Print Checks
-Print Setup
-Exit

Edit
-Undo
-Cut
-Copy
-Paste
-Delete Transaction
-Void Transaction (or Unvoid)
-Split Transaction
-Schedule in Future
-Mark as Cleared
-Find

List

-Account List
-Payee List
-Category List
-Other Classification
*-1. (Other)
*-2. (Other)
* If created

Report

-Register report
-Summary report
-Income & Expense
-Tax report
-Budget report
-Net Worth

Options

-Balance Account
-Pay Bills
-Calculator
-Top Line View (or Entire
    Transaction View)
-Settings
-Password

Window

-Account Book
-Checks & Forms
-Future Transactions

Help

-Index
-Keyboard shortcuts
-How to use help
-Windows basics
-Previews
-About Microsoft Money

C
APPENDIX

Business and home category lists

BUSINESS CATEGORIES PROVIDED BY MICROSOFT

Category	Shortcut	Tax
INCOME CATEGORIES		
Interest Income		T
Other Income		T
Rental Income		T
Revenue	Sales	T
EXPENSE CATEGORIES		
Advertising	Ads	T
Automobile/Truck	Car	T
Gasoline	Fuel	T
Maintenance	Fix	T
Payments	Pmt	T
Bank Charges	Fee	T
Entertainment		T
Meals	Dine	T
Other		T
Freight	Ship	T
Insurance		T
Automobile	Car	T
Health		T

Category	Shortcut	Tax
Liability		T
Life		T
Interest Expense		T
Late Payment Fees		T
Miscellaneous	Etc	T
Office Expenses		T
Equipment		T
Furnishings		T
Rent		T
Repairs	Fix	T
Supplies		T
Payroll		T
Bonus	Bn	T
Commissions	Cm	T
Federal W/H	IRS	T
FICA W/H		T
Overtime	OT	T
Salaries & Wages	Pay	T
State W/H		T
Purchases	Buy	T
Discounts	Less	T
Returns & Allowances		T
Services		T
Accounting		T
Legal		T
Taxes		T
Federal Income Tax	IRS	T
Other Taxes		T
Permits		T
Property & Use Taxes		T
Sales Tax		T
State Income Tax		T
Travel	Trv	T
Airfare	Plane	T
Ground Transportation	Cars	T
Lodging	Hotel	T
Utilities		T
Electricity	Power	T
Heating Oil/Gas		T
Telephone	Phone	T
Water/Sewer/Garbage	WSG	T

INCOME CATEGORIES

Category	Shortcut	Tax
Business Income	Biz	T
Investment Income	Gains	T
Dividends	Dv	T

Category	Shortcut	Tax
Interest		T
Long-Term Capital Gain	LTCG	T
Short-Term Capital Gai	STCG	T
Tax-Exempt Interest	Ex	T
Other Income		T
Alimony Received	Alm	T
Gifts Received		T
Loans Received		T
Lotteries		T
Tax Refund	Refund	T
Unemployment Compensat	UEC	T
Retirement Income		T
IRA Distributions		T
Pensions & Annuities		T
Social Security Benefi	SS	T
Wages & Salary		T
Bonus	Bn	T
Commission	Cm	T
Gross Pay	Pay	T
Overtime	OT	T
Tips	Tp	T

EXPENSE CATEGORIES

Category	Shortcut	Tax
Automobile	Car	
Gasoline	Fuel	
Maintenance	Fix	
Payments	Pmt	
Bank Charges	Fee	
Charitable Donations	Donor	T
Childcare	Kids	T
Clothing	Wear	
Education	School	
Books		
Fees		
Supplies		
Tuition		
Food	Eat	
Dining Out	Out	
Groceries	In	
Furnishings		
Appliances	Apps	
Art		
Carpeting	Rugs	
Cookware	Pans	
Furniture		
Home Electronics	AV	

Category	Shortcut	Tax
Lighting	Lamps	
Linen		
Repairs	Fix	
Gifts		
Healthcare		T
Dental	Teeth	T
Eyecare		T
Hospital		T
Physician	Doctor	T
Prescriptions		T
Housing		
Gardening		
Improvements	Add	
Maintenance	Fix	
Mortgage Principal	Pmt	
Rent		
Insurance		
Automobile	Car	
Health	Med	
Homeowner's/Renter's	House	
Life		
Interest Expense		
Mortgage Interest	Home	T
Other Interest		
Job Expenses		T
Non-Reimbursed		T
Reimbursed		T
Leisure		
Books/Magazines	Read	
Cable Television	CATV	
Cultural Events	Educ	
Entertaining	Party	
Movies	Film	
Photography	Camera	
Sporting Events	Sports	
Sporting Goods	Equip	
Tapes/CDs	Music	
Toys & Games	Play	
Video Rentals	VCR	
Miscellaneous	Etc	
Accounting & Legal Fee	Expert	T
Casualty & Theft Loss	Loss	T
Newspapers	Paper	
Pet Care		
Supplies		
Personal Care	Care	
Cosmetics	Makeup	

Category	Shortcut	Tax
Fitness		
Hair Care	Cut	
Manicures	Nails	
Taxes		T
Federal Income Tax	IRS	T
Property Tax		T
Social Security Tax	FICA	T
State & Local Taxes		T
State Income Tax		T
Utilities		
Electricity	Power	
Heating Oil/Gas		
Telephone	Phone	
Water/Sewer/Garbage	WSG	
Vacation	Trip	
Lodging	Hotel	
Travel		

Afterword

So much to say, and so little time! We will end here, but you will go on using Money for many productive years. Although we couldn't explore all the fine details of Money, I hope I have provided a sound spring board so you can use this wonderful program effectively to gain better control over your finances. Best of luck to you in all of your computing efforts!

Index

reminder messages, 122
reports, 116-120, 125-128
restoring customized views to
    standard views, 116
screen attributes, 121, 128-129
screen views, 111-116, 123-125
settings, Money environment,
    36-37, 120-123

D

data entry
    accounts payable, 188
    accounts receivable, 193
    budget data, 133-134
    customization techniques, 122,
        129-130
    SmartFill and SuperSmartFill,
        45, 56-57
dates, 7, 55
    custom formats, 122-123
depreciation of assets, 205-206,
    213-214
detailed budget reports, 136-137,
    145, 146
dialog boxes, 18, 24
    customization techniques, 117
    quick keys, 240
document icons, 30
document windows, 19
dragging, 29

E

Edit menu, 23, 241
editing, quick keys, 240
equipment as assets, 204-205
errors, 7
exiting Microsoft Money, xviii
expense categories, business, 69
expense reports, customization
    techniques, 119
exporting, 225-229
    File Import and File Export,
        229
    reports exported for word proc-
        essing, 225-228, 236-237
    reports exported to spread-
        sheets, 228-229
    tutorial, 235-237

F

File menu, 24, 241
    Import and Export options, 229

files, 46-47, 62-63
financial management, 65
financial ratios, budgets, 133
financial statements, 77, 89-90
Find feature, 61
focus on button, windows, 22
fonts, customization techniques,
    120, 127
future transactions, 51-53, 58
    accounts payable, 189, 197-198
    depreciation, 214
    maintaining future files, 52-53
    reminder system, 52, 122, 171,
        178-179
Future Transactions window,
    Money window, 43-44

H

help buttons, windows, 22
Help menu, 242
Help tutorial, 5-6
home categories, 244-246

I

icons, 30-31
    Money window, 41-42
    windows shrunk to icon-size,
        35-36
importing, 229
income categories, business, 69
income reports, customization
    techniques, 119
income statements, 77-79, 89-90,
    209, 211
    printing, 142
installation of Microsoft Money,
    xvii-xviii

J

journals, 79-80

K

keyboard reference, 4, 239-240

L

landscape orientation, wide-report
    printing, 127
liabilities, 207-209, 214-218
    net worth calculation, 209,
        210, 218

taxes payable, 207-208, 214-218
list boxes, 25
List menu, 242
lists, 91-109
    account lists, 91-97, 106-107
    browsing, 104-105
    category lists, 99-101, 108-109
    classifications, 101-103, 105-
        106
    payee lists, 97-99, 107
    tutorial, 104-109
loans
    auto loans, 75
    mortgages, 75
    payments, business loans, 74-
        75, 85-87

M

menu map, 241-242
menus, 23-24
    option selection, 23-24
    quick keys, 23-24
Money window, 3, 39-63
    Account Book window, 43
    accounts, 46
    backup files, 55, 63
    calculator, 45, 57-58
    categories, 46, 47-50
    Checks & Forms window, 42-
        43
    classifications, 46, 47
    data entry, SmartFill and
        SuperSmartFill, 45, 56-57
    dates, 55
    files, 46-47, 62-63
    Find feature, 61
    future transactions, 51-53, 58
    Future Transactions window,
        43-44
    icons, 41-42
    new account creation, 94-95
    prompt lines, 41
    selected transactions, 40
    splitting transactions to multiple
        categories, 49-50
    subcategories, 48-49
    Toolbar, 41
    transaction-entry, 59-60
    transaction-entry windows, 50-
        51
    transfers between accounts, 53-
        55, 59